THE GREEN CAMPING BOOK

CONWAY
Bloomsbury Publishing Plc
50 Bedford Square, London, WC1B 3DP, UK
29 Earlsfort Terrace, Dublin 2, Ireland

BLOOMSBURY, CONWAY and the Conway logo are trademarks of Bloomsbury Publishing Plc

First published in Great Britain 2024

This book is a guide for when you spend time outdoors. Undertaking any activity outdoors carries with it some risks that cannot be entirely eliminated. For example, you might get lost on a route or caught in bad weather. Before you spend time outdoors, we therefore advise that you always take the necessary precautions, such as checking weather forecasts and ensuring that you have all the equipment you need. Any walking routes that are described in this book should not be relied upon as a sole means of navigation, so we recommend that you refer to an Ordnance Survey map or authoritative equivalent

This book may also reference businesses and venues. While every effort is made by the author and the publisher to ensure the accuracy of the business and venue information contained in our books before they go to print, changes to such information can occur during the production and lifetime of a publication. Therefore, we also advise that you check with businesses or venues for the latest information before setting out

All internet addresses given in this book were correct at the time of going to press. Bloomsbury Publishing Plc does not have any control over, or responsibility for, any third-party websites referred to or in this book. The author and the publisher regret any inconvenience caused if some facts have changed or sites have ceased to exist, but can accept no responsibility for any such changes

A catalogue record for this book is available from the British Library

Library of Congress Cataloguing-in-Publication data has been applied for

ISBN: PB: 978-1-8448-6679-3; ePub: 978-1-8448-6680-9; ePDF: 978-1-8448-6681-6

2 4 6 8 10 9 7 5 3 1

Designed and typeset in Silva Text by Austin Taylor
Printed and bound in Germany by Mohn Media

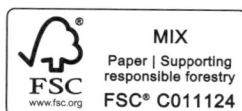

MIX
Paper | Supporting
responsible forestry
FSC
www.fsc.org
FSC® C011124

To find out more about our authors and books visit www.bloomsbury.com
and sign up for our newsletters

THE GREEN CAMPING BOOK

HOW TO CAMP SUSTAINABLY, ETHICALLY AND RESPONSIBLY

MARTIN DOREY

CONWAY

LONDON · OXFORD · NEW YORK · NEW DELHI · SYDNEY

↓ Going camping is good for the soul. As is doing anything outdoors, whatever that may be. We know this from the pages and pages of research that tell us that reconnecting with nature, forest bathing, walking in meadows, swimming in clean seas is good for us.

Contents

Foreword

Doom, gloom, and indeed, more doom.

It can all look a bit bleak at times right now, can't it? I'm not going to go through an exhaustive list of things that make us feel awful, every day, because you don't have to look very far. Just shift your eyeline very slightly to either side, up or down, and you will make contact with the bit of technology that's inevitably waiting there. It will tell you about the woes of the world, most of which you can't do anything about. Whether it's your corner of the world, or a bit thousands of miles away that you'll never visit, we've invited misery into our homes and lives through black mirrors and smart tech to the point where even a visit to the fridge can require a thorough digesting of the darkest of headlines before you get to choose a chutney. A side order of global guilt and shame? A spoonful of pervading anxiety with that? Our pleasure. And only the occasional picture of a cat chasing a reflection to lighten the mood. The wonderful thing is that we are paying for these devices, often as upgrades to things which once simply kept our food fresh, our floors clean or our bills paid. We maybe even took out credit to allow them to dollop out a dose of grief with each glance. Have a little look around the room and you can see them, winking away at you, on charge, just waiting to ladle out a bit more jittery sadness. Basta! Enough!

You know who saw all this coming? George Bloody Orwell, that's who, the utter genius. He spotted 80 years ago that we would end up welcoming the means of our own despair into our living rooms. But do you know something that people don't often recognise about Orwell? He was the world's biggest nature nut. If it grew, swam or flew then George loved it, and would spend as much time trying to understand it as he could. Read any of his books, even the grimmest and bleakest of them, and you'll hear, gently pulsing under the

surface, the heartbeat of the natural world, waiting to break through the man-made monochrome to surround us with roses and riverbanks, with crab apples and kingfishers, sandbanks and Cypress trees. All we need to do is give it space to let it happen; to take the hand of someone we love and trust, to walk out, be quiet and still and let nature take over.

What I love about my friend Martin Dorey is his ability, through his brilliant writing, to show who he is 24/7 – that generous, forgiving, trusted companion holding out a hand. The book he's written here is a gift – part of the process of allowing yourself the space and peace away from the bleeps, alerts and notifications to hear nothing, shortly followed by everything; the symphony of nature. The echoing still of the night, the shimmer of wind in trees, the ride-cymbal pattern of a stream: it's all there, and to get to it you don't have to be part of the problem. He's showing us not only that camping is inherently an environmentally responsible way to spend our free time (which, as a camper I think I knew) but that there are ways to do it that keep companies on their toes and make them play nice with Mama Earth. You can spend your money and your time with the right people so that you know that when you go, you go with God or Gaia, and not with the markets and Mammon. That feels good to me. Thanks, Martin. You're the best.

I also like simple solutions to complex-seeming problems that make us all feel powerless. It turns out there is one that we had at our fingertips all along:

Go Camping! Enjoy the book!

Matt Allwright

↓ 'I believe everyone, regardless of their ability, should have the opportunity to experience the outdoors and camping under the stars. It's about reasonable adjustment, then anything is achievable. Daisy loves the outdoors, swimming, camping and walking, and with a little support she manages to do the things she loves.'
LYNNE GREEN, DAISY GREEN'S MUM

Introduction

The view from here
(Is awesome)

Hello campers.

The idea behind this book is very simple. This is to help campers like you and I to continue to do what we love in the greenest way possible and to help those who are new to camping to do it in the greenest way possible, too. There is a little more to it than that, but that's the basic premise.

In many ways a book about making camping greener is like preaching to the choir because camping – whether it's car camping, backpack camping, glamping or bikepacking – is already a far greener way to travel, when compared with flying off to Mauritius in a private jet, for example. Likewise, travelling on foot creates less pollution, congestion and CO_2 than driving. These are given.

Staying in a tent is also much better for the soul and humanity than staying in a hotel, although I would say that because I've been camping since I was a little kid and come from a long line of campers. Plus, when you camp you are in control of where your food comes from, what energy you consume and what you throw away (or recycle), unlike in a hotel.

Going camping is good for our well-being, too. As is doing anything outdoors, whatever that may be. We know this from the pages and pages of research that tell us that reconnecting with nature, forest bathing, walking in meadows and swimming in clean seas is good for us. And I believe it. I really do.

However, camping is just like any other modern activity in that it has become an industry where people and brands make money out of supplying kit and space to camp in. And because of that, for some, it becomes an opportunity.

I hope this book will help you to make the kind of positive choices we all need in order to be able to continue to go camping without it destroying the very thing we camp to enjoy. In many cases, I also hope those positive choices will help you to help nature flourish, as well as yourself.

On a very basic level I assume that, as a camper, you may also be an environmentalist. You might not think you are. However, the way I see it, going

↑ You smell the earth, feel the grass beneath your feet, hear the birds sing, taste the salt on the wind and see beauty all around. How could you not be an environmentalist?

camping puts you in such close contact with the natural world that it is impossible to ignore. You smell the earth, feel the grass beneath your feet, hear the birds sing, taste the salt on the wind and see beauty all around. You sleep under the stars, under canvas or under the thin metal skin of a tiny house on wheels. You cook and eat in the open, over coals, eating melted, sticky sugar from pointed sticks. You play in nature, remembering all those things you learned as a child: how to skim a stone or make a blade of grass screech between your fingers like a barn owl. As you lie awake, just before dawn, you listen for the sounds of the birds, the rushing stream, the wind in the trees, the knock of the woodpecker. You sleep on granite that is millions of years old, with just a sleeping mat to keep the cold away, or park so you can wake and throw open the van's doors to a vista that's been shaped by natural forces beyond your imagination. When you get caught out by showers on a hike you shelter beneath trees that scrub the air clean through photosynthesis. You plunge into seas that provide over half of the oxygen we all breathe. You kick off your shoes and feel sand and rock beneath your feet. The sun warms your face as you peel back the awning and stare out into the new day.

How could you not be an environmentalist?

Good for the planet
(Great for the soul)

Camping, by its very nature, is a 'green' activity. Its sole purpose – unless you have no choice but to sleep out – is to get you away from the house and into nature to do something that makes your heart sing.

I love camping, and always have. Often it has been out of necessity because I didn't have the money to stay anywhere else, but mostly it's been because I want to be in the thick of it. As a result, I have spent nights lying awake listening to the sound of crashing surf or animals scuttling about outside. I felt connected. Come the morning I loved the fact that I could unzip my sleeping bag and step out into a fresh, new world where anything – usually surf-related – could happen. Catching waves made me happy and camping by the beach, either in a tent or in a van, made that possible. Camping and being happy are so intricately interlinked that it's difficult to separate the two.

Later, when my kids, Maggie and Charlie, were small, I would take off with them for a few days to explore some wayward part of the UK. Our little gang of three would pitch up and go exploring. We flew kites on the beach, hid from midges under our sleeping bags, picked up litter from golden, sun-flooded beaches, and disappeared on long, impossible cycles. It makes me so happy that they both camp today, at festivals or just because they can.

There was a danger that I would be put off camping during wet trips to Wales with my parents in the 1970s. I don't remember family camping trips being joyful – life never was – but I never felt like I missed out on luxury, and I do remember my Uncle Peter cleaning his teeth with a stick. It was the ultimate in survival for me and I was so very impressed. But then I was about seven years old. The blue and orange family tent we owned – it was marked up with a series of paint splodges to aid construction – was destroyed in a storm in the mid-1980s.

My grandfather was a Scoutmaster and lifelong adventurer, even though he was a mild one who never went anywhere except the West Country. He made kites and rode bikes, painted very English watercolours and told tall tales of adventures with his brother in the years after the First World War. He didn't go far or discover anything new but his cycle touring made him, at that time, a pioneer in his own way. Despite everything, life under canvas, and out in the natural world, was good. Very good. And it still is.

According to Mind, the mental health charity, getting out into nature can 'improve your mood, reduce feelings of stress or anger, help you take time out and feel more relaxed, improve your physical health, improve your confidence and self-esteem.' It also claims nature can 'help you meet and get to know new people, connect you to your local community and reduce loneliness.'

It has long been proven that exposure to blue and green spaces can improve physical and mental health. The NHS has employed thousands of link workers in the past few years to prescribe people of all ages to projects that take them outside or allow them to connect with nature to improve their overall well-being. They do this because people who are healthy and happy tend to turn up at A&E less frequently than those who aren't, so putting less pressure on resources. In some ways you could see it as your civic duty to get out there and get consumed by nature so that those who really need our NHS can get easier access to it!

But how should we be giving back? Nature gives us our very existence, makes us feel good and yet it is often seen as a resource to be used up for our own satisfaction. Even the language we use around sport implies we are there to dominate the natural world instead of working in harmony with it, as if nature was a force to be defeated. We conquer peaks and destroy the waves on our surfboards. Sometimes, all we do is take. Camping is no different. We must not forget that even just to get there we have made an impact, whether that's from driving to the campsite, buying our kit or burning fossil fuels to cook our dinner.

So, how do we make up for that? The team at Trash Free Trails[1], for example, encourage mountain bike riders to leave a positive trace by getting involved with natural spaces, because just picking up our own litter or even the litter of others can, in some ways, encourage us to continue with business as usual. And it's not enough any more.

I am the same. I try to live a decent, low-impact life but it's hard. Society is set up for us to accept consumerism, waste, litter – and even litter picking – as business as usual so we can continue to consume. This book is my effort to help us all, me included, to break that cycle.

But what power do we have? Believe me, as consumers we do have power, because, at a basic level, we can withdraw our money from businesses we don't think espouse our own values. Other choices might be harder to make, but they still matter.

We can choose campsites carefully. We can choose our kit carefully. We can adjust our behaviour. We can connect with people and landscapes. We can encourage others to love nature. We can support each other. We can welcome everyone, irrespective of their colour, ability, background or sexuality. We can get involved in environmental projects. We can even take to the streets. All these

↓ It has long been proven that exposure to blue and green spaces can improve physical and mental health. People who are healthy and happy tend to turn up at Accident and Emergency less frequently than those who aren't, so putting less pressure on resources.

↓ Trash Free Trails encourage mountain bike riders to leave a positive trace (by getting involved with natural spaces) because just picking up our own litter, or even the litter of others, in some ways, can encourage us to continue with business as usual.

small but important steps – you might call them marginal gains – can add up to make a bigger difference.

Of course, you don't have to feel that you need to take every step or feel bad because you were unable to. Do what you can, be happy that you have done enough and let the power of that thought allow you to slide into your next positive action.

The first, most important step, I believe, is to fall truly, madly, deeply in love with nature.

Teetering on the brink
(Of something brilliant)

We exist in a time when our very existence is on a knife edge. Everything we do can have a positive or negative effect, whether it's picking up someone else's plastic bottle on the trail or driving our camper vans on to the machair in the Outer Hebrides. Our impact matters.

Whether we like it or not, or believe it or not, climate change is happening. Extinctions are happening. Nature is being marginalised by developments and industry, our governments are taking oil money, and our rights to the land are being eroded and restricted by power and more money. (Did you know, for example, that we have a right to roam on just 8% of land in England and Wales?)

If we use (and colonise) the outdoors – whether it's a campsite or 'wilderness' – to make ourselves feel better when the modern world becomes too much, we need to think about what *it* needs too. Is it a resource to be tapped into when we feel like it?

The struggle is real
(Let's not forget it)

We know the struggle for nature goes on long after we've packed up our tents and taken the train home. It doesn't go away just because we have left. The birds will still struggle to find enough food because since 1945 we have lost 90% of our wildflower meadows to intensive, industrial agriculture. Parcels of land that may have been a home to nature will still be developed. Monocultures will still be creating green deserts out of places like Cornwall and Devon. Uplands given over to shooting estates will still cause flooding downstream or offer little habitat for anything other than game, in the name of 'conservation'. Pesticides and weedkillers will still be poisoning bees, insects and birds – and the habitats and ecosystems we need for our existence.

So, what can we do to help, even after we get home? I don't want to be like a politician flying into a disaster zone to make himself look good in the short term but who fails to take the message home with him or do anything about it. I want to be better than that. I am sure you do too.

Climate change – the impact

'Human activities, principally through emissions of greenhouse gases, have unequivocally caused global warming, with global surface temperatures reaching 1.1°C above 1850–1900 temperatures in 2011– 2020. Global greenhouse gas emissions have continued to increase, with unequal historical and ongoing contributions arising from unsustainable energy use, land use and land-use change, lifestyles and patterns of consumption and production across regions, between and within countries, and among individuals (high confidence).

Widespread and rapid changes in the atmosphere, ocean, cryosphere and biosphere have occurred. Human-caused climate change is already affecting many weather and climate extremes in every region across the globe. This has led to widespread adverse impacts and related losses and damages to nature and people (high confidence). Vulnerable communities who have historically contributed the least to current climate change are disproportionately affected (high confidence).

Climate change is a threat to human wellbeing and planetary health (very high confidence). There is a rapidly closing window of opportunity to secure a liveable and sustainable future for all (very high confidence). Climate-resilient development integrates adaptation and mitigation to advance sustainable development for all, and is enabled by increased international cooperation including improved access to adequate financial resources, particularly for vulnerable regions, sectors and groups, and inclusive governance and coordinated policies (high confidence). The choices and actions implemented in this decade will have impacts now and for thousands of years (high confidence).'

INTERNATIONAL PANEL ON CLIMATE CHANGE (MARCH 2023)[2]

→ What power do we have? We can choose campsites carefully. We can choose our kit carefully. We can connect with people and landscapes. We can encourage others to love nature. We can support each other. We can welcome everyone, irrespective of their colour, ability, background or sexuality. We can get involved in environmental projects. We could even take to the streets.

↓ I hope that the joy and gratitude you feel while out in nature doesn't wane when you leave it. When you get home after a camping trip you are still part of nature. Your weekday self might not see meadows or mountains again until Friday but you still need clean air to breathe, clean water to drink and healthy food to eat.

The greatest challenge
(Is not being overwhelmed)

I hope this book will be inspiring and informative. You may find it challenging at times and that's OK because the subject is challenging. It's easy to be paralysed by problems that are so big and overwhelming you cannot see the end of them. Feeling anxious is a normal reaction; guilt at feeling like you are not doing enough is pretty standard, too. I have felt that.

When I started the #2minutebeachclean[3] project in 2013 I faced a beach that was littered with so much plastic I could never have picked it all up. I felt so overwhelmed and sad that I felt paralysed. But my love for that beach drove me to make a start, two minutes at a time, and to try and inspire others to do the same. In the end we got it done. Imagining that beach in a pristine condition made it easier to start than imagining myself removing every single item of rubbish. All I needed to do was to turn the tables.

As we search for ways to tackle the crisis in nature and ourselves, we will have to visit some uncomfortable truths about the state of the planet. No book about anything green would be complete without a problem for us to solve. That problem is how we are going to continue to enjoy the outdoors while also allowing it to thrive and flourish, on the basis that when it flourishes, we do too.

I hope that the joy and gratitude you feel while out in nature doesn't wane when you leave it. When you get home after a camping trip you are still part of nature. You might have to get up on Monday and face a new week at work, at home with the kids, mending cars, chasing dreams or being a captain of industry, but you are still an inhabitant of Planet Earth. Your weekday self might not see meadows or mountains again until Friday, but you still need clean air to breathe, clean water to drink and healthy food to eat. Dare I say it, you also need dreams of meadows and mountains to sustain you mentally until the next time.

Love what you do
(The rest will follow)

While I was writing this book, I spoke to a number of people in the camping and outdoor industry to find out what they do, why they do it, how they do it, and how they feel about the industry as a whole. There was one thing that I noticed they all had in common: their love for nature and the outdoors.

These inspiring people proved to me that they are driven more by a love for their sport – and the mountains, waves, hills, bridleways and open spaces that make them possible – than they are for money. Their love for the outdoors influences the decisions they make every day. During their working days they act to protect the spaces that give them the good times away from their desks. Their relationship between desk and leisure becomes blurred to such an extent that the two are inseparable.

- **Adam Hall**, former Sustainability Director of Internet Fusion Group, is a surfer and passionate advocate for cleaner seas. He was a trustee of The 2 Minute Foundation and helped set up North Devon World Surfing Reserve. His boyhood, in rural Devon, was spent looking for otters.
- **Andy Middleton**, founder of TYF Adventure in Pembrokeshire and the DO Lectures, is a world-class kayaker and surfer who invented coasteering and pioneered kayaking The Bitches off Ramsey Island in Wales. His love for the natural world is infectious and irresistible.
- **David Hanney**, CEO of Alpkit, left London to live in the Peak District so he could be there to help the company make pioneering moves in the open-water swimming, gravel biking and bikepacking markets.
- **Kevin Bird**, who owns a campsite that set the benchmark for The Greener Camping Club, took a risk to do his own thing so he could present his land in the way that he felt would inspire others.
- **Dom Ferris**, founder of Trash Free Trails, inspired me with his intelligence and passion for coming up with ways of looking at the world that are entirely positive. I find his drive to undertake purposeful adventures deeply moving.

Love can make us do all kinds of mad things. It can be selfless and kind, all-consuming and without limits. With love though, compromise is never a dirty word. It can guide you to make difficult decisions easier and drive you with an unstoppable, heartfelt belief.

Before I spoke to these people, I had a fixed view of the outdoor industry. I figured that it was just like other industries and that, as consumers, we should accept that, because big business will always be business first. Of course, some brands and manufacturers work hard to protect the things they love, but there are many more who don't.

I saw business as being separate from the natural world because many of them use it as a resource that can be turned into profit. In my work as an anti-plastic campaigner, I came across plenty of big corporates – including some of the biggest companies in the world – who were only interested in the natural world, and looking after it, as a PR exercise or as a way of enhancing the bottom line. At least that's how it seemed to me. Nature was just another tool to make money or to make themselves look good so they could make more money. When it came to *actually* putting their hands in their pockets to finance beach clean-ups or to effect lasting, positive change, they tended to disappear faster than a rat up a drainpipe (if you are an executive for a global corporation and you think that's unfair, feel free to prove me wrong. Put £50k into the 2 Minute Foundation with no strings attached and then drop me a line). We called that greenwashing and it was hard to avoid, especially as the CEO of a small environmental charity.

However, when it came to the outdoor brands and talking with the people who run them, it felt very different. I enjoyed a connection with these people that was deeper than boardroom banter or backslapping smugness. The love was apparent from the very beginning. And that love is what I believe will be our salvation.

These people – and you – prove that love can make a difference when it comes to camping and the outdoors. If you love what you do, everything else will follow.

What to look for
(In a camping business or brand)

When it comes to buying stuff for your camping adventures, it's good to look at the people behind the brands. Who are they? What motivates them? How do they act? How do they treat their employees? Would you like to have a drink with them? Would they be good people to go on a hike with? Can they *actually* surf? Have they camped recently?

Generally speaking, businesses that have jumped through difficult hoops to get serious, well-respected accreditation have proven already that their hearts

→ Dom Ferris, the founder of Trash Free Trails, inspired me with his intelligence and passion for coming up with ways of looking at the world that are entirely positive. I find his drive to undertake purposeful adventures deeply moving. © Ian Lean

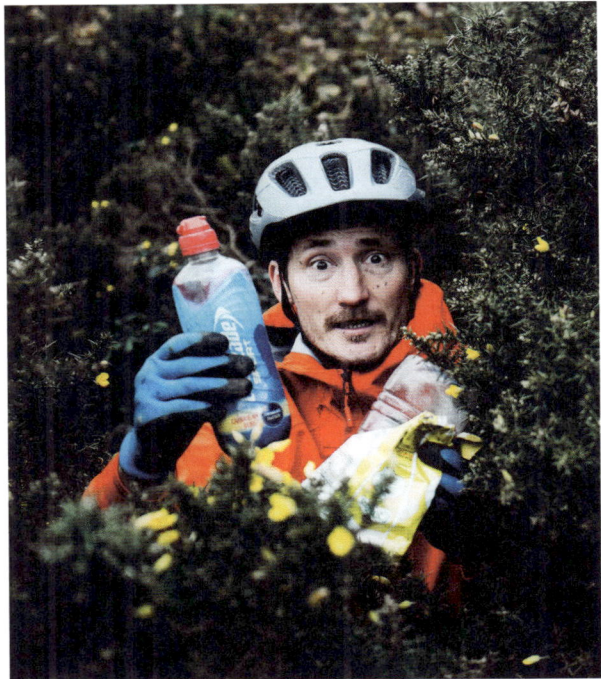

are in the right place. Placing your trust in them can be a good starting point for your adventures. Two accreditation standards to take note of are:

1. **1% for the Planet:** This is an initiative in which companies donate 1% of their turnover to the planet. That money then goes to environmental causes. In some cases, the companies that are certificated may actually be giving more, but 1% is the minimum.
2. **B Corp Certification:** This is a designation that ensures companies meet standards of societal and environmental impact. The standard requires companies do no harm, treat people and places as if they matter, benefit all, and share a collective responsibility for the future.

There are other certifications, of course, such as being Fairtrade or paying a living wage, and some of them are mentioned later, but these two are a great place to start.

← It's easy to be paralysed by problems that are so big and overwhelming you cannot see the end of them. I have felt that. When I started the #2minutebeachclean project in 2013 I faced a beach that was littered with so much plastic I could never have picked it all up.

→ 'In the world of adventure – mountaineering, kayaking, surfing – you always set out to be prepared. You work out the risks and prepare for them. The outdoor industry, and industry in general, isn't looking out for the risks that are heading their way. Businesses are refusing to engage with risks when it comes to sustainability. Kayaking has 6 classes of water. If you are unprepared for Class 6 you face death. The climate crisis is at least a 5.' ANDY MIDDLETON, FOUNDER OF TYF.

↓ As a lifelong camper and, in the last 15 years, an environmental activist, I have become ever more aware of the damage my life and work can inflict on the natural world. Like everyone, I am in a period of transition and am working hard to make things right. It is the only thing to do, because without nature and the outdoors, I would be nothing. © Clive Symm

1

Why this book?

You are the last hope
(Please don't forget it)

The simple answer to the question of 'why this book?', of course, is that we are really, royally, properly, way beyond reasonable doubt, totally screwing up our home – shitting on our own doorstep you might say – and, given what we now know, we need to act with the utmost urgency, at every level, in everything we do. That's it.

Camping and the outdoor industry are just as much a part of this problem as everything else, even though they are leading the way. That said, it is entirely possible that we, the lovers of the outdoors, camping and campervanning, are those who climate change will affect more than those who choose to stay at home. We are the ones out there, in the field, up the mountain, on the water and under canvas. The mountains, moors, beaches and meadows are our playground (and life support) and if we fuck it up, or let others fuck it up for us, that will be the end of it.

We need to be there for nature as much as it is for us. Never mind the small matter of the survival of the human race.

So that's why this book.

Green is good
(Unless you faked it)

When the idea of writing this book popped into my head and wouldn't go away, I knew it felt right. For me, writing a book about camping from an environmental point of view would bring parts of my life together, which, so far, I have kept largely separate. I have spent the best part of 15 years writing books about camping and camper vans, and have written travel guides and books about van life. I have included messages about being responsible where I could, but it was never about environmentalism.

I have also written books, as a green activist, about ocean plastic and waste, as well as climate change and extinction. I started an environmental charity and was even awarded an MBE for my environmental work. Seeing the world through a green filter has become how I live.

Therefore, it made so much sense to put the two things together. Why not? They already make good bedfellows – you go camping to enjoy being in nature. However, I did wonder what more I had to say beyond asking you to buy good-quality gear and making it last.

Then I remembered that I have a sneaky feeling that somehow big business has crept in and that the outdoors has been taken over by corporates and hedge-fund managers, who buy up outdoor companies to add to their portfolios. Maybe it's got too big to be simply about camping any more?

The camping & outdoor industry

Tents & caravan awnings sold **£6.6M** in 2021

In **2019**, tented campers spent **12.5M** nights under canvas

The industry is worth **£9.3B** to the UK economy, employs **130,000** people

I have been a regular visitor to camping and caravan shows. I love them but there are some aspects that I find shocking. Some shows are huge, taking up several halls of big exhibition centres, every inch of which is laid with nylon carpet. It arrives on gigantic rolls and gets laid the day before the show, cut to size to fit the stands. When I think of all the hundreds of thousands of feet that tramp over this during the show it makes me fear for our waterways – so many microfibres.

Walking around shows sometimes gives me the eco-creeps. While it's great for the industry, and amazing for people who love camping to see many of the larger players in one place, it is a sea of planet-fucking long chain carbons, from the nylon tents to the extruded plastic caravans to the fake grass, plastic hedges, vinyl banners, and lanyards on show IDs. Somehow, at this end of the business, the connection with nature seems to be faked and forgotten. And that's a part of what this book is also about.

While I don't want to decry the industry for commercialisation, it helps me to remember that we often exist in a paradox: we are outdoor people and yet we occasionally go to vast indoor arenas to choose our camping gear. Camping becomes as much a part of the exhibition industry as it is a part of its own.

The solution? Go camping.

↑ Have we forgotten that we are a part of nature? Sometimes it seems as if we have, especially when it is used as a commodity to sell an outdoor lifestyle. Even then, we create out own version of it.

↓ Completing routes like the NC500 in a few days is to miss the point of going to northern Scotland. Go for the beauty, the landscapes, the adventures, but don't do it just to tick it off your bucket list.

The NC500 is
(Not a racetrack)

At about the same time I was starting to worry that camping was becoming more about money than stars and sunsets, I had the feeling that my chosen form of camping – travelling by camper van – might not be the best thing to do any more. It perpetuates the car and fossil fuel industry and puffs out huge amounts of carbon. Shockingly, vans made up 16% of the UK transport emissions in 2020. Admittedly, the majority are delivery vans, but even so, unless we change our habits, we are part of that problem.

Seeing posts on social media about people 'doing' the North Coast 500 (NC500) in a few days made me recoil in horror. Given the climate crisis it seemed crass to drive to Scotland to appreciate the beauty of the landscape but then whizz through it without really stopping to look at it (or even getting out of the van to be in it). It's no wonder the locals get pissed off because no one stops to buy their marmalade! It's not a racetrack.

It would be easy to accuse me of hypocrisy at this point when you consider my books are about driving routes. I hold my hands up. In my defence, though, they are about *slow travel*, which is far from racing around Scotland in two days. The solution to this I will go into later but it's basically about slowing down, pitching up for longer and getting more involved in where you are. Carry on camping, sure, but for goodness' sake, stop haring about.

Feeling awful about climate
(Is just temporary)

Unless you are an oil company executive, a politician, or a Tufton Street lobbyist in a state of denial because you are in the pocket of the oil industry, you will have felt the shadow of eco-consciousness washing over you in recent years. You may have resisted – or given in – and felt a heavy mass pressing down on you: we need to be green because, well, climate change, existential crisis, save the planet and all that; KeepCups and Morsbags. The pressure is on all of us to do better. And we all know we can.

The tsunami of guilt you feel – or feel that you should feel – when you book a flight or pass an empty plastic bottle on the street is a real thing. You might feel anxious that you didn't do the thing you should have. Did you put out the recycling? Remember that it is possible to own a car or a phone and care about the planet; or even wear trainers. Don't listen to those who are only interested in 'greenupmanship' or who are greener than thou. And, for fuck's sake, don't ever feel bad if you attend a protest and someone says 'How did you get here? By car?' Those people are just jerks. So, no, don't worry. All the planet needs right now is your love. And that's easy. Go camping. Nature won't judge you.

Less hysteria
(More hoots given, please)

The human race is facing an existential crisis of its own making and it's going to take a lot of other plants and animals with it. Nature is being marginalised: the ice caps are melting; forest fires are raging after extensive dry periods; and coral reefs are dying because the water temperature is rising. We are facing the sixth mass extinction. Our soil is being depleted by agriculture. Worms, Earth's great architects, are in decline. Our jungles and forests are being cut down to feed farm animals to feed our hunger for meat. Human development and activity is marginalising the natural world. The seas are rising. And global weather patterns are going absolutely bonkers. Our life support system – the magical, wonderful, beautiful, amazing Planet Earth – is in the middle of an absolute shitshow of a crisis and we are the cause of it. And it seems, sometimes, as if no one actually gives a hoot.

The outdoor industry, as I have found out, is one that, thankfully, does give a hoot. Which is a relief I must say, because I was very cynical until I started talking to the people in it. The reason for this, I believe, is because of the connection with nature. Businesses that have their roots firmly in the soil, rock or snow – and who remember that – understand the relationship between them and nature. Their business model relies on, for example, enabling people to stay dry while hiking, and so they understand that their customers care about the environments they choose to hike in. So why wouldn't they want to protect those environments? It stands to reason, right?

> **The human race is facing an existential crisis of its own making and it's going to take a lot of other plants and animals with it.**

It seems strange, though, that some elements of the outdoor industry still can't get their heads around being green and don't see it as essential. Skiing companies that don't engage with climate change or the climate change activists in their sector (step forward Protect Our Winters[1]) are on the edge of a business precipice. With the ski season getting shorter (in some places it has shortened by as much as 30 days), ski resorts below 1,200m (3,937ft) facing going out of business, and a customer base that actually cares about climate change, I can't see how it's morally possible to still take money out of the sport if you don't fight for it. That's fire sale business ethics. It's the same for surfing businesses that ignore ocean plastic and don't contribute towards the clean-up, continuing to package their products in plastic. Did they not see this coming? Or how about companies that sell tents and yet aren't, apparently, doing anything about the thousands of them being left at festivals each year?

↓ Forest fires is Spain are burning more intensely due to long dry winters, and are starting earlier than usual. According to Statista, 3,060 sq km (306,00 hectares) — more than three times the previous year — were lost to wildfires in Spain in 2022.

↑ Some ski resorts are facing a shorter season and a bleak future. So why isn't everyone involved in the ski business doing all they can to mitigate climate change when it threatens their very existence?

On a positive note, tent-selling mega-giant Decathlon has announced a takeback scheme for festival tents, which means you can exchange your tent for vouchers to the value of the tent when you return it after a festival. This is good. As someone who has physically picked up tents from a festival site, I can tell you that (in my experience) Quechua tents (Decathlon's own brand) are among the most popular to be discarded, possibly because they are so cheap they are considered almost 'disposable'.

It seems crazy to say this, but I have heard stories from executives who have only got into sustainability because their children told them about the plight of the ocean after learning about it at school. How lacking in self-awareness is that? I could go on and on.

Maybe it's because the executives of these businesses have forgotten what it's like to go camping or that the holding company's board of directors is made up of people who are more interested in money than going outside. They have lost contact with their customers, what their customers like to do and how their loyal custom pays for their mortgages. This kind of disconnect is what is killing us.

It's up to us to shake it up. We can choose to make the good guys rich and put the bad guys out of business. All we have to do is stay cool, drop the hysterics about climate change and give a hoot. Then go camping.

If this doesn't move you
(I don't know what will)

Right then, let's get into some of the specifics of this climate change/eco disaster/ biodiversity hysterics I've been banging on about.

For as long as I can remember, people have been raging against the destruction of nature while others have been waging war against it. It is a deep rabbit hole to dive down, but needs must. Don't forget to give oxygen to your fury if you feel the same fury as I do. Come up for a breather every so often.

According to industry documents, ExxonMobil, the oil giant and once the world's biggest company, knew about climate change in 1977, well before it became a public issue, thanks to its own team of climate scientists. It also predicted, with stunning accuracy, the upward curve of global temperatures and its relationship with rising CO_2 emissions. It then chose to spend billions of dollars refuting the science of its own scientists, in order to protect its business.

Oil company shills and client journalists in the media, funded by Tufton Street thinktanks, are still paid to cast doubt on the legitimacy of climate science. The doubts they cast are attracting conspiracy theorists in droves, who tweet all kinds of nonsense against respected climate scientists and academics. One person I confronted on X (formerly Twitter) claimed climate change was a ruse to contain us all in 15-minute cities and to tax us with ULEZ (Ultra Low Emission

Zone) and congestion charges. As if the amount ULEZ brings in (in London, ULEZ accounted for £34 million in 2022) compared with what the oil companies are making (Shell made £40 billion profit in 2022) would offset the gravy train that the oil, automobile, aviation, war, plastic and chemical industries have been on for the last 100 years.

If there are doubts about the climate crisis you can bet they have been funded by the same oil companies who are looking to protect their vast profits.

Anyhow...

Global warming, caused by the greenhouse effect of additional CO_2 in the atmosphere, which creates a barrier that heat cannot escape through, might well just be the tip of the very quickly melting iceberg, because there are so many other pressures on our planet, all of which are manmade. However, it really is the 'BIG ONE', which is driven by and exacerbated by all the other environmental pressures together.

I mean. How big a problem does it have to become for us to act?

Our climate is changing as a result of global warming and we are already experiencing the effects. In the UK, we have had record cold temperatures and record hot temperatures. The seasons are now, on average, warmer than at any time since records began in 1659. Sea levels have risen by 16.5cm (6½in) since 1901. In comparison to the 1960s, birds are now breeding earlier by anywhere between three and 21 days. Bees have declined by 30% since 1980. Storms, like the massive Storm Eunice, which brought the strongest winds in 30 years to the UK in 2022, are stronger, last longer and are more powerful than ever. Fires rage on.

> It's up to us to shake it up... All we have to do is stay cool, drop the hysterics about climate change and give a hoot. Then go camping.

Light pollution, which has increased greatly over the last 25 years, means that connections made to the night sky are now unavailable to most of us in our everyday lives.

Somehow all of this is too big and too abstract for us to take urgent action. We feel numbed and oppressed by such huge ideas and losses. It's easy to be frightened or unable to act. It's hard to be able to connect cutting our electricity usage to a storm that is raging outside. We can't see how our own actions could possibly make a difference. We feel eco or climate anxiety and suffer stress, sleep loss, and even depression or a sense of suffocation and panic as a result.

I write books about it to ease the stress and guilt (while also trying to live a good, green life). You might do something else. Or you may not know what to do at all. My answer? Go camping.

↑ Let's face it, nature will always find a way. It's our existence we need to worry about.

It's getting hotter
(So what?)

Rising temperatures are easy to see and feel. It's fine when it's the UK hitting the heady heights of 30°C (86°F), but what about when it creeps up to 40°C (104°F) (as it did in 2022)? What about when it starts to creep up above 45°C (113°F)? Aside from the threat to human life, infrastructure will barely cope. Skin cancer rates – I have had it and can assure you it's no joke – will rise too.

The effects of rising sea levels are also easy to see. Around 200,000 coastal homes were at risk of flooding in 2023. My home town, Bude, in North Cornwall, is one of the most vulnerable places in the UK to sea level rises. The house my kids own will have Atlantic surges licking the front door in 50 years' time.

Storms, likewise, are easier to understand. Their ferocity is a measure of the changing weather patterns. If your fence blows down it will cost you money to repair. And if it doesn't now, it will in the long run, as your insurance costs will go up. We will all pay in the end!

↓ Seek out the places, like the RSPB Reserve at the Mull of Galloway, where nature is allowed to thrive, to find out what the countryside around us should be like.

It's harder to see how habitat loss, a decline in pollinators, the increased use of plastics, global production and all the other environmental pressures will affect us. But affect us they will, whether through increased pressures on infrastructure, through increased migration of displaced people, or worsening global temperatures.

Even the local loss of a mature tree will have an effect that we may not see directly, other than the loss of species associated with it, and the ecosystem it supports. Trees, as reported in late 2022, have a value, in terms of carbon capture that is 'almost incalculable'[2], according to Professor Mat Disney of UCL, an author of 'Laser scanning reveals potential underestimation of biomass carbon in temperate forest'.

It has long been reported that the loss of our pollinators may lead to a collapse of food crops. This would mean food prices rising, the loss of birds (who feed on pollinators) and a loss of the entire food chain that relies on these insects. We've already seen food shortages in the UK blamed on weather events.

The supply, treatment and disposal of water is another one. It amounts to about 1% of UK emissions and about 6% of a household's, so it's not irrelevant. The immediate effect of water becoming more of an issue – due to droughts – is higher water bills and rationing. Without any water, all life dies. But even so, that's unimaginable in our society, for now. It isn't if you live in the Global South.

The point I am trying to make here is that all environmental issues have a cost to us at some point or other, whether it's today or tomorrow, and we need to do all we can to mitigate this. And that includes when we go camping.

Cry long and hard
(For what is gone)

When it comes to detecting the scale of change that is happening, we need to ensure we do not become the victims of shifting baseline syndrome, a condition whereby our basic benchmarks for pollution, weather events and loss of habitat are so low – and lower further over time – that they normalise a lack of biodiversity or the presence of litter, for example.

In order to measure and mourn what we have lost we may need to trawl our collective memories to recall the beauty and abundance of nature from, say, 1945. I will talk a little about looking back to look forwards in Chapter 7 but for now, here's something:

England has lost 97% of its wildflower meadows since 1945 as a result of changing land use, agricultural practice and the use of pesticides and soil 'improvers'. What this means is that when you sit on a train and look out of the window and see acre upon acre of green, glowing grass, especially in Devon or Cornwall, it's not normal. It's most likely been ploughed up, 'improved' with pesticides and nitrates (that may pollute rivers) and planted with nothing but the kind of grass that grows quickly enough for the farmers to get a couple of cuts a year out of it to feed to his cows. The cows may even live in a barn and never see the light of day. It really isn't normal. However, if you have never known any different, it is normal.

In 1945, those fields may have been a wildflower meadow bursting with yellow rattle, southern marsh orchids, red clover, knapweed, bird's foot trefoil, Devil's scabious and wild carrot, among other species. It would have been a riotous place, buzzing with insects and bouncing with hares, scuttling mice and swooping birds. The grasses, insects, worms and invertebrates would have provided a good diet for the birds, the grasses food for the mice, the mice and shrews a tasty morsel for owls and the flowers lots and lots of pollen for bees and pollinators.

England's meadows would have been a very different place. We need to remember that (not in a nationalistic, nostalgic, Elysian, blue birds over Dover kind of way), if we can, and make that our aim for restoration and rebalance. If we remember the fields

All environmental issues have a cost to us at some point or other, whether it's today or tomorrow, and we need to do all we can to mitigate this.

of England as they were 10 years ago it will mean remembering England with many decades of decline already well underway.

The best way to mourn our loss is to seek out those places where nature still thrives. Fortunately, because land isn't given over to agriculture on campsites, they are often places where there are areas of uncut meadow where you can see nature, as it should be, as it was and as it could be.

It's the same with light pollution and the night sky. Streetlights, billboards, shop windows and offices that leave the lights on overnight when there is no one to use them, make it impossible to see the night sky in its full glory. Dani Robertson, in her book *All Through The Night* (HarperNorth, 2023), says 'In our biggest cities, people can hope to see around ten to twenty stars, out of the 5,000 that should be visible to the naked eye. If we don't make an effort to find the night sky and see it in its full glory we are at risk of normalising pollution – and cutting ourselves off from the universe.'

Look up to the dark skies. Seek out the meadows. Find the wild places. Go camping. Make a connection. Then take action.

→ Dani Robertson, in her book *All Through The Night* says 'In our biggest cities, people can hope to see around ten to twenty stars, out of the 5,000 that should be visible to the naked eye.'

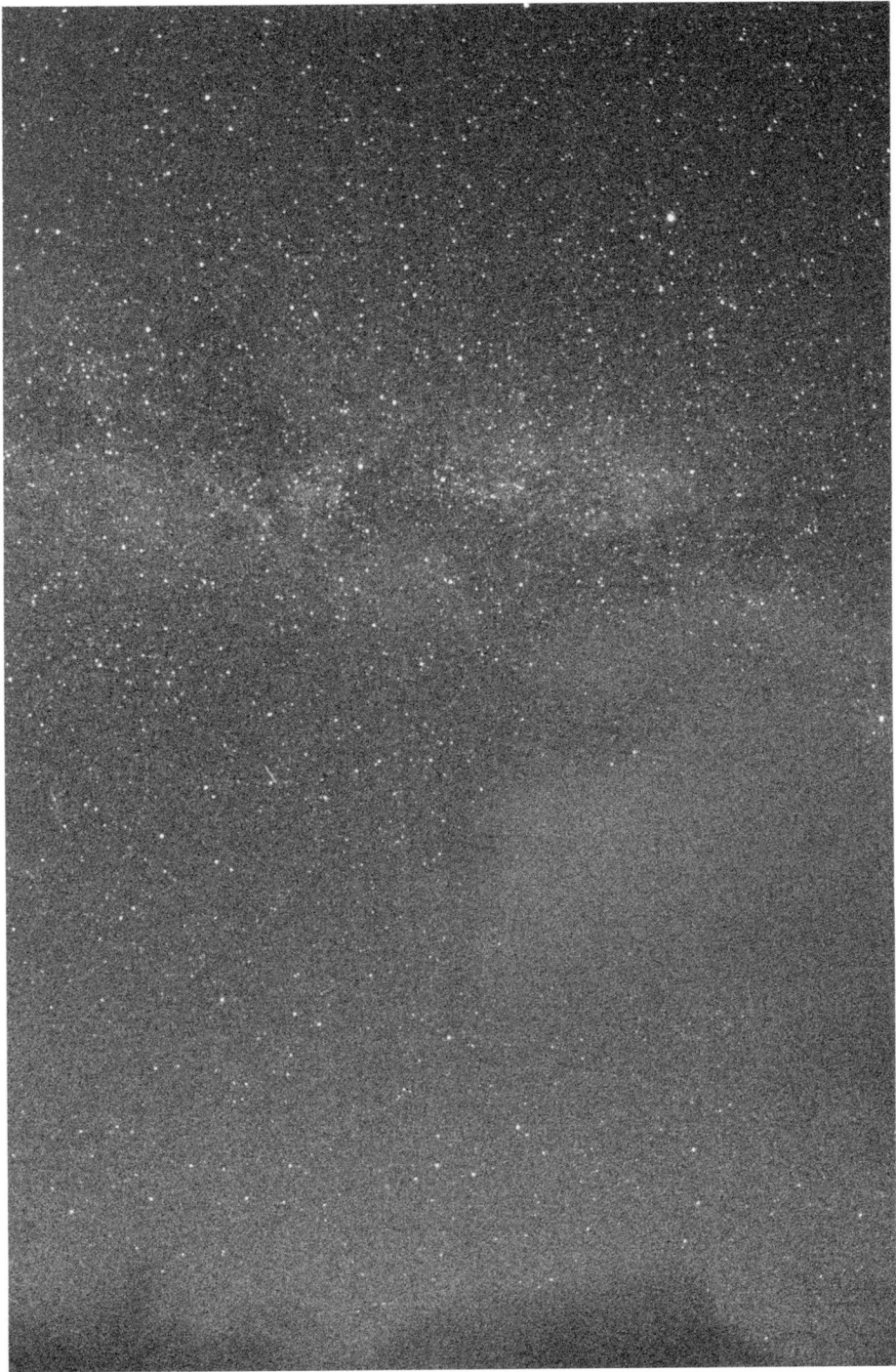

↓ Loving your stuff for longer is by far the greenest option when it comes to your gear, making repair a radical act in the face of increasing pressure to buy more stuff constantly.

2

Trying to do the right thing

First up, here's a mini chapter about doing the right thing to get you thinking about your camping journey and how the brave new world of green thinking might affect it. It's never easy to navigate or understand what is happening with green thinking – and that's OK, it changes all the time and there are dead ends and diversions at every turn.

There is money to be made from being green, even in the camping and outdoor world, and that can attract less than perfect practice. So, here's the skinny on a few of the pitfalls I have discovered as an environmental activist and anti-plastic campaigner over the last 15 years.

When it comes down to it, however, being a greener camper will often take a little more effort than simply going with what you are used to doing or taking the path of least resistance. There are choices to be made at every step in the journey. Some of them are hard, some are easy, some will save you money, and some will cost a little more in the short term. You may not even see the benefit of your actions, so it's important to remember that they do matter and that it is important.

The most eco thing
(Is the thing you already own)

I will talk about tents, clothing and kit later, but there is one general rule to being green when camping – and in everyday life too – stop consuming! Here are some other tips:

- The greenest thing is the thing you already own, be it a tent, rain jacket or stove.
- If you can repair your stuff to keep it serviceable then that is by far the greenest option.

- If you don't own stuff then the next best thing is to borrow it. Saves a few quid too.
- If you can't beg or borrow, buy second hand if you plan to use it a lot.
- After buying second hand, renting is the next greenest option. Rented items get used and don't sit in garages and lofts for 50 weeks of the year.
- Continuous growth and consumption just isn't sustainable, and contributes huge amounts of carbon to the atmosphere, whether from manufacturing, transport or disposal.

↓ Going to a waste-free shop can be a really rewarding experience. It's a different way of shopping where you get to talk to people who care. Often it can work out comparable to going to the supermarket. In some cases, items may cost more but will last longer, so making them more cost-effective in the long run.

Buying plastic free
(Doesn't always cost more)

- If you visit a plastic-free shop to buy staples like rice, cornflakes, pasta or nuts for your camping trips, it isn't always more expensive than the supermarket, even though the preconception is that it may be.
- Take a trip to your local waste-free shop before you go on your next camping trip – compare prices. You may be surprised.
- Going to a plastic-free shop can be intimidating but, in my experience, plastic-free shopping can be a really good experience. People who run the shops will want to help if they can. It can be a really good way to shop and can bring communities closer.
- Some items are more expensive at plastic-free shops, but if you consider their lifetime of use, or durability, compared to the alternative, there are often savings to be made.

The recycling
(Is not always recycled)

- You can put stuff in the recycling but it doesn't always get recycled. Sometimes it ends up as 'energy from waste' and that means it gets burned to make electricity.
- Only about 45% of plastic waste in the UK gets recycled.
- Some recycling gets exported to countries that do not have proper recycling facilities and consequently it often gets burnt. They frequently have poor human rights records, too.
- Recycling a bottle doesn't always mean that it will get turned back into a bottle. Plastic can only ever be 'downcycled', which means it is of a lower grade than virgin plastic.
- It is better to reuse or reject plastic than to rely on the recycling system.
- Aluminium can be infinitely recycled, but still takes energy to do so.

Bioplastic
(Is just plastic)

- Bioplastic is plastic-like material made from non-fossil fuel sources, like corn starch or potatoes. While it is better to use organic materials than to use fossil fuels, if the end result is to produce a material that has plastic-like qualities then it may well be just as bad. The big question is about 'end of life'.
- Even bioplastics can cause harm to animals in the environment and in the ocean if they are ingested or they get entangled in them. Promising that they will break down 'in five years' is not good enough. Five years is enough time to do irreparable damage.

- Some bioplastics still release toxins when they break down.
- Bioplastics can ruin recycling streams if they get into them, so rendering the whole batch useless, and require their own specialist recycling. This was particularly prevalent with foodware. A lot of recycling facilities will not accept bioplastics.

Degradable plastic
(Is still flipping plastic)

- Degradable plastic is plastic that has had an agent added to it that will allow it to break down in water. When it breaks down it just breaks down into smaller and smaller pieces.
- It is still plastic and still has all the toxic properties of plastic.
- Watch out for 'photodegradable' plastics, too, as they are the same but degrade in sunlight.

Recyclable is not the same
(As recycled)

- Lots of manufacturers are calling their products 'recyclable' these days. This means they can be recycled.
- However, recyclable doesn't necessarily mean an item will get recycled, unless the manufacturer is offering some kind of takeback scheme for the item.
- Putting a recyclable item in the recycling doesn't always mean it will get recycled.
- It is better for the environment to try to avoid any kind of plastics, especially single-use plastics.

Compostable stuff
(And compostable stuff)

- You will, by now, have come across the term 'compostable'. This is a term that is used when an item (a wet wipe, for example) can be composted back to its non-toxic ingredients.
- Magazine wraps from organisations like the National Trust and The Camping and Caravanning Club, which are home compostable, should come with instructions on the packaging as to what needs to be done with it.
- If an item is defined as 'compostable' the manufacturer should include information on disposal and a timeframe for biodegrading. Putting something in your home compost is not the same as putting something in your food waste bin for collection: the environment in your home compost is not the same as industrial composting facilities where food waste goes.

- If an item is described as compostable it may not necessarily be safe for it to be left or buried on your camping pitch. Items rot down at different speeds and under different conditions. Some items may take up to six months to rot down completely under industrial conditions and yet are still described as compostable by European standard EN 13432.
- If something is compostable it doesn't necessarily mean it will compost down on its own in the natural environment. Compostable items often don't compost down in landfill, either, because there is no oxygen and no turning of the matter – so they last a lot longer. Some items need specific conditions only found in hot box or industrial composting.

↓ Just because plastic can be recycled, it doesn't mean it gets recycled. Around 12 million tonnes of plastic finds its way into the oceans each year. Single-use plastic is avoidable.

↓ Recycling a bottle doesn't always mean that it will get turned back into a bottle. Plastic can only ever be 'downcycled', which means it is of a lower grade than virgin plastic. It is better to reuse or reject plastic than to rely on the recycling system.

- Many 'compostable' items need time, heat, microbes, oxygen and agitation to become compost. These elements are present in industrial composting facilities, where the whole lot is turned by a JCB before being left to rot down. It's like a huge version of your home compost, except more powerful and hotter.
- You should be able to put items that are 'home compostable' in your home compost. These items should contain instructions for safe and effective composting.

Read the label
(Properly)

Be aware of what labels/symbols mean. Recycling labels can be confusing, with the one that you will see regularly – the green dot – being a little misleading as this is not a recycling symbol. There is also a 'home composting' label and a 'compostable' label. For more details on what the labels/symbols mean, see overleaf.

↓ The greenest option when it comes to camping gear is the thing you already own. After that it's the stuff you rent or borrow.

Chart of common symbols

RECYCLE: Easy, isn't it? This means the item can be recycled. Sadly, it may not be the case, depending on where you are and what your local council's policy is towards recycling – it may get shipped offshore or burnt for energy recovery. Common recycling requirements include:

• Rinse and recycle – for food tins and yoghurt pots, so they don't contaminate other recyclate.
• Lid on and recycle – because bottle caps cannot be recycled separately.
• Recycle at supermarket – most likely to be soft plastics that are collected at supermarkets and not at the kerbside.
• Remove sleeve and recycle – because the sleeve is a separate type of plastic that cannot be recycled.

DON'T RECYCLE: This stuff can't be recycled and may even ruin a recycling stream if it is recycled. Avoid.

NOT YET RECYCLED: This is such a load of twaddle. It means that it cannot be recycled but it is the supermarket's way of making you think they are 'working on it' and it matters to them. It doesn't. Avoid like a badger with a migraine.

PLASTIC RESIN CODES: These are present on most plastic packaging and explain what type of plastic the item is made of, and therefore gives you an idea of whether it can be recycled.

1   PET: Used for drinks bottles and some food packaging and widely recycled.
2   HDPE: Cleaning product bottles, milk cartons, etc, and widely recycled.
3   PVC: Car parts and window fittings; not easily recyclable.
4   LDPE: Used for plastic bags and wrapping and can be recycled at specialist points (supermarkets and recycling centres).
5   PP: Used for some tubs and trays and widely recycled.
6   PS: Polystyrene, used for takeaway boxes, etc, and not easily recyclable.
7   Other: Crisp packets, rice packets, etc. Only recyclable at specialist points.

GLASS: We all know this one. Drop it in the bottle bank, leave at kerbside. Don't get seen by your neighbours or do multiple trips.

PAPER, CARD AND WOOD: Usually recyclable in all the usual ways, although it's not recommended to recycle food-contaminated packaging. The FSC logo means it comes from well-managed forests independently certified in accordance with the rules of the FSC.

RECYCLABLE ALUMINIUM: Infinitely recyclable, unlike plastic, so a better choice.

COMPOSTABLE PACKAGING: Products that are certified to be industrially compostable according to the European standard EN 13432/14955. Do not put compostable packaging into the recycling with other plastics. It contaminates recyclable plastics. Should be recycled with your garden waste through your local authority.

HOME COMPOSTABLE PACKAGING: Suitable for home composting in your compost heap at home, if you have one. Does not need to be turned or composted industrially. Do not put it in with your plastic recycling.

MOBIUS LOOP: This means that an object can be recycled or is made from recycled material, but that it will not always be accepted in all recycling collection systems. You may see a percentage in the middle, which indicates how much of the material is recycled. Not always helpful but may affect buying choices.

THE GREEN DOT: Don't be fooled by this lovely green symbol. All it tells us is that the manufacturer has contributed to the recovery and recycling of packaging in Europe. It does not mean it is recyclable or recycled. Smells a bit greenwashy to me.

↓ 'We have lots of biodiversity on the land and it is a truly special place to come. We stood our ground and did what we felt was right, not what we felt campers and the camping industry expected of us. It's worked out ok.'
ANNA, OWNER OF BAKESDOWN FARM, CORNWALL.

3

Where are you staying? Campsites and touring parks

'About ten years ago we were on the cusp of going with what we thought everyone wanted out of a campsite. But somehow is just didn't feel right for us. We decided we would do things the way we wanted. If people turned up and didn't like it, then I figured they simply wouldn't come back. But people did. We made a real effort to explain to our customers why we didn't mow everywhere and why the site is like it is. We were amazed that we didn't see a drop in bookings at all. As a result, we have lots of biodiversity on the land and it is a truly special place to visit. We stood our ground and did what we felt was right, not what we felt campers and the camping industry expected of us. It's worked out OK.'

Anna, owner of Bakesdown Farm Camping, Cornwall

Get out there
(While you still can)

This chapter is about campsites and touring parks. It is also about which campsites have good eco credentials, what those credentials are and how you can find them.

Campsites are really important spaces. As land that is used for leisure they are not affected by agriculture, industry or the need to make money besides providing a camping experience. That means they are not subject to agricultural policy, pressures to improve yield or to feed the nation. Even when they are the product of diversification and are part of a farm, the land they use can be treated in any way the landowner or campsite owner wants.

This means campsites have huge potential to become wildlife havens. They are dotted all around the country, which means, with the right approach to management, they could become a series of vibrant, exciting islands of biodiversity within a sea of development, industrial agriculture and housing.

The importance of campsites to the people who stay on them cannot be ignored either. Often, campsites are the first places where people come into direct contact with nature. For people who live in inner cities, even a large

↓ Campsites are often the first places where people come into direct contact with nature. Those touch points are vital and the responsibility of the campsites to make camping holidays truly special, educational and 'best in class' is greater than ever.

touring park may contain more opportunities to learn about nature than exist in their everyday lives. These touch points are vital and the responsibility of the campsites to make camping holidays truly special, educational and 'best in class' is greater than ever. With a positive view of sustainability, the camping industry can lead the way in the fight against climate change, biodiversity loss and access to nature. What an amazing, unmissable opportunity to have a positive effect on a huge number of people!

- During the Covid-19 pandemic, 4.5 million people in the UK went camping for the first time.[1]
- 42% of British adults went on a camping or caravanning holiday during the three years ending November 2021.[2]

If you are otherwise too busy, stressed, introspective or scared to be engaged by green issues, going camping may give you an opportunity to learn about nature in a friendly, easy, relaxed way – just by being a part of it. This is the camping industry's chance to inspire you.

The chances are that you are already quite green (because you are reading this book), but imagine if you were an inner-city kid or member of a family that lives in a neighbourhood where there is little access to nature. If you rarely get the chance to go outside of your neighbourhood, a campsite could be the first place where you get to be in nature in a safe and controlled manner. The campsite helps you feel comfortable in nature. You get introduced to birds, insects and plants. You begin your journey to understanding nature. You are inspired to protect it.

I feel very strongly that campsites, touring parks and certificated locations can work together to improve our connections with nature and the nature within them. They have the potential to become a network of mini-wildlife havens – islands in a sea of degradation.

To that end this chapter, I present to you my 'Charter for Campsites', a basic 20-point plan for campsites to improve our connections with nature. Campsite owners can use it – if they don't already have policies in place – to create more nature-friendly places. You, as a camper, can use it to make choices.

'Everything we have done for sustainability
in the last ten years has paid off.'
Charlotte Veale, Wooda Farm Holiday Park, Bude

Your responsibility as a camper
(Make the good guys rich)

As a camper, you can choose to stay at sites that are trailblazing greener camping experiences. By supporting them you are also supporting best practice in the industry (and giving yourself a more authentic experience at the same time). Even if you are a first-time camper, you can choose touring parks and holiday parks that are doing great things for nature. This means you don't have to feel that you need to go full-on, wee-in-a-bucket-type camping just yet. That's the best thing about it – a camping holiday can be anything you want it to be. You can stay in a chalet, a caravan, a yurt, a camper van, a tent or even a bivvy if you like, and that's absolutely fine. Choose the trip that suits you – but make sure you do it with people who also care about the environment.

There are ways of finding good places to stay, although it's not quite as easy as you might think to select sites based on their eco credentials.

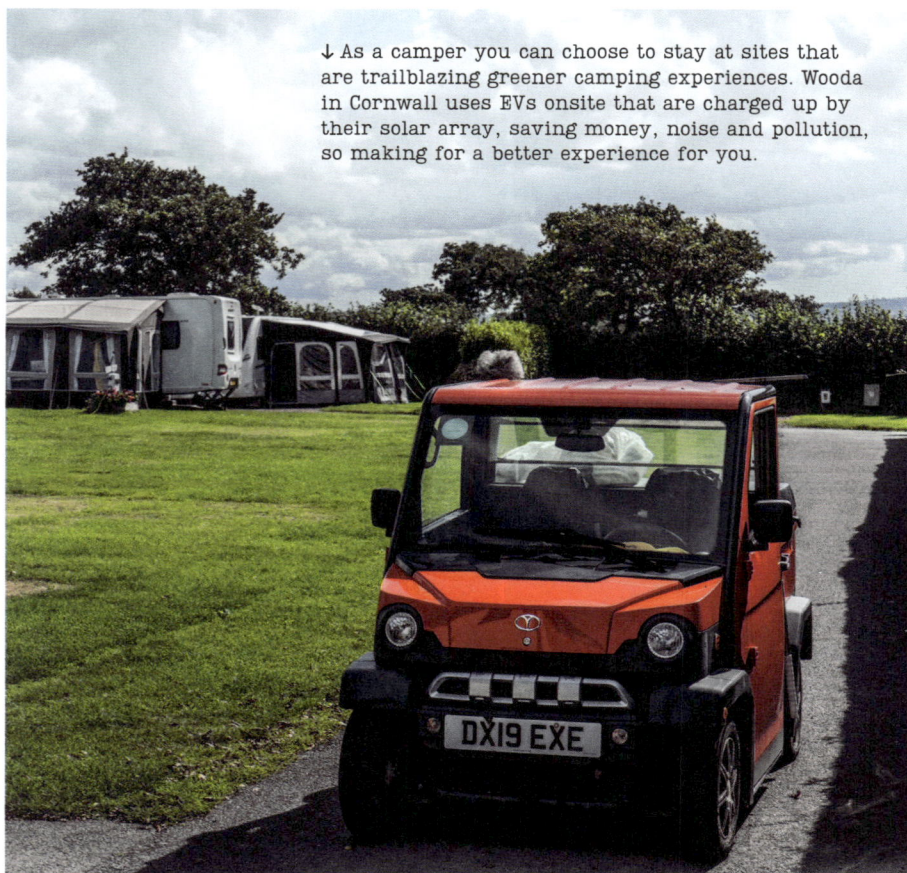

↓ As a camper you can choose to stay at sites that are trailblazing greener camping experiences. Wooda in Cornwall uses EVs onsite that are charged up by their solar array, saving money, noise and pollution, so making for a better experience for you.

And a little reminder
(For those who go off-grid)

You may be one of the many thousands who choose not to stay on campsites and backpack camp, bikepack or stay off-grid in motorhomes or camper vans. Doing this responsibly, as you know, is of the utmost importance if we are to be welcomed in the future and if we are to leave a positive trace wherever we go. There are some rules to making as little impact as possible and you'll find them later on in Chapter 4.

Find the right site
(For amazing adventures)

If you want to camp legally in England and Wales and don't have the permission of a landowner to stay on their land, then you are going to have to stay at a campsite. There are thousands of them in the UK and they range from big, multi-use holiday parks to small certificated locations. Choosing them can be a case of simply finding one that's near where you want to go – if you are touring, for example. However, if you are going to spend a week on holiday in one location, then getting the right site is important. I would argue that choosing a site that enables you to camp in a nature-friendly way is vital. Given that the climate crisis is happening, and that you are trying to enjoy a vacation with a low impact, it's ever more important to make sure you stay at a campsite with good green credentials or support a camping organisation that takes green issues seriously.

All new campsites are required by the Environment Agency, or as a condition of their planning permission, to undertake an Environmental Impact Assessment. These look at soil health and erosion, water and flood risk, air quality, flora and fauna and socio-economic impacts, and suggest mitigation measures for each. What it means is that new campsites must have basic measures to be greener in place, even if they don't shout about it. Older campsites, on the other hand, may not have been through such measures.

How to choose a greener campsite
(It ain't easy)

There are several ways to find a greener campsite, but surprisingly it isn't that easy. There is no universal accreditation or scheme that judges and rates all campsites on their sustainability credentials. This is a shame as it would make it very easy for anyone to choose a site based on how much they care for their environment and their community and, in that, push others into best practice. So there's an opportunity there.

However, you can choose a camping club to book with based on their environmental principles or you can find individual campsites. Again, surprisingly, few of the main campsite listings websites (or club websites) will allow you to search for campsites based on their environmental credentials, apart from Pitchup, which will allow you to search based on the David Bellamy Conservation Award (although it's buried a little in the menu).

Searching for eco campsites

ALAN ROGERS: Alan Rogers, an independently operating directory owned by The Caravan and Motorhome Club, is the first directory site to create new submenus in the facilities filters of its website that enable campers to search for sites that employ sustainable practices or have environmental awards. This is industry-leading work and means that you can search (at the time of writing) from around 700 sites based on their eco credentials. The site now makes it possible to search for campsites based on energy/resource management, waste management, nature management and eco awards.

Alan Rogers lists sites based on their quality and covers sites from clubs as well as some Certified Locations (CLs) and independents. It does not charge a fee for listings, which means it remains independent. www.alanrogers.com

DAVID BELLAMY-ACCREDITED SITES ON PITCHUP: Pitchup will allow you to search for David Bellamy Conservation Award sites, as well as sites that offer wild camping, wildlife havens or forest camping. www.pitchup.com

CAMPSITES.CO.UK: This campsite aggregation site will allow you to search for various criteria, including eco campsites. www.campsites.co.uk

CAMPSITED.COM: Another aggregation site that is a relative newcomer but still riding high. It is in the process of looking at its internal structures to become greener as a company, plans that may include search criteria. Watch this space. www.campsited.com

→ You can stay in a chalet, a caravan, a yurt, a camper van, a tent or even a bivvy if you like, and that's absolutely fine. Choose the trip that suits you — but make sure you do it with people who care about the environment too.

↓ The Caravan and Motorhome Club's new England Club Site is one of the most biodiversity rich on the club's network.

Choose award winners
(Start with Bellamy)

The David Bellamy Blooming Marvellous Pledge for Nature is a new 'award' scheme for sites belonging to the British Holiday & Home Parks Association, an organisation that represents and serves those who own or manage holiday, residential, tenting, touring and glamping parks. It replaces the David Bellamy Conservation Awards, a scheme that ran for over 25 years, which offered sites the opportunity to win Gold, Silver and Bronze awards based on three criteria: ecological management of the park, sustainability of their offering, and their standing as good neighbours to those around them.

It was hugely successful and is still regarded as a benchmark within the industry. However, then, as now, parks were only eligible if they were members of the British Holiday & Home Parks Association, which means hundreds of ineligible campsites that may be doing great work were not listed. Parks were vetted by more than 60 assessors and between 500 and 600 parks won awards.

Following David's death in 2019 and the Covid-19 pandemic, his son, Rufus, has simplified the idea and replaced it with the David Bellamy Blooming Marvellous Pledge for Nature. This new scheme asks parks to make a commitment to improving their existing habitats for wildlife, creating new wildlife habitats where possible, managing their green space in as environmentally friendly a way as possible, involving their guests and staff in wildlife conservation and engaging with local conservation bodies and projects. Each year, the parks must also commit to starting at least one big project to help nature. In the first year (2022) the challenges were, in true Bellamy style: 'Everyone

> **Choosing a campsite with good green credentials is vital for enjoying a low-impact vacation amidst the climate crisis.**

Active' (create environmental activities for everyone to enjoy); 'Home Sweet Home' (set up bird boxes and other artificial wildlife homes); 'Horti-heroes' (manage your green space in a way that reduces environmental impact); 'Pollinator Patch' (create a part of their park where bees, butterflies and other insects can get food); 'Special Species' (choose an at-risk species and give it a helping hand); 'Super Signage' (provide environmental information and interpretation to help everyone enjoy the wildlife on your park); 'Tree-mendous' (plant native trees and make their woodlands work for wildlife); and, finally, 'Wonderful Wetlands' (boost the wildlife value of their ponds and other freshwater habitats).

To find a park that has taken the David Bellamy Blooming Marvellous Pledge for Nature, see www.ukparks.com/bellamy-parks.php. You can also find and book all of the Bellamy Conservation Award-winning campsites, rated Gold, Silver and Bronze, on www.pitchup.com

Green tourism awards
(UK-wide accreditation)

The Green Tourism award is a scheme that is worldwide. It accredits tourism businesses for best practice. However, at the time of writing, only seven campsites in the UK were listed as being accredited, although they have been working with The Caravan and Motorhome Club to accredit 160 sites. www.green-tourism.com/members/awards

Green key campsites
(In 40 countries worldwide)

The Green Key certificate scheme, which started in Denmark more than 25 years ago, is a 'leading standard of excellence in the field of environmental responsibility and sustainable operation within the tourism industry.' In England, Green Key is run by Keep Britain Tidy.

↓ It's not always easy to find a green campsite using traditional methods. Alan Rogers, an independently operating directory owned by The Caravan and Motorhome Club, are the first directory site to create new submenus in the facilities filters of their website that will enable campers to search for sites that employ sustainable practices or have environmental awards.

The scheme requires campsites and holiday parks to meet a range of criteria to qualify, with further criteria expected for the length of membership of the scheme. This is to ensure year-on-year improvement. Criteria include:

- The management must appoint an eco-manager from among the staff and hold meetings with staff, as well as providing training, to ensure policies are upheld and that improvement is continuous.
- The campsite must formulate a sustainability policy with reference to chemical pollutants, water usage, energy usage, protecting local biodiversity, reducing carbon emissions and also committing to the principles of the circular economy.
- The policies must also include a commitment to equality, anti-corruption, anti-exploitation and support for the local community.
- Other requirements are that the campsite informs guests about the environmental policies in place and encourages them to get involved with initiatives.
- There are lots of other criteria, which include using eco liquids for cleaning; fitting water-saving cisterns; separating waste (and educating staff about it); reducing single-use packaging and food waste; supplying organic, local or Fairtrade food items; the use of tap water over bottled water and protecting local biodiversity on site.

It all sounds too good to be true, and I am all in favour of education, improvement and responsibility, but the drawback for us in the UK is that, while there are hundreds of campsites and holiday parks in Europe with Green Key accreditation, there are only ten locations in the UK, with the majority of those being holiday parks.

This may be due to the popularity of the David Bellamy Conservation Award Scheme or that, in the UK, we just don't get it. So, while it's not much to us at home, use it to find a site in Europe! www.greenkey.global

Camping clubs
(And their green credentials)

Camping clubs are membership organisations, like the Camping and Caravanning Club or The Caravan and Motorhome Club. Their governance may be slightly different but many of them are not-for-profit, which means they invest money made back into the club and do not (and cannot) pay dividends to shareholders. They exist solely to benefit the membership.

Campsites and, perhaps more importantly, camping clubs are in a unique position because they can apply any policy they like for the benefit of the planet. It is up to them to decide what they think is more important – a few noisy members or the pollinators, soil health, biodiversity and nature.

The Caravan and Motorhome Club

In 2020, the Caravan and Motorhome Club employed a sustainability executive to help push forward the sustainability agenda at every level within the organisation. This included, in 2022, working with Green Tourism (see above) to assess all 160 club sites according to its criteria of people, places and planet. Most sites gained Silver or Bronze awards, so there is still work to do, but the club acknowledges this. Currently it is not possible to search for club sites according to their award, but it is under consideration. It is possible, however, to search for sites according to car charging, proximity to RSPB reserves and accessibility.

In February 2023, the club launched a 'sustainability hub' on its website (www.caravanclub.co.uk/sustainability-and-green-tourism) to highlight the work it is doing. This hub contains information about sustainability targets and programmes across the network.

The club has a policy for charging electric vehicles on site and has installed chargers at eight club sites, so far, and will be installing them at future developments, along with other 'green' measures, such as ground source heat pumps and solar panels in toilet blocks. The club diverts 94% of waste from landfill, 73% of which is recycled and 23% of which is recovered.

The club is, generally speaking, doing a good job of transitioning. However, it has to tread a fine line between being a motoring organisation, being answerable to its members and doing what one might consider to be the right thing. www.caravanclub.co.uk/uk-holidays

'The club, like any business, must take sustainability seriously.
We operate campsites in some of the most beautiful places in the UK
and we need to ensure these are protected for the future.'

Camping and Caravanning Club

Like other clubs, the Camping and Caravanning Club recognises its responsibility to the environment and is acting accordingly. With 100 club sites, around 1,200 Certificated Sites and 750,000 members, its slice of the camping pie – and the land that is used for campsites – is not insignificant. The club has recently audited its business from a sustainability point of view and has a plan to focus on three core pillars – carbon reduction, biodiversity, and reusing and recycling – with initiatives within those pillars. Plans include updating infrastructure to include solar, plus EV charging in an appropriate way as technology moves forward, working to improve and understand biodiversity on its sites and educating site managers and campers about wildlife – something it has done since the club was founded in 1901.

The club magazine features regular articles about sustainability issues,

↓ Sites that have pet farms or allow kids to get to know domesticated animals may well be giving them their very first chance to fall in love with nature and the natural world. It is a big responsibility.

↓ Members of some clubs will complain that leaving verges uncut looks scruffy or is wet and shows laziness instead of understanding that it is good for biodiversity. This is a battle that will rage on for a while until those who prefer neat lawns understand why it's important for all of us to let them grow.

CARAVAN AND
MOTORHOME CLUB

No-mow zone
to give wildlife a home

as well as the excellent, long-running Eat Local campaign, which encourages campers to cook from locally sourced ingredients. As you'd expect, on a local level site managers provide campers with information on where to hire bikes, where to find footpaths or local shops, and where to catch public transport.

The club commissioned the Outjoyment Report in 2022. It was undertaken by Liverpool John Moores University and Sheffield Hallam University and looked specifically at camping, spending time outdoors and well-being. Perhaps unsurprisingly the report highlights that, compared to non-campers, campers are more likely to flourish, with strong motivators for going camping being feelings of happiness and enjoying nature.

Currently there is no function on the club's website to search for sites with the best environmental credentials; however, it is possible to search for accessible facilities and there are plenty of other searchable criteria. www.campingandcaravanningclub.co.uk

'As you would expect, there is a lot that is already done at a site-specific level to support biodiversity. Our plans are to take this much further by looking at things like wildlife corridors, ensuring only native tree and plant species are planted at club sites, and ensuring each location has rewilding areas. The chances are you will also see things like bug hotels at our sites. We are also piloting a scheme at one of our club sites whereby students from a local college are auditing the wildlife on a small nature reserve on the site with the intention to carry out supporting work to help wildlife thrive. This is seen as a long-term partnership with subsequent years of students using data shared by their predecessors and helping the area to thrive over a number of years.'

Freedom Camping Club

The Freedom Camping Club has over 400 certificated sites operating under its supervision in England and Wales. The club has a bold ecological mitigation document that requires owners of certificated sites to mitigate against damaging ecosystems while offering camping. Environmental assessments are made during the application process for new sites. As such the club considers its role to promote and encourage recreational camping and caravanning, engagement with the natural landscape and appreciation of nature.

The Freedom Camping Club was the first to offer seasonal pitches on certificated sites in order to reduce the amount of traffic, pollution and congestion before and after weekends during the camping season, as well as lessening damage to sites. It also helps to decrease the carbon footprint of caravanners as it reduces the need to tow. www.freedomcampingclub.org

Greener Camping Club

In 2015, two campsite owners from Wales, who had felt restricted by the rules of one of the larger camping clubs, decided to set up something different. They wanted to put sustainability at the forefront of the camping experience – something that, surprisingly, isn't always at the forefront of the camping experience.

The camping club model allowed the Greener Camping Club to certify sites for member-only use without needing planning permission, working with campsites that could offer 10–15 pitches for tents and pitches for five caravans or motorhomes. Some of their over 160 sites offer glamping as well as tent pitches.

The club encourages landowners to put sustainability first so that the camping experience is more natural, with less density than other campsites, more biodiversity and opportunities for wildlife. All sites are assessed for their suitability and how they fit with the ethos of the club.

Each year, 20% of the club's revenue gets spent on environmental projects and each membership pays for tree planting. In 2022, they planted 18,000 trees on their sites.

Some of the ideas employed by the club include:

- Compost toilets.
- Mowing pitches but leaving other areas to grow as meadow to encourage biodiversity.
- Direct contact with campers to foster better relationships.
- Allowing campers to borrow leisure gear such as wetsuits, boogie boards, chairs, and kayaks to remove the potential waste.
- Special rates for campers who arrive on foot or by bike.
- Acting in a fair and ethical way, with clear terms, conditions, site rules and great customer service.

Unlike with some other clubs, searching for a Greener Camping Club site will automatically guarantee a greener, more sustainable experience because all sites are assessed from the word go with strict green criteria.
www.greenercamping.org

Nearly Wild Camping

Nearly Wild Camping was set up by ecologist Steve Evison, and like Greener Camping Club, it is a club that's operated as a non-profit co-operative with 280-plus sites and a membership of 6,000 in the UK. Its sites have a wilderness rating for the facilities they provide, with a 5-star campsite offering no facilities other than space to pitch your tent. This means you can enjoy a 'wild experience' without having to run the risk or stress of being moved on. Booking is done through the owner.

↓ The Caravan and Camping Club's Outjoyment Report highlights that, compared to non-campers, campers are more likely to be flourishing, with strong motivators for going camping being feelings of happiness and enjoying nature. Campers are happier and less anxious, have significantly higher levels of psychological well-being, feel significantly less stressed and have significantly higher levels of nature connectedness than non-campers and are likely to spend slightly more time in nature.

The organisation encourages the 'leave no trace' ethos and is big on education to allow campers to fall in love with nature and the outdoors. www.nearlywildcamping.org or search for sites on www.campsites.co.uk/search/almost-wild-camping

Sanctuary Camping Club

This small camping club operates in the same way as many other clubs, except it is exclusively for sites in East Anglia, England. The club believes in recreation with a purpose and that by encouraging, helping and supporting campsites, those sites can develop into a means of enhancing the environment, promoting well-being and become beautiful, educational pockets of repair. It encourages recycling, repair and upcycling in order to reduce the carbon footprint of the organisation and has a biodiversity consultant who can advise site owners on introducing wild flowers, grasses and trees. The club encourages sites to grow things like fresh herbs for campers to use, fruit trees and even simple salad vegetables, as well as providing mud kitchens, bean tepees and room to play for younger campers.

www.sanctuarycampingclub.co.uk or search for sites on www.campsites.co.uk. The site allows for searches under different criteria, including quiet, woodland and forest campsites.

Campsites as a hope for nature
(And campers too)

When I started this book, I had an idea that I would find out the area taken up by campsites in the UK. The reason behind this was to prove a point that, taken as a whole, the campsites of the UK make up a significant enough area to be relevant as an 'ecosystem' in their own right, with a unique opportunity to make a genuine difference to wildlife and biodiversity. I felt that knowing the power their collective area could have on the landscape, the campsites, camping clubs and farmers offering their fields for CLs might be inclined to flex their eco muscles and become a shining example of good practice. After all, they are stronger together than apart.

As far as the number of campsites goes, some estimates put it as high as 9,000, but a conservative estimate from The Expert Camper puts it at 7,297, which is good enough for an initial calculation. To work out the rough area I found a selection of campsites that I already knew, from the tiniest to the largest (not including Shell Island's 1.21 sq km (121 hectares), as I felt it would skew the average), measuring their approximate area using Google Earth. The average area of these sites was 0.06 sq km (6 hectares).

This gave me a *very* rough area of 438 sq km (43,782 hectares), which is around 170 square miles – that's a little bigger than the Isle of Wight.

The UK's land area is 243,610 sq km (24,361,000 hectares), and while

↑ The Greener Camping Club encourages landowners to put sustainability first so that the camping experience is more natural, with less density than other campsites, more biodiversity and opportunities for wildlife. All sites are assessed for their suitability and how they fit with the ethos of the club. And that includes composting loos.

campsites cover only around 0.18% of this (according to my rough calculations), it's still not insignificant and gave me a great deal of hope. Britain's campsites, given a little more care, could easily become super-havens for wildlife and biodiversity, and positively affect the surrounding areas: a network of mini nature reserves spread across the whole country; bright islands of life in a sea of biodiversity loss.

For comparison, there are currently 219 National Nature Reserves in the UK, covering an area of 986 sq km (98,600 hectares). This is just over double the land area given over to camping.

We know that where Marine Conservation Zones (MCZ) like Lundy Island off the north Devon coast introduce no take zones, the protected species thrive and spill out into the surrounding area. According to a study of the MCZ around Lundy[3], conducted five years after it was established, there was 'an increase in abundance and average size of landable-sized lobsters, both within and adjacent to the protected area'. The same could be said of nature reserves: nature cannot be contained and spills out from the places where it is protected. On land, protected places and small parcels of wilderness act as wildlife corridors or sanctuaries, offering food and shelter to many species of birds, mammals, insects and invertebrates. In a world where nature is constantly being marginalised, campsites can offer hope. Unlikely to be developed, they are permanent green

↑ We need to get over the idea that all of a campsite needs to be neatly mown. The days of the neatly clipped lawn — an elitist 18th-century country house construct — should be behind us. Now that we know that long grass captures carbon better, provides a better habitat for all kinds of biodiversity and keeps the soil cooler, it's time to stop clutching the pearls and let nature in.

pockets that can be optimised easily in favour of nature and wildlife, while still offering a quality camping experience. In some ways, they could offer a superior camping experience, allowing campers to fall in love with nature.

This does not mean I consider campsites to be devoid of nature. Many of the hundreds I have visited over the years are already teeming with wildlife – and that's incredible. However, it is important to note that there are still sites that are more tarmac than grass or which employ vicious mowing regimes in order to appear neat and tidy. This is something we need to get over. The days of the neatly clipped lawn – an elitist 18th-century country house construct – should be behind us. Now that we know that long grass captures carbon better and provides an improved habitat for all kinds of biodiversity it's time to stop clutching the pearls and let nature in.

Think of the benefits of being able to camp on sites that are part of a countrywide network of mini wildlife havens! They include:

- Opportunities to observe, get to know and fall in love with nature.
- The chance for the next generation to learn about nature, wildlife and garden conservation.
- The opportunity for 'wildlife tourism' for campsites with exceptional biodiversity.
- Carbon capture from grass and trees to 'offset' the effects of vehicles on site.
- Protection for mature trees to contribute to carbon capture.
- Improved soil health leading to an increase in invertebrates and insects, so attracting birds.
- Opportunities to create mini wildlife zones, such as ponds to attract aquatic species, like frogs and newts.
- Stargazing on clear nights without light pollution.

The campsite manifesto
(What you should be able to expect from a green campsite)

Learn while you camp

Campsites are great places to learn about nature or to make small changes that will add up to make a big difference. Campsites that make an effort to educate campers about why things are the way they are will make swift progress. For example, if the site is allowing the grass to grow long it will help if the site explains to all campers why it is doing this. Regular campers who are used to neatly mown grass, for example, might get upset about seeing it unmown, mistaking it for laziness or lack of care. A simple notice explaining the change, why it's necessary and what benefits they will experience from it will help all of us to accept it.

Being excited about wildlife

When I turn up to a campsite, I love to hear about the wildlife I can expect to see. And we know that if campers are able to fall in love with the natural world, then they will be more inclined to help you protect it, and also to take that love home with them. A warden's enthusiasm and delight at nature will inspire everyone. Good education should tell you about what you can expect to see and give you opportunities to record what you have seen. It's great for getting the kids involved.

Giving nature a voice

It might sound bonkers but businesses that make an effort to reserve a place at the table for nature or ask a member of staff to speak for nature at meetings will naturally consider sustainability at every turn. It's a simple thing that can help everyone to focus on aspects of decision-making other than money or convenience. Giving a voice to the voiceless is a powerful message.

Less mowing, more long grass

Results from the charity Plantlife's 2019 No Mow May citizen science project[4] showed that leaving lawns to grow for a month in May can result in a tenfold increase in the amount of nectar available to bees and other pollinators. In the experiment, lawn owners 'saw an increase in the growth of daisies, germander, speedwell and creeping buttercup, as well as a resurgence of white clover, selfheal and bird's foot trefoil' after two months of not mowing. An American study in 2019[5] also showed that urban grassland that is mowed just once or twice a season increased biodiversity by at least 30%. Leaving grass to grow also sequesters more carbon, reduces weeds and produces more oxygen through better photosynthesis. Pathways mown into grassland are a good way to see them without getting wet feet.

Making space for meadows

Since the 1930s, 97% of Britain's wildflower meadows have been lost to intensive agriculture.[6] What were once vitally important habitats have been ploughed, sprayed and replanted with monocultures in the interest of industrial food production. The wildflower meadows weren't just beautiful to look at, they also supported hundreds of species of birds, flowers, insects and invertebrates. They helped to sequester carbon, hold back water, lock up pollutants and provide a home for more pollinators than other ecosystems. Leaving areas of meadow can help to restore this imbalance and will attract more species, providing lots more opportunities for you to observe birds and insects.

No pesticide use

Pesticides and weedkillers, including neonicotinoids and glyphosate, are having a devastating effect on nature and may also have a detrimental effect on people.

↓ If campers are able to fall in love with the natural world then they will be more inclined to help you protect it, and also to take that love home with them. A warden's enthusiasm and delight at nature — and the way they show it — will inspire everyone.

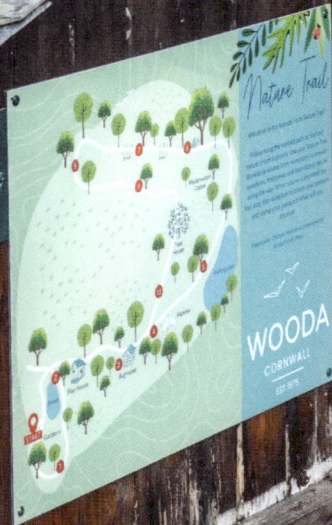

Nature Trail
Start Point

WOODA
CORNWALL
EST 1975

↓ The thing about native plants is that they are suited, generally, for the climatic and soil conditions in the UK because they have evolved to take their place in the ecosystem. This means they need less maintenance and are also more suited to the insect and invertebrate life they may support — the relationship is symbiotic.

Neonicotinoids, which following Brexit are being reintroduced for some uses, are pesticides that also kill bees and insects, and indirectly the birds that feed on them, too. Glyphosate, which is included in weedkillers like Roundup, has been recorded as having a detrimental effect on human health. In 2015, according to the Soil Association, 'the International Agency for Research on Cancer (IARC), a branch of the World Health Organization, concluded that glyphosate products have the potential to cause cancer.'[7]

Importance of trees

According to the Met Office, 'four of the five warmest summers on record for England have occurred since 2003, as the effects of human-induced climate change are felt on England's summer temperatures'.[8] If this tells us anything it is that we need to be prepared for more high temperatures and the associated problems that go with them. The Forestry Commission advocates the use of trees for urban spaces for the cooling effect they can have by providing shade and reflecting solar radiation. On sites where there is a lot of hardstanding this could be an important way to mitigate the effects of more heat. Trees also suck up carbon dioxide, produce oxygen and moisture, and provide habitats for wildlife. A study in 2022 from the University of Ghent[9] claimed that mature trees are twice as good at sequestering carbon than previously thought, making them 'of incalculable value' when it comes to adapting to climate change. As previously stated, mature trees also provide cover and roosting and nesting sites for birds, as well as supporting their own ecosystems.

> A hedge that is 1,000 years old may have as many as ten or 12 different species within it.

Protected ancient hedgerows

Hedgerows are protected by law because of their importance to wildlife and biodiversity. However, they are sometimes exempt from protection if they are on private land or are less than 30 years old. The 'Hooper Formula' can be used to determine the approximate age of a hedgerow. Count the number of shrub species in a 30m (98ft) stretch. Each one represents, roughly, the age in 100 years of the hedgerow. A hedge that is 1,000 years old may have as many as ten or 12 different species within it. Sites that retain and plant new native hedgerows will have a positive effect on biodiversity, providing cover and nesting sites for birds, as well as an ecosystem for their food.

Planting native species and fruit trees

Native plants are those that belong in a landscape or ecosystem. They may include plants that have migrated here from Europe or those brought here

Life Around the Pond

This thriving habitat is abundant with life, from bugs and amphibians to mammals, birds and many plant species. Take a look and see if you can spot any of the below creatures whilst you relax by the water.

We are lucky to see lots of beautiful dragonflies around the Wisley pond. Dragonflies were one of the first types of insect to appear on the planet around 300 million years ago, pre-dating the dinosaurs. Fossils show that some had wingspans of up to 60cm!

The common pond skater is predatory, feeding on small insects by detecting vibrations in the water's surface.

Possibly our most familiar amphibian, the common frog is a species found throughout Britain and Ireland, and much of northern Europe. Frogs are often found close to fresh water in habitats that shelter them throughout the summer as they can breathe through their skin as well as their lungs. Outside of the breeding season they can roam up to 500 metres from their pond.

Common frogs are carnivores so feed on a variety of invertebrate prey including slugs and snails. Despite their wide mouths, frogs drink by absorbing water through their skin and swallow using their eyes, they retract them into the head to help push food down their throats.

Male frogs make a low purring sound in the breeding season to attract females, which are largely silent. Their spawn (group of eggs) is laid in freshwater in clumps. Tadpoles generally take up to 16 weeks to grow back legs, then front legs before they metamorphose into tiny froglets, ready to leave the water in early summer.

→ Bees are struggling due to the loss of habitat and nesting sites as well as the devastating effect of pesticides and fertilisers. Give them a helping hand by planting flowers that are bee friendly, set up 'bee hotels' for solitary bees and consider even setting up a hive on the grounds — as long as it's away from campers.

← Taking stock of the kind of species you have present in your campsite will not only provide a talking point for campers (and a starting point for wildlife watching), but will also provide a management action plan if the species highlighted turn out to be at risk or need protection.

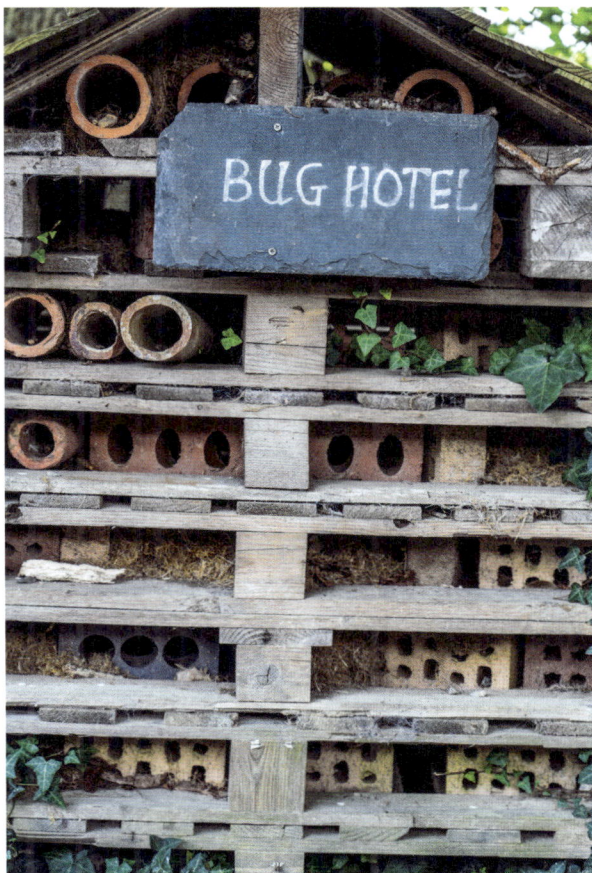

by people thousands of years ago. Generally, they are suited for the climatic and soil conditions in the UK because they have evolved to take their place in the ecosystem. This means they need less maintenance and are also more suited to the insect and invertebrate life they may support – the relationship is symbiotic. Native UK fruit trees, however, are fast disappearing, leaving us with a witheringly narrow selection. Sites that plant fruit trees will allow these to thrive, and provide food, a talking point and, in spring, blossom for the pollinators.

Feeding birds

Birds are in decline in the UK, with species such as the tree sparrow declining by 95%.[10] This is due to a number of factors, including hedgerow loss, changes in farming techniques and the use of fertilisers and pesticides. Feeding birds in winter can be very positive for populations. According to research from Exeter University in 2016, people living in neighbourhoods with more birds, shrubs and trees are less likely to suffer from depression, anxiety and stress. Feeding birds can bring many species to campsites and provide a focus for education and recording species.

Knowing what to see

Taking stock of the kind of species you have present in your campsite will not only provide a talking point for campers (and a starting point for wildlife watching) but will also provide a management action plan if the species highlighted turn out to be at risk or in need of protection. Having an ecology survey can also help you to set a benchmark from which you can grow. As you continue to manage the site for nature you should notice a gradual increase in the number of species.

Stay with good people

Paying decent wages is the first step to getting good staff. Treat them well and train them well and they will be engaged and will do well by you. Being a living wage employer is a good start. Treat people with fairness and equality; hire without prejudice; develop a good crisis and risk assessment plan, and be good people to work for.

Renewable power

Changing to renewable electricity suppliers is easy. You just have to switch. The stuff that comes down the pipes is the same, does the same stuff and keeps your campers equally happy, but with the added bonus of not being generated by burning fossil fuels, which, as we know, is one of the main drivers of climate change. A simple, easy fix – why don't we all do it?

Alternative technologies

Alternative technologies such as solar thermal, solar PV, air source heat pumps, ground source heat pumps and wind can help to reduce costs, as well as the impact of any building or business. Solar thermal, for example, is most effective during the spring, summer and autumn when there is more heat from the sun to warm the water in the elements. Solar thermal can be used with other forms of water heating, which can be called upon if there isn't enough strength in the sun (for example in the winter). This could be an ideal fix for campsites as there is zero cost once the installation is complete; they can be mounted on the roof of toilet blocks; and the hot water is 100% green. Of course, it requires investment, but it will pay for itself eventually.

Campers' charter for recycling

I'm not generally in favour of blaming consumers for the ills of the packaging industry, but, having seen the lack of care with which campers approach recycling on many, many occasions, I believe this is something that campsites can do better. The idea is to ensure that all campers are educated on arrival

↓ Employing alternative technologies produces clean, free energy and can help to reduce the energy demands as well as saving a huge amount of money on energy bills. Solar panels are a clear signal to campers that you care about the environment.

↑ Light pollution can affect all kinds of animals in their hunting, migrating and sleeping patterns, wreaking havoc on their natural rhythms. It can also affect our ability to see the stars in the sky on clear nights, so disabling our connection to the universe.

about the use of recycling bins and where they are on site, and that they sign a form to say they will recycle properly. Make it easy too – mark bins clearly.

Mend and lend camping equipment

Waste is a big problem when it comes to the leisure industry. Items like windbreaks, boogie boards, buckets and spades, wetsuits and even tents get discarded as if they are 'single-use'. The simple solution to this waste – and to get rid of the demand for such items – is to mend and lend them. It will save you sending it to landfill (and paying to dispose of it) and save your campers from having to bring it, especially if they travel by train.

Reductions for cyclists and walkers

Some sites do this already and some won't be able to do this because they don't allow tented camping, but where it is possible it can really encourage campers to arrive in the greenest way possible and to think about how they travel. Rewarding them will encourage it.

Bee-friendly sites

Bees are struggling owing to the loss of habitat and nesting sites, as well as the devastating effect of pesticides and fertilisers. Give them a helping hand by planting flowers that are bee-friendly, set up 'bee hotels' for solitary bees and even consider setting up a hive on the grounds – as long as it's away from campers. Reducing mowing will also help, especially in the spring – dandelions are considered weeds but are nectar for emerging bees in the spring.

Help to buy local

Buying local produce puts money back into the local economy instead of sending it to the pockets of the multinationals. It can help to reduce food miles, supports local businesses and puts your campers in touch with local produce, crafts and people. This can help to create a more authentic experience for campers and allow them to get to know the area better. This could be a list of locally owned shops and independents where campers can buy supplies, or stocking the campsite shop with local produce.

Low-level lighting to reduce light pollution

Light pollution can affect all kinds of animals in their hunting, migrating and sleeping patterns, wreaking havoc on their natural rhythms. It can also affect our ability to see the stars in the sky on clear nights, so disabling our connection to the universe. This disconnect ruins the camping experience. While we might think that we need light at night, we really don't. Some sites remain dark, with a minimum of light at toilet blocks or on pathways. If you have to have lighting – which you don't by law – then keep it low-level so it doesn't spill, and even consider motion-sensitive lighting. It may save money, too.

↓ Wild camping is and can be a cathartic exercise in survival, disconnection from the digital world and reconnection with the natural world. It can make an overnight near home feel more like an expedition and can boost self-esteem — because — amazeballs — you survived!!!! Wild camping makes you self-sufficient, and there is no better way to get closer to nature.

4

Where are you staying? Wild camping

Into the wild
(Carefully does it)

If you are not camping at a campsite or holiday park, then you must be camping 'wild' or staying on someone's land with permission – without facilities. That's what this chapter is about.

Wild camping has long been the Shangri-La of the camping world. It's seen as the ultimate way to escape the constraints of the modern world and is lauded by many as the gold standard of back-to-nature camping. The appeal of wild camping – and by that I mean lightweight camping, done with a backpack or on a bike – is obvious. You escape everything, pitch up where you want, have nothing but nature for company, all done under your own steam, with a minimum of kit and without all the vapid, meaningless crap you left behind at work, at home or at school. There are no campsite fees or rules to obey and no internet or social media to erode your mental well-being.

Wild camping is and can be a cathartic exercise in survival, disconnection from the digital world and reconnection with the natural world. It can make an overnight near home feel more like an expedition and can boost self-esteem because – amazeballs – you survived! Wild camping makes you self-sufficient, and there is no better way to get closer to nature. I get it, totally, have done plenty of it in my life and will always advocate for it because of the benefits it can bring.

Of course, wild camping is not for everyone and no one should feel like they aren't a good enough camper because they prefer campsites. It's your choice.

Similarly, wild camping isn't suitable for just anywhere. Even in places where wild camping is legal there are considerations, especially if you plan on leaving the places in which camp as you found them (the basic level of the leave no trace philosophy), or better. Some environments are more sensitive to camping and trampling than others and should be avoided in order to minimise the disruption to flora and fauna. Even the lightest of camps can have an impact. As the butterfly effect proposes, you may not even see what your impact has been.

But first, let's start with the law. And those who think they're above it.

Fly camping
(Is not wild camping)

Fly camping used to be used as a term for people who walked away from their base camp for a night under the stars with minimal kit. Sadly, following Covid-19, and problems associated with 'camping on the fly', the term has taken on a new meaning in the UK. Now it means people who camp without permission, away from campsites and who leave their kit, along with their rubbish, after they have left. The term, I believe, comes from fly tipping.

Fly camping is not camping. It's basically just trashing the environment and acting as if your actions don't matter. They do, and they will destroy any hard-won relationship that any of us might have had with authority, whether that authority is National Park management, landowners or the National Trust. Fly camping is the reason that is most often cited by landowners as the reason we (the camping public) shouldn't be allowed free access to the countryside.

Just to be very clear: we are not them. Fly camping should be condemned in the strongest terms, and anyone caught abandoning tents in the countryside deserves the full force of the law.

Wild camping and the law
(It's quite simple)

As many will already know, wild camping (and by that I mean camping in public-access areas or on private land without needing the permission of the landowner) is illegal in England and Wales, but legal in Scotland under areas covered by the Open Access laws in the Land Reform (Scotland) Act of 2003. Trespass, for the moment, it should be noted, is a civil offence.

Wild camping is defined by many as lightweight or backpack tent-based camping with small numbers of people staying for one or two nights. You hike in and hike out, or bike in and bike out. No mess, no damage, no problem. Simple. Or is it?

In some places in England and Wales, while not technically legal, wild camping is tolerated, particularly when done discretely and out of the way, often above the fence or enclosure lines on high ground. Some National Parks offer very clear guidance on this, which follow the usual rules:

- Camp away from houses and farms.
- Pitch late and leave early.
- Stay for one night.
- Leave no trace.
- Don't light any fires and do not use disposable barbecues.
- Toileting should be at least 30m (100ft) away from any water source or path, and waste buried at least 15cm (6in) deep and covered over.
- Take all rubbish and food scraps with you.
- Move on if asked to do so by a landowner.
- Don't dig ditches, trample plants or move rocks.

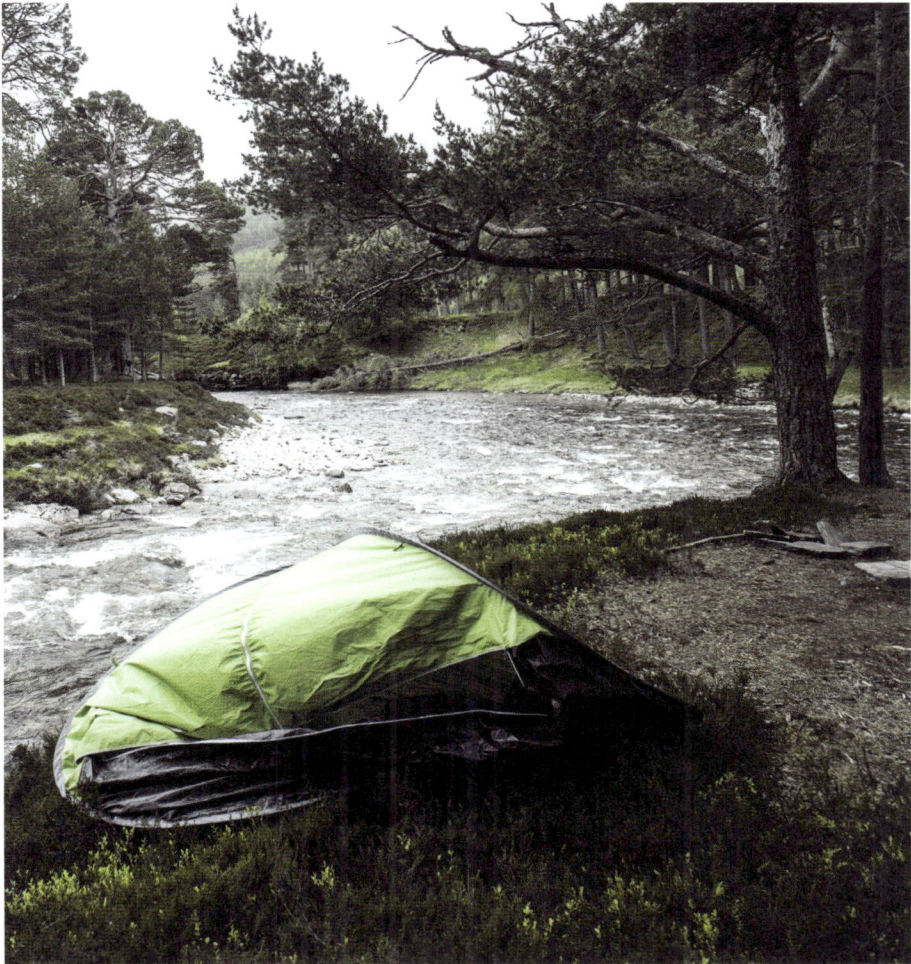

↑ Fly camping is not camping. It's basically just trashing the environment and acting as if your actions don't matter.

Wild camping and you
(Being out there)

No one is going to ridicule you if you don't like the idea of wild camping. Some people can't cope with feeling unprotected and alone and that's absolutely OK. We are programmed to be wary of nature, wild animals and other humans so it's a natural reaction to be cautious.

While there aren't many bears or wolves about these days, there are still humans to worry about and there is always the possibility of being disturbed. That may be by landowners or gamekeepers who want you to leave, by others who just make you feel uncomfortable or someone who poses a genuine threat to your safety. Whichever it turns out to be, their presence can shatter the idea of a peaceful night under the stars and make wild camping unbearable. The only solution, when it comes to personal safety, is to go with people you can trust. Soloing takes a special kind of courage.

I can speak from personal experience that drunk and rowdy humans can be absolutely terrifying for a solo traveller. I spent a night (with permission) in my van in a pub car park in a tiny village near Carlisle in 2021. I was woken by a group of drunken young men shouting, throwing bins about and walking around the van. At one point one of them used a hose to spray the van. I was terrified. I thought about confronting them and asking them to stop but felt that it could have turned nasty at any moment. I couldn't drive away, so just had to lie low until they went away, after about an hour. I wouldn't wish that on anyone. Even inside a locked van it was frightening.

↓ There is no allowance for vehicles — and that includes motorhomes and camper vans — in the Scottish Outdoor Access Code, which means that you cannot just park up anywhere for the night in Scotland, although many believe you can. The Land Reform (Scotland) Act does not cover motorised vehicles and the open access laws do not allow vehicular access.

While you are far less likely to be met by an axe-wielding psychopath or a gang of drunken yobs if you are camping above the treeline in the mountains, the worry can still make you feel deeply uncomfortable. Don't fret about it – if wild camping isn't for you, it isn't for you.

That said, if you can do it and feel comfortable, do it. It may well be the most liberating experience of your life.

Camper van Shangri-La?
(Not quite)

It is worth noting that there is no allowance for vehicles – and that includes motorhomes and camper vans – in the Scottish Outdoor Access Code, which means that you cannot just park up anywhere for the night in Scotland, although many believe you can. The Land Reform (Scotland) Act does not cover motorised vehicles and the open access laws do not allow vehicular access. The Road Traffic Act of 1988 also states that it is an offence to drive on land that is not a road or track without lawful authority. That means you will need permission from the landowner if you intend to go off-road with your camper. Let's not forget that every scrap of land is owned by somebody. The law allows you to drive up to 13.7m (15 yards) away from a road for the purpose of parking, but you still need the landowner's permission.

What this all translates to is this: there is no blanket permission to wild camp in a motorhome or camper van in Scotland. What exists in Scotland is a historical tolerance for motorhomes and camper vans and, it must be said, there are times when that gets stretched. It is up to us, as motorhomers and campervanners, to change people's minds. This means observing the following:

- Take all you need from nature in terms of mental health and well-being, but do not exploit it.
- Give back when you can by litter picking, volunteering or contributing to conservation.
- Get permission from the landowner.
- Do not drive off-road unless you have permission and only in places that can handle it.
- Never empty waste of any kind, black or grey, into the countryside.
- ONLY empty your tanks at approved stops or *aires*.
- Leave your pitch nicer when you leave – pick up your litter and pick up others' litter too.
- Do not light fires unless you have an off-the-ground firepit.
- Bring your own firewood.
- Be nice and move on if asked.

The lost moor (The last wilderness)

In January 2023, a court case brought by hedge fund manager Alexander Darwall against Dartmoor National Park Authority to remove the right to wild camp without the landowner's permission succeeded in the High Court.

In doing so, the court effectively outlawed wild camping in the last place in England and Wales where it was permitted without the permission of the landowner. For campers everywhere, this was tragic news, even for those who had never camped on Dartmoor. As someone who has, using my right to do so, I enjoyed it immensely, feeling empowered by being able to use those rights. Even though I might not wild camp on Dartmoor regularly, I felt deeply saddened by the loss.

Wild camping, and the legal ability to be able to do it, is a notional freedom that symbolises our ability to roam, unhindered by fences, barriers, class, race, gender or sexuality. It is the sense of belonging to the place we call home and of inclusion and fairness. When this last right was removed it felt, to me, like the walls had finally closed in. The enclosure of the Commons, a landgrab by the wealthy that started in the 1300s and resulted in the removal of rights of the common people (to use land to subsist, forage, collect firewood or hunt), was complete.

NOTE: The High Court overturned the ruling in July 2023, so normal camping rights have been returned.

Your right to roam
(And where you can't)

Today, you, as a commoner, camper and outdoors lover, are only allowed on around 8% of the land in England without fear of committing trespass. These limited rights were enshrined in the Countryside and Rights of Way Act (CRoW) of 2000. That includes National Parks, mountains, coastlines, commons, heathland and moors. However, these areas are often remote and out of easy reach of most of the population. As the Right to Roam campaign says on its website: 'access to this land has become a postcode lottery, available to those who live next to it, or who can afford the cost of travel and overnight stays. We urgently need access to nature, its beauty, its space, its flora and its fauna, for our health, our creativity and our peace of mind. In a world of steel, glass and concrete, of stress, ecological detachment and screen-based lifestyles, the countryside is a natural health service that can heal us.'

The other 92% of land in England is in private ownership and is covered

↑ 'We urgently need access to nature, its beauty, its space, its flora and its fauna, for our health, our creativity and our peace of mind. In a world of steel, glass and concrete, of stress, ecological detachment and screen-based lifestyles, the countryside is a natural health service that can heal us.' RIGHT TO ROAM. © Elizabeth Kay

by trespass laws, which, broadly speaking, means that you can be prosecuted in a civil court for damages you may have done to that property (for the value you have taken from the trespass) if you enter a property, with or without knowledge of the ownership, without permission. There is a lot more to this, so do check out Nick Hayes' *The Book of Trespass* (Bloomsbury Circus, 2020) if you want to know more.

How that ownership breaks down has been examined by another writer, Guy Shrubsole, in his brilliant book *Who Owns England?* (William Collins, 2019). To sum it up briefly, he says 'The aristocracy and landed gentry still own around 30% of England, while the country's homeowners own just 5% of the land. The public sector owns around 8% of England; the country's 24 non-royal dukes own a million acres of Britain.'

↓ Wild camping, and the legal ability to be able to do it, is a notional freedom that symbolises our ability to roam, unhindered by fences, barrier, class, race, gender or sexuality. It is the sense of belonging to the place we call home and of inclusion and fairness.

We need access
(We need love)

It seems cruel to me that we, as commoners (with no commons to call our own), are denied this access to nature at a time when we need to fall in love with it. How else will we fight to protect it? It's arrogant of the rich and powerful to assume that they are always the best custodians of the countryside. Those who have created monocultures out of the countryside for industrial agriculture, grub ancient hedgerows, poison raptors, blame and butcher badgers for bovine TB, kill foxes for sport, populate their land with pheasants for shooting, and retain grouse moors as playgrounds for top-rate paying guns are not always the best stewards of nature (or even a part of it) for the benefit of everyone. They can be thugs and vandals, too.

But of course, the law is on their side because we, the commoners, are the ones painted as thugs and vandals, intent on littering and causing damage because, well, we don't understand the ways of the countryside. Ironic? If anything, this makes me want to work even harder to protect nature.

The Outdoor Access Code
(And your duty to it)

Happily, there are places where it is legal to wild camp in the UK, namely Scotland. This is governed by the Scottish Outdoor Access Code 2005, a set of guidelines for users and guardians of the countryside based on the Land Reform (Scotland) Act of 2003. It is a 130-page document, and it is very clear about what we can and can't access and when.

The code sets out the main responsibilities of those using public access rights as follows:

- Take responsibility for your own actions.
- Respect people's privacy and peace of mind.
- Help land managers and others to work safely and effectively.
- Care for your environment.
- Keep your dog under proper control.
- Take extra care if you are organising an event or running a business.

The code makes special mention of respecting Scotland's natural heritage and talks about being careful not to disturb plants and ecosystems. What it doesn't do is refer to specific types of ecosystems or give advice on what kind of ecosystems are more sensitive to camping than others. For more details, see www.outdooraccess-scotland.scot

↓ Happily, there are places where it is legal to wild camp in the UK, namely Scotland. This is governed by the Scottish Outdoor Access Code 2005, a set of guidelines for users and guardians of the countryside based on the Land Reform Act (Scotland) of 2003.

The perfect pitch
(Might not be all it seems)

Wild camping, where permitted, still requires careful consideration if you are to avoid damaging sensitive environments – like the butterfly effect in chaos theory, which says even small actions can have a far greater effect on the world, even though you might never see it. The world is deeply interconnected, and your actions have a profound effect, whatever you do.

The first person to use the term 'ecology' to describe nature as a whole was a botanist called Arthur George Tansley, who stated in his 1935 article, *The Use and Abuse of Vegetational Concepts and Terms* (*Ecology* 16, 284–307), that 'Though the organisms may claim our prime interest, when we are trying to think fundamentally, we cannot separate them from their special environments, with which they form one physical system.' This tells me one simple thing (again): everything you do matters.

The environmental organisation Leave No Trace has recommendations around pitching tents in wild places and suggests, as a basic minimum, camping on 'durable surfaces', such as sand, soil or rock. The rule of thumb is to camp in already impacted areas, especially in places that see a lot of camping, as the impact (and any damage) will already have been made by previous tents. Your presence, as long as you pitch in the same place, will do little to make the damage much worse than it is already.

If you cannot use the same footprint as a previous camper, pitch in places where there is little vegetation or just sand, rock or earth. If there is no bare ground, stick to areas where there are short grasses and plants that are resistant to grazing, such as dandelions and other 'rosette' species (these types of plants are capable of growing back from the root when grazed or trampled).

> **The world is deeply interconnected, and your actions have a profound effect, whatever you do.**

It is the same principle as 'sticking to the path'. Paths are designated as spaces where the collateral damage we make by walking is offset by the benefit we get from travelling to the environment in the first place. It may be a casualty of being trampled by walking boots, but it takes the pressure off the rest of the environment – as long as everyone sticks to it. Using the path avoids lots of boots trampling all over an area and, in doing so, causing more overall damage.

While reading around the subject of making camp in sensitive environments I was pointed towards a 2012 paper from the High Weald Area of Outstanding Natural Beauty in the South Downs National Park of England[1] that discussed 'eco-camping' and the impact of camping and setting up camp in environmentally sensitive areas. It made really interesting reading.

← There is never an excuse to leave litter or to expect someone else to pick up your mess. It's not camping. It's just being a big, entitled, selfish baby.

→ Lighting fires or using disposable barbecues can cause irreparable damage to ecosystems. If there is a firepit there already, use it. If there isn't, make sure your fire or BBQ is off the ground where it cannot damage grass, peat or vegetation.

Pitching your tent on a 'fresh' parcel of land might seem like the romantic thing to do, but it will have a much more profound impact than using a site that someone else has used before. Lots of vegetation, such as bluebells and wood anemones (ancient woodland indicator species), are very susceptible to trampling and can take a long time to recover. The High Weald paper noted research found the worst impact was made by the first to pitch, with those coming after causing little significant damage.

Trampling is cited as the main cause of disturbance on ecosystems, with deep-diving David Cole, an American researcher quoted in the paper, claiming that 'just one night of camping by three people generated 4,000 steps in 100 square feet – an intensity that resulted in each 1m² of ground being trampled 406 times.' This, the High Weald report says, represented an impact 'in excess of the carrying capacity of many plant species found among the ground flora of British woodlands.' Basically, the land may not recover in the same way it was before, so upsetting its balance. Resilient species that favour trampled ground will be quick to recolonise, for example, so forcing out the less resilient species and creating a subtly different woodland than was there before.

On top of this, there are other environmental considerations. Birds are disturbed by the presence of humans and the light pollution and noise we create when we camp. In some extreme cases nest sites may be abandoned, with ground-nesting birds being among the most vulnerable. The RSPB has reported

that during the Covid-19 pandemic, when there were increased pressures from wild camping, several endangered osprey pairs failed to breed due to the proximity of wild campers to their nest sites.

Likewise, mammals can be affected by camping. Compacted earth can make foraging for grubs and insects more difficult and long-term disturbance can cause badgers, for example, to desert their setts or emerge later, so finding it harder to forage for enough food.

The report concluded that camping should be avoided in ancient woodland, lowland heath, and unimproved grassland (meadows) because of the time it can take for these ecosystems to recover.

Perfect pitch
(Do not disturb)

Some thoughts on choosing a wild pitch:

- Pitch in areas that have already been pitched in. Do not disturb fresh ground for your pitch as it only creates more damage. There's no point in reinventing the wheel: a good pitch is a good pitch.
- Pitch in low-grade environments like improved grasslands (grassland that is not species-rich or that has been 'improved' by fertilisers or pesticides) or managed forests (plantations). Avoid environmentally sensitive areas like unimproved meadows, ancient woodland, and heathland, nice as they may seem. They are more vulnerable to damage and less resilient than grassland and wooded plantations.
- Pitch in places where there is less plant ground cover, preferably where there is very little. The fewer plants there are, the less there is to disturb.
- Pitching in open grasslands where the grasses are short, tussocky, possibly grazed (like high moorland) and where rosetted plants grow (low-growing, grazing-proof plants like dandelions) will create less disturbance than pitching in woodland where there are tall, easily damaged grasses, bushes and roots.
- Do not use deadwood to burn for fires as they are habitats in themselves and can support insect life. They are great stores of carbon. Leave them be.
- If you intend to light fires, bring wood with you from managed sources. Only light fires in places where there is no chance of damaging grass or setting light to roots, peat or undergrowth. Use firepits that are raised off the ground to avoid damaging the ground.
- Never use disposable BBQs. They are dangerous, wasteful and cause forest fires every year.
- Avoid camping near setts, nesting sites or roosts to minimise disturbing animals, birds or insects. This tip is also useful if you want to avoid being overrun with ants or badgers, for example.

↓ Pitching your tent on a 'fresh' parcel of land might seem like the romantic thing to do, but it will have a much more profound impact than using a site that someone else has used before. Lots of vegetation, such as bluebells and wood anemones (ancient woodland indicator species), are very susceptible to trampling and can take a long time to recover.

↓ If you intend to wild camp away from organised sites, it helps to know your way around the countryside. Telling the difference between an ancient woodland and a plantation is the most basic of this kind of knowledge. This is where access is important: if you have never known either, how will you know?

- Look for animal routes through undergrowth, to water for example. Avoid pitching on them and you'll ensure they can still be used, plus you'll minimise the chances of being woken by rustling mammals in the night!

What I found interesting about this research is that it gives us very good guidelines for making wild camping *even more* responsible, even when we camp in a way that is lightweight and has minimal impact.

Where we pitch *does* matter and to choose the flattest piece of ground is not really enough any more. Sites should be chosen carefully and with consideration and thought. It might seem to be against the principles of the wild camping ethic but perhaps the best place to pitch your tent isn't just somewhere that someone has pitched before, but somewhere that is actually dedicated to pitching tents. Like a campsite!

That said, if you intend to wild camp away from organised sites, it helps to know your way around the countryside. Being able to identify types of environments is essential because it will enable you to work out where your impact will be minimised. Telling the difference between an ancient woodland and a plantation is the most basic of this kind of knowledge. This is where access is important: if you have never known either, how will you know? You would, of course, be forgiven for not knowing. It isn't necessarily your fault. The blame lies with those who wish to keep you out of the countryside and who see no benefit from it other than to line their own pockets.

Understanding the countryside is something we can all aspire to. Knowing one habitat from another is important when it comes to pitching your tent, lighting your fire, and laying out your bivvy bag. If we camp without regard for the damage we may be doing then all we are doing is 'colonising' nature. We are taking from it without giving back.

> **Actively working to defend [the countryside] is the final, great leap into activism and conservation.**

Being mindful of where you sleep and tread is one move you can make to redress the balance. Being able to identify types of landscapes, plants, birds and animals comes next. Actively working to defend it is the final, great leap into activism and conservation.

Knowing what's what isn't something that's exclusive to people who have grown up in the countryside. Anyone can learn to tell the difference between an oak tree and an ash tree. And it's fun: learning to identify plants can lead you down a long and winding road towards a kitchen bursting with free food, for example. Being able to tell one bird from another can lead you to all kinds of exciting landscapes and places. The first step is having access. And then, of course, learning to fall in love.

↓ Thousands of tents are abandoned at festivals every year. Some may get donated to charity and some may get turned into beach-cleaning bags, but most will end up in landfill or get incinerated for energy recovery.
© Camplight

5

Where are you staying? Festival camping

Rock and roll camping
(Take it home)

In 2019, as part of my work for the 2 Minute Foundation, I worked with Leopallooza Festival in Cornwall to give new life to tents that had been abandoned. The festival was one of the most eco-minded in the UK and had amazing credentials, and the team worked incredibly hard on education, but even so, we still packed away over 50 broken and abandoned tents the morning after the three-day event. They were taken to a workshop in Bude – Rooted Ocean – where they were turned into beach-clean bags. Ironic really, that these 'disposable' items were used to clear up disposable plastic.

The Association of Independent Festivals (AIF), a not-for-profit that represents festival organisers in the UK, estimates that around 250,000 tents are abandoned at festivals every year. Some of those may get donated to charity, some (a very few of them) will get turned into beach-cleaning bags but most of them (around 900 tonnes of plastic) will end up in landfill or get incinerated for energy recovery. Those that sit in landfill will break down over many hundreds of years, leaching chemicals into the ground and generally being really, really shit for the planet.

If you ever wondered why your festival ticket costs so much, this may be part of the reason. Clean-up crews work their socks off clearing up and sorting tents, sleeping bags, inflatables and litter that festivalgoers can't be bothered to sort out, so that all environmental rules and regs are adhered to.

So what can we do about it?

The disposability problem
(With the industry)

There is a big problem with the tent-selling industry. And that is that tents are often marketed as 'festival tents', with the assumption that this means they, like barbecues, plastic cups and plates, are somehow 'disposable'. It's easy to go to a giant outdoor specialist or supermarket and pick up a tent, a couple of sleeping bags and mattresses for under £100. It's even easier to buy them online: search 'festival tent' and you'll come up with plenty of cheap options. Interestingly, only GO Outdoors had a notice about taking your tent home on its search results for 'festival tents'. Chapeau.

Anyhow, this cheap camping stuff is all very good, until your mattress goes down, your sleeping bag is cold and the tent leaks and then breaks. Then maybe you wish you'd spent a little more, huh?

Generally, cheaper, poorly made items are not fit for purpose, and are made thousands of miles away, possibly in factories without brilliant human rights records. Mattresses will puncture, sleeping bags won't be warm enough, tent poles will snap, the nylon will tear and the zips will jam. Come Monday morning, when it's cold and wet and you're hungover and tired and just want to go home, the easy thing is to leave the lot and let the clean-up crews take care of it. After all, it's broken, right?

All this does is contribute to the needless waste that is choking our planet. Oil is being used to make nylon and plastic. It's being manufactured in the Far East and then shipped to you, only for it to be left in a field and then, ultimately, to go into a hole. What a shame it is for all of us that this can happen.

Take it home
(And grow up a little)

That's all there is to it really. Just take it home. There is never any excuse to abandon tents or any other camping equipment. It's not that difficult to pack it up and take it home, so take it home. And if you can't, don't go camping.

← Generally, cheaper, poorly made items are not fit for purpose and will break. Come Monday morning, when it's cold and wet and you're hungover and tired and just want to get home, the easy thing is to leave the lot and let the clean-up crews take care of it. After all, it's broken, right? © Jack Lowe

↑ The Association of Independent Festivals estimates that around 250,000 tents are abandoned at festivals every year. Most of them (around 900 tonnes of plastic) will end up in landfill or get incinerated for energy recovery. © Anna Richards

The pre-pitched rent-a-tent
(Rent-a-mob)

These days, lots of festivals offer tented accommodation that is pre-pitched, so saving hassle but possibly adding to your festival bill by quite a few hundred quid. Glamping pods, bell tents, cubes and geodomes are the order of the day, with bedding extra. The advantages are that you don't have to buy a tent, which will sit in storage until the next festival, or that you might be tempted to leave it behind when you go home. If a pre-pitched tent gets damaged it will be repaired and returned to active service, whereas a lot of cheaper 'festival tents' will just end up in landfill.

Another obvious advantage is that your tent is pre-pitched, which means you will have your own designated space and don't have to fight for a little patch of ground in the free-for-all that are the camping fields.

→ Camplight are a company that take old, abandoned tents from festivals, mend them and then rent them to festivalgoers so they don't have to bring their own tent or spend money on them, so saving money and waste. Genius!
© Camplight

↙ Camplight's model saves waste and can often get you closer to the heart of the action in a pre-pitched field. Campers have less to carry and less to worry about when it's time to pack up on Monday morning. Genius!
© James McCarthy

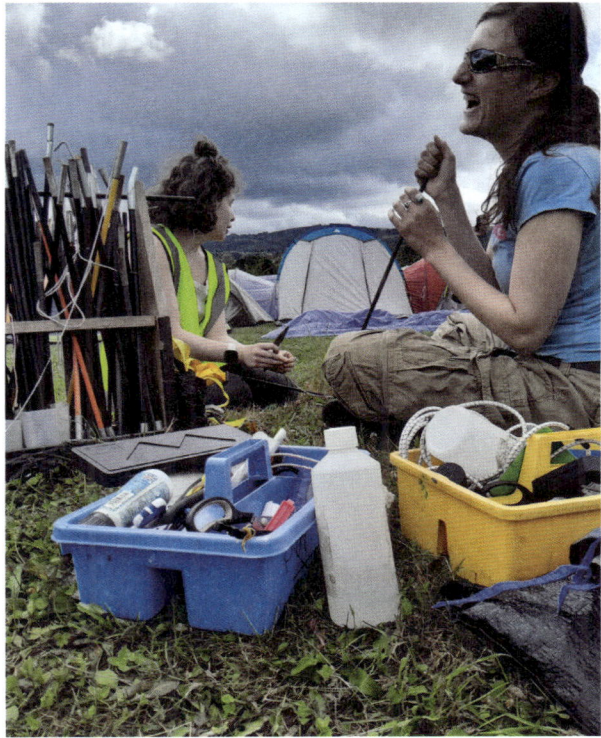

Camplight tent recycling

I spoke to Kieran, the founder of Camplight, one Friday night when he was on his way back from an event in Bristol. After a couple of minutes' small talk, I felt as if I was talking to a kindred spirit. Although from different backgrounds, we had both begun similar journeys by picking up discarded, unwanted stuff. While I was litter picking on the beaches in Devon and Cornwall he was at Glastonbury, cleaning up after festivalgoers. That was in 2010. In the intervening years he's been working hard to turn that waste into something that can help end the waste, and pitching thousands of tents in the process.

He's a recycling wonder and has offered tents for hire at various festivals, including Glastonbury, since 2012. The idea is very simple: he collects tents from festivals, repairs and cleans them and then rents them out at other festivals to festivalgoers who don't want the hassle of carrying and pitching their own tents. The sites are usually close to the action and save you from having to haul heavy camping gear, including chairs, →

sleeping mats and sleeping bags, from the car park to the campsite. If you want to camp with friends in a group, Camplight will pitch your tents all together. You can also hire an event shelter and campfire to gather around when not watching bands. Genius! I love everything about this.

While it is possible to rent tents at other festivals and from other hire companies, what makes Camplight so different is that all the equipment is salvaged, repaired and cleaned, making one festivalgoer's waste another festivalgoer's gold. Prices are typically lower, too. www.camplight.co.uk

Campeazy offers a similar service for events; however, the tents are not salvaged. www.campeazy.com

Tangerine Fields offers 'boutique camping experiences' at some of the UK's major festivals, with geodome tents, Bedouin tents and 'bubble' tents, as well as cubes and bell tents. www.tangerinefields.co.uk

Cardboard tents
(That are good in the rain)

Cardboard tents have been around for a while and have been used at festivals like Glastonbury. They make sense in that they are 'sustainable' and do not contain plastic. The company that makes many of them has put them through a car wash and they can be decorated to make them more fun or easier to identify. At the end of the festival, they can be left and recycled into more cardboard. A neat idea that has its place.

I like the fact that this is a solution that doesn't involve plastic, so from that point of view it's truly excellent. However, the problem I have with this is that while the cardboard tents do save people the hassle of carrying a nylon tent into the festival site – all you need to do is bring a sleeping bag – they still perpetuate the disposability myth that someone else will clear up, that it's OK to leave it, and that recycling is the answer. Recycling isn't the answer. Far from it. Recycling should be the last resort. Reuse is the answer.

Search for cardboard tents at www.kartent.com

← Tentshare is a scheme set up by Rebecca Heap to help reduce the number of tents going to landfill or sitting unused in people's garages. Tentshare allows the owners of tents to rent their tents to campers for festivals or camping trips. Tents can be rented all over the UK. © Camplight

↓ Going glamping makes things a lot simpler.
It means you can go without a tent. Often it will
mean you can do without a cooker, utensils and
plates, too. At the more luxury end of the market,
you can do without bringing a sleeping bag or
sleeping mat. In some places, where there is on-site
catering or where you can order groceries or hamper
in advance, you may not even need to bring food.

6

Where are you staying? Glamping, eco resorts and luxury outdoor hospitality

'However people get into nature, it doesn't really matter.
The more people that get out the better. So many of us have lost the
connections that are vital for our mental health and physical well-being.
Glamping helps us to build love for nature, begin to understand it
and therefore be more likely to protect it.'
Sarah Riley, Inspired Camping

Since I started this book, I have had the nagging feeling that glamping (glamorous camping, as it was coined) might just give us an answer we need to the problem with overconsumption and waste in parts of the outdoors sector.

Going glamping makes things a lot simpler. It means you can go without a tent. Often it will mean you can do without a cooker, utensils and plates, too. At the more luxury end of the market, you can do without bringing a sleeping bag or sleeping mat. In some places, where there is on-site catering or where you can order groceries or a hamper in advance, you may not even need to bring food.

This is when hotel stays start to cross over with camping. It might not be right for all of us, but it has its place in this story. Glamping is big business. As the UK's leading glamping aggregation site, Canopy & Stars (www.canopyandstars.co.uk), itself a B Corp company, said in its 2023 market report that it had increased revenue by over 180% since 2017, doubling in the period from 2019 to 2022.

Glamping can be as simple as renting a wooden hut on a campsite – The Caravan and Motorhome Club offers 'Experience Freedom' breaks on some of its club sites – or as indulgent as staying in a luxury eco resort where there is access to luxury add-ons – like spas, pools and wild swimming. Extras like retreats, experiences and courses may introduce traditional crafts, wellness, knowledge sharing, yoga or outdoor activities like hiking, running or surfing.

The important link in all of these – and all other forms of camping – is that there is a connection with nature. You still get to wake up in nature, hear the birds singing, smell the earth and get to appreciate the beauty of the outdoors. There is still a little of the experience that might be outside your comfort zone that makes it feel genuine.

That this side of the camping industry has increased so much is excellent news for both camping and nature. Glamping, while insulating us from some of the harsher realities of other forms of camping, still offers an opportunity to get closer to nature than you might manage by staying in a bricks-and-mortar rental or a hotel.

Research proves that we need wilderness in our lives to destress and reconnect. And if glamping enables us to start a journey to personal wellness, getting to know and learning to love nature, then it's all positive.

Another positive side of glamping (and camping in general) is that it gives opportunities to landowners to gain an income from their land if they want to rewild it instead of using it for intensive agriculture. Land that might previously have been given over to agricultural practices that discourage biodiversity, use pesticides or fertilisers, which may cause damage to rivers or watercourses, may be managed

Research proves that we need wilderness in our lives to destress and reconnect.

for nature while still bringing in an income. And at the same time those parcels of land are helping people to fall in love with nature, and therefore make them more likely to protect it. In many ways it's a win-win.

Other benefits are that campers can travel light – perhaps by public transport or by bike – or can leave their car at the site while enjoying a car-free unwind. As I have said previously, you don't need kit to go glamping, which means you can spend money on experiences and not things – something that helps to curb wanton consumption and waste. Why would you spend £500 on a tent that you'll use just once a year when you could stay in a bell tent, a yurt or a luxury cabin?

↓ Other benefits are that campers can travel light — perhaps by public transport or by bike — or can leave the car at the site while enjoying a car-free unwind. You don't need kit to go glamping, which means you can spend money on experiences and not things — something that helps to curb wanton consumption and waste.

↑ Luxury camping works as it acts as a cushion between nature and those people who aren't quite ready to go camping yet. But with intentional inconveniences still abundant, glamping reminds us we are in nature and amongst the extremes of it, which makes us feel alive and brings extraordinary life-changing experiences with it.

Why we need to go glamping

By Sarah Riley, founder of Inspired Camping

Now more than ever, we *need* the wilderness! There is heaps of research to prove this is the case. From happier office workers who are given something green to look at, to forest bathing to reduce blood pressure – nature-focused techniques have proven benefits for our health.

However, we are prehistorically hardwired to be outside, camp and move from place to place. It's how our ancestors first survived.

Glamping is an experience that's designed to be enjoyed year-round, in unique and awe-inspiring structures. With accessories to keep us warm in the winter and cool in the summer, such as wood burners, heated blankets and fans, it gives a comfort level for even the least outdoorsy among us.

It offers a hotel-style stay, with a view, under canvas, and if you're really lucky you'll experience something that goes way beyond just accommodation. Many glamping guests have returned home wanting their experience to never end, so it has become completely transformational.

With my work, I am fortunate enough to see things from different perspectives. From the campers' point of view as well as the owner of a unique destination. Great businesses and their owners have a restorative vision about why they are operating and how much they want to give back. Building something amazing in the wilderness, which provides a gateway into nature without harming it, is difficult but it is possible. It just takes a lot of effort.

Luxury camping works as it acts as a cushion between nature and those people who aren't quite ready to go camping yet. With intentional inconveniences still abundant, glamping reminds us we are in nature and among the extremes of it, which makes us feel alive and brings extraordinary life-changing experiences with it.

There's no doubt we are in uncharted waters right now as the human race didn't exist at a time when global temperatures were reaching such heights. In fact, we don't know what's going to happen next. This is a voyage of discovery, and like any voyage there will be tough and difficult times ahead, as well as new beginnings.

But we can make a difference if we do it collectively.

In my opinion, new business owners in luxury outdoor hospitality are the pioneers who are revolutionising the travel industry so a larger number of people can make more sustainable choices about how they spend their leisure time. It's pioneers like this that will nurture future generations of Earth protectors and advocates and help us move towards a more sustainable future.

↓ Part of the joy of camping is the simplicity: getting away from the modern world and its vapid trappings. We go camping to find ourselves in nature, look at the stars above and find something within ourselves that may have been lost. We reconnect with each other, ourselves and the wider world.

7

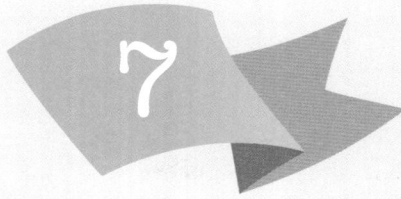

Where have we been?

How the past can inform the future

I'm not a big one for nostalgia. I'm certainly not one for seeing the past through rose-tinted spectacles. Some of it was awful. Some of the camping trips I went on in the 1970s were truly horrific. I spoke to my mother about how we used to camp as a family, and she reminded me of a disastrous trip to Wales in the 1970s when she ended up in hospital with an insect bite and my cousin cried all week because he felt ill. It rained all the time and, inevitably, someone brushed up against the side of the tent and it leaked.

It goes like that sometimes. And it's exactly how I remember it. Definitely no rose-tinted spectacles here!

When it comes to sustainability, however, I have always felt that we should look to the past in order to imagine a better future. Some of the practices that were normal in the past, like growing vegetables in our gardens, will help us to become more resilient in the future, if we can find the time and effort to relearn how to do it.

Growing vegetables is a really good example of how what was normal in the not-too-distant past can help us in the future. After the Second World War, food was scarce and so people gave over their gardens to growing in order to have fresh, seasonal fruit and vegetables. With home-grown produce there are no food miles or packaging to dispose of or recycle, therefore there are no greenhouse gases produced to transport that food to you. You don't rely on supermarkets so much, you save money and you learn how to work with the seasons.

It's such a no-brainer, if you have a garden, of course. Admittedly, however, it takes commitment to turn over your world to 'The Good Life'. And the big supermarkets would probably rather you didn't.

The point is that past practice can give us a steer going forwards. But what about camping?

In many ways, depending on the type of camping we do, it is all about going back to nature, rediscovering roots and reconnecting with the land. Part of its joy is the simplicity of getting away from the modern world and its sometimes-vapid trappings. We go camping to find ourselves in nature, look at the stars above and find something within ourselves that may have been lost. We reconnect with each other, ourselves and the wider world. We are halfway there already. Or are we?

From what I have seen on campsites all over the UK and Europe, some of us may have forgotten to disconnect from our home lives when we go camping. There are lots of us – I'm included in that, too, to some extent, although I draw the line at watching TV – who drag around our home from home with us when we get away to such an extent that the point of getting away seems to have been lost. What's the point of driving all the way to a campsite just to put the telly on? I can't understand that. It's the same with doomscrolling social media, although I understand the need to stay connected. Sadly, it means we always have to be connected, either to the grid or to the internet. Does that umbilical cord stop us from immersing ourselves, truly, in the very best a camping experience can offer us?

Looking back
(To look forwards)

I wondered if there were any aspects of camping in our past that we could learn from. Coming from a long line of campers, I only had to pick up the phone to talk to my mother, herself a veteran camper and the daughter of a Scoutmaster, my Grandfather, who camped all his life. As well as recalling the horrors of our Welsh camping trip she also told me about the types of tents they slept in and that her lilo always seemed to go down in the night. They used canvas bell tents and A-frame tents. Kit was heavy and meant that they travelled by car or, in the extreme cases, by bike.

Bikes and camping
(The golden age of touring)

The 19th century saw the birth of the bicycle, first as the dandy horse, then as the penny-farthing, then, in around 1880, the forerunner of the modern bike, the safety bicycle. There are records of people riding from London to Brighton for the first time, of cycling to London from Liverpool (and being pelted with stones in Wolverhampton), and even cycling the Col du Tourmalet in the Pyrenees some 30 years before the Tour de France first climbed it.

At around the same time (1879), the Bicycle Touring Club was created. Bicycles made touring to places much more accessible, even democratising what was, at first, a rich man's pastime. Bicycles were relatively cheap, and almost

↓ Cycling produces no emissions, gets you closer to nature, keeps you fit and can help you to fall in love with the natural world because you have more time to see it and more chance to really move through a landscape — without hindrance - rather than covering miles in a vehicle.

↓ The Association of Cycle Campers — the forerunner of the Camping and Caravan Club – was founded in 1901 thanks to the pioneering work of Thomas Holding. Cycle camping meant, for the first time, that campers could carry heavy equipment and be truly independent.

anyone could use them, so bringing recreation to the masses.

Interestingly, photography was having a boom at around the same time and according to an essay by Jack Thurston[1] (author of the *Lost Lanes* series) cyclists were quick to jump on the medium. Kodak even brought out a camera that could be bike-mounted for convenience.

After the advent of the motorcar the cycling market crashed, leaving the bike as transport for enthusiasts, or, perhaps fittingly, for the less well-off. As such, the bicycle became a mainstay of the outdoor movement of the 1920s and 30s, along with rambling, gymnastics, swimming and, of course, camping.

My partner, the inimitable Dr Lizzy Kay, spent much of her twenties cycle touring in Europe and South America. She crossed the Andes twice on her Kona mountain bike and finished a tour of Argentina at Tierra del Fuego in the far south. She also cycled through Norway in the early spring – a feat that should not be underestimated. She camped wild most of the time, pitching late and leaving early. She never bought water, perhaps because it was less available, but also because public spring water was readily available in many places, in town squares and at the side of the road. Food was bought daily so as to avoid carrying heavy weights.

Lizzy cooked with a meths or multi-fuel stove because it was light, creates very little waste and could be transported abroad easily without carrying gas cannisters. It also worked in cold conditions, unlike Campingaz, which will not work below around 3°C (37.4°F).

So, what can we learn from this? Cycle touring has always been popular because of its ability to transport you and your luggage without too much difficulty, free of charge, to places you might not otherwise reach. Cycling produces no emissions, gets you closer to nature, keeps you fit and can help you to fall in love with the natural world because you have more time to see it and more chance to really move through a landscape – without hindrance – rather than covering miles in a vehicle. Off-road cycling – bikepacking – can also get you to places where a motor vehicle can't.

Admittedly, the dangers of traffic today are much greater than they were in the 'golden age' of cycle touring. In fact, the figures from the UK government are shocking to say the least. In 2021, 111 cyclists were killed on UK roads, which is about 40% fewer than in 2020 but more than most years since 2008. That said, cycling has had a boom since 2020, with bike sales peaking at 3.1 million, a rise of around 15% on the previous five years, according to the Bicycle Association[2]. Today's bikes are also better equipped to go off-roading than ever before, kit is lighter and safer, and off-road cycling routes are more numerous, and better planned and signposted.

If you have a bike, use it. If you are scared of cycling on the road, tell your MP or local council. Campaign, if you can, for better cycle lanes. Only then will cycling become safer.

Boating and camping
(It was a thing)

In his essay 'River Thames and the Popularisation of Camping, 1860–1980', Oxford historian Simon Wenham claims that boating and camping on the River Thames preceded the formation of the Association of Cycle Campers (1901) and perhaps even the Cycle Touring Club (1878).

In the late 1800s, boating and camping on the upper reaches of the Thames became very popular, with lots of boaters choosing to camp on the riverbank or in boats with canvas awnings stretched over them. Renting boats and equipment from Oxford, many would make their way down the Thames, camping as they went. The essay suggests that lots of the campers caused havoc (or consternation) along the riverbanks as they allegedly caused damage, chopped trees and bushes for fires, left litter and there was even, as Simon claims, 'surreptitious milking of cows'. As you can imagine, this caused tension with landowners along the river and, I am conjecturing, may have been part of the reason why riparian rights have now made 97% of Britain's waterways off limits to swimmers and boaters.

The Thames Preservation Act of 1885, which was seen as an act of preservation, actually prevented free use of the river by making it a requirement of law to register boats and to ban boaters from camping in all but approved places.

What do we learn from this? First, that camping was a heavy activity and the notion of backpacking camping had yet to emerge. Boats were a great way to travel and explore and still be able to carry a heavy tent and equipment. Tents like gypsy benders, patrol tents and bell tents were popular but heavy! They still are.

Paddling a kayak or a SUP down a river is a really great way to travel and gives you a completely different perspective. You can carry a good amount of kit, too. Having SUPed 42km (26 miles) down the Thames in 2021, I loved it but was concerned about restricted access. We felt free, but hemmed in. Even so, perhaps we should reconsider this as a way to travel, considering it creates zero emissions and gets us closer to nature. With careful planning, river trips can be fantastic. *Paddling Map of Britain* (Rivers Publishing, 2022) by Peter Knowles is a great place to start.

Second, the Thames, and camping, were seen as a great escape from Victorian London, enabling men and women to engage in a healthy pastime and 'converse' with nature. Getting out into nature, for the purposes of restoration and enjoyment, is nothing new to us. It was as important to the Victorians as it is to us now and it is vital that we continue to recognise this need in ourselves.

Finally, the message seems to be very clear: that we need to learn from our mistakes. We need to fall in love with the places we go to enjoy to such an extent that we are prepared to fight for the right to continue to enjoy them, otherwise

↑ In the late 1800s, boating and camping on the upper reaches of the Thames became very popular. Renting boats and equipment from Oxford, campers would make their way down the Thames, camping as they went. This isn't so different from latter-day SUP adventurers taking on challenges that also involve wild camping.

↓ Meths stoves (Trangia) are still used because they are light, work in all conditions and run on readily available fuel, methylated spirits, so do not rely on fossil fuels. They are one of the most environmentally friendly ways of cooking in the great outdoors – and are easy to use.

an Act of Parliament will change everything. That means respecting nature, taking everything in and out and leaving it nicer than you found it, if you can – in that way the rich and powerful landowning minority will have no reason to complain that the rabble are not the best custodians of the countryside or to create rules that exclude us in the name of conservation or preservation.

Kit from yesteryear
(And why it's still good today)

Primus stoves and multi-fuel stoves

The Primus stove is a pressure stove that uses heat and pressure to ignite kerosene. It was first sold and advertised in 1892 as the wickless and smokeless stove because it burned clean and without soot. The Primus stove is still available as a multi-fuel stove, although it looks very different today.

The advantage of the Primus stove was that it could be fuelled by kerosene, petrol or diesel, which meant it could be used anywhere in the world without having to worry about transporting gas or using gas in cold climates.

Today, it is still possible to buy multi-fuel stoves that work using the same principles of heat and pressure. They are controllable and versatile, and especially useful in cold climates. However, they do use fossil fuels, and that means the carbon footprint of extraction, processing and transport needs to be considered.

Meths stoves

Meths stoves are favoured by ultra-light campers because there is barely anything to them. They run on methylated spirits so do not rely on fossil fuels – which makes them one of the most environmentally friendly ways of cooking in the great outdoors – and are easy to use, if less easy to control.

Bell tents

The origins of bell tents lie with Indigenous communities in the northern hemisphere, who used skins to cover wooden staves, so creating tepee-shaped lodges. These temporary, triangular dwellings have long been used by militia and itinerant people in Europe and Asia. However, in 1856, an American called Henry Hopkins Sibley is credited with creating the first patent for a bell tent-type design (called the Sibley tent), which was made following his experiences in the North West Frontier. His design, which was easy to put up and easier to carry than a tepee, had just one single centre pole but no vertical sides. Sibley sold this design to the US Army, who used it during the War of Independence.

There is also another side to the story, which is that British military were using bell tents, similar to those in use today, during the Crimean War (circa 1855). They had no interior fire but still used the principle of one pole.

Which came first? Who cares? What this legacy gives us today is a tent design that's spacious, easy to put up, is made from tough, long-lasting canvas and sheds rain well. At the end of its life, it can return to the earth (if made with canvas and wood). Bell tents are cool, are the ultimate in glamping luxury and can last for years if treated properly. Something for the future?

A-frame canvas

So you put up an A-frame with a ridge pole, lob a load of ferns, grasses, leaves over it and, hey presto, you have the first tent. Thereafter you might use animal skins or canvas over the frame and make it into something that can be erected easily, can be used at scale, and will keep you warm and dry when you are on the move. Ta-da. The A-frame tent.

Tents have been used, so historians say, since forever. Romans used them, hunter-gatherers used them, Vikings used them, my grandad used them.

The A-frame design is so well used and loved because it works. Modern designs might include fly sheets and inner tents, but the basic design – two A-frames and a ridge pole – hasn't changed much over thousands of years. Lots of companies still make these kinds of tents although many of them are now made in nylon.

The problem with traditional A-frame canvas and steel-pole tents is that they are heavy (10g/22lbs or more), which makes them impractical for lightweight hiking, trekking and cycle touring. However, they do have their uses, last a long time, and are recyclable and degradable at the end of life.

Ventile

Ventile is a material made from 100% organic cotton that was developed during the Second World War to improve survival rates of pilots who ditched into the sea. The brief for it was to be comfortable and flexible in the cockpit but waterproof when in the sea. As a result of the fabric, which went into mass production in 1943, survival rates of airmen who ditched into the sea increased by 80%. In 1953, Sir Edmund Hillary used Ventile fabric in his garments for the first ascent of Everest.

Ventile is light, quiet, waterproof and strong because its weave is so tight. The fibres, which expand when wet, make it waterproof, too. Ventile is still used in outdoor garments, and is often made from recycled cotton or blended with hemp and linen. It's expensive and has faced criticism for not being as squeaky clean as one might think (for example, containing water-repellent coatings) but it's not plastic, and at the end of its life, which will be long, it will rot down.

I have owned Ventile garments for some time and love the way they feel, even when wet.

↓ The A-frame design is so well used and loved because it works. Modern designs might include fly sheets and inner tents but the design — two A-frames and a ridge pole — haven't changed much over thousands of years. Vango's Force 10 tent, the cover star of this book, continues the tradition with aluminium (infinitely recyclable) poles and cotton canvas.

↑ 'For those who are too scared to ask about disability, I would say keep asking. What can I do? How can I help? What do you need from us? It's becoming easier to tell who is asking these questions when you see innovations like track mats laid across field sites for people in wheelchairs, having quiet sensory spaces at outdoor events, or even just events and owners showing they have collaborated with their local disability group. Seeing things like this – proudly displayed – is what will make people with disabilities more willing to participate. We don't expect instant change or these providers to have all the solutions. But we do want to see that these places have tried.' ALEX GIBBON, COMEDIAN

8

Where are we going?

What we can do to create a better future

This chapter is about the future. It's about where we think we are going as campers, nature lovers and outdoor people. What do we need to do to create a world with sustainability at its heart where everyone is included, has equal opportunities, and can achieve greatness and greenness without being discriminated against because of their background, physical or mental abilities, skin colour or sexual orientation?

So, what do we need to do to ensure that the forests we walk in, the rivers we swim in and the oceans we play in are clean and healthy for everyone, for ever more?

According to my wise, self-classifying, 'wokeist, lefty' mate Sian, 'Historically, enjoying the countryside is massively embedded with classism, ableism, racism and heteronormativity that is only just starting to be deconstructed in a meaningful way. Lots of marginalised communities lag behind in the way they react with the great outdoors. That's not to say that marginalised communities don't participate but visibility is lower so it's a classic self-fulfilling prophecy of privilege and visibility. You can't be what you can't see.'[1]

'Sustainability, too, is another angle that is visibly championed by privileged sections of society.'[2]

Finally, as if to give me the answer we all need, 'If people are provided with the space to give a shit they will (and do) but it's all about environments being inclusive, not exclusive.'

Nature and the outdoors don't discriminate. The benefits of cold-water swimming, forest bathing, camping, cycling, hiking, climbing mountains and being in the outdoors can be just as meaningful for me as they are for the next person. But that assumes that the next person is able to access nature in the same way I can. And we know that not everybody can.

It could be as simple (or frustrating) as not being able to physically get a wheelchair on to Dartmoor, or it could be something else: racism or fear of racism, feeling out of place or unwelcome, being unable to access natural spaces because of transport, overwhelm, money, access to equipment – the list goes on.

Camping shouldn't be a white, middle-class occupation for people in good health, although, if you read the stats you might believe otherwise. Of the many thousands of campers surveyed (around 15,000) in The Camping and Caravanning Club's 'Outjoyment Report', 95% noted their ethnicity as English/Welsh/Scottish/Northern Irish/British (against 74.4% 'white British' in the 2021 Census). Only 14.5% came from households with a household income of less than £20,000, and only 3.5% said their health was poor (against 9.6% in the 2021 Census). The Camping and Caravanning Club are doing well in addressing this, it must be said, but it seems that there is still much for all of us to do.

According to the 2021 report from the Campaign to Protect Rural England (CPRE), which looked at access to the English countryside, not everyone enjoys equal access. 'Data shows that ethnic minorities have on average 11 times less access to green space. And, of the time people from BAME [the term used for identification in the original research] backgrounds spend in green spaces, only 15% of it is in the countryside. This is compared to 38% for people from white backgrounds. For children, we see the same pattern: of their visits to the natural environment, 20% of children from a BAME background visit the countryside compared to 40% of white children.'[3]

While nature won't discriminate, the climate crisis can and will. In a press release from London City Hall in 2022 it was stated that 'analysis from City Hall shows Black, Asian and Minority Ethnic Londoners are more likely to be affected by the impact of the climate crisis.'[4]

It is well documented, too, that those with the smallest carbon footprints, who have the smallest impact on the natural world, will be those worst affected by the climate crisis. It is the stupid, selfish, rich white men who run the fossil fuel companies, water companies and agricultural, pharmaceutical and chemical corporations who are doing the real damage to our society, not the gay couple doing a beach clean, the Asian kid riding his bike in the Peak District or the physically challenged girl who just wants to go camping.

It shouldn't be this way. Everyone has the same rights to the planet – and the rights to camp and benefit from nature – because it belongs to all of us. At least it should belong to all of us. As we know from campaigns like Right to Roam, and of course the small matter of the last thousand years of British history, this is just not the case. Money and power control the land, and that controls the access and therefore the ability to benefit from, and care for, nature.

For thousands of people who may be disadvantaged, live in deprived areas or who have access issues, going camping may be the only time they have a chance to get to know and fall in love with nature and the natural world. That makes

↓ Nature and the outdoors don't discriminate. The benefits of cold-water swimming, forest bathing, camping, cycling, hiking, climbing mountains and being in the outdoors can be just as meaningful for me as they are for the next person. But that assumes that the next person is able to access nature in the same way I can. And we know that not everybody can.

↑ 'I have bad knees and poor eyesight but I love being outdoors. I am doing my Gold Duke of Edinburgh award and this makes me really happy. My instructor is helping me. My mum always says "It's about what you CAN do that matters." I would like all my disabled friends to be able to go camping just like me.' DAISY GREEN

the responsibility of the camping and outdoor industry even greater than it has ever been to do the right thing. The opportunity – to welcome everyone – is an opportunity that we cannot miss if we are to have a positive influence on the planet. When it's done right, the lessons learned in nature and in the countryside will be taken back home. Those lessons, and the actions that follow, will benefit all of us. A spark, lit by a campsite that's doing its best to welcome nature, a manufacturer that's focused on sustainability, a charity that inspires a love for nature or a person who welcomes everyone with a smile when it's needed most, could turn into the kind of raging, hopeful firestorm that we desperately need if we are to turn things around. Inspiration is sometimes all it takes.

We have much to do
(And not all of it is that hard)

When it comes to clean air, water and countryside, there is much to do, too, especially for those who might suffer more from the effects of congestion, pollution or poor air quality than those with privilege (people who live in deprived areas are more likely to suffer as a result of air pollution, for example).

As campers, we can choose to spend our money with campsites that are doing the right thing (see Chapter 2), love our gear for longer, repair gear that is broken, buy, if we must, from companies that are also doing the right thing (see Chapter 2), rent out or donate our unused gear, support camping clubs that have strong sustainability goals (and have actually achieved them), and behave impeccably ourselves.

We can pick up litter, contribute to local community projects, support the communities in which we travel, volunteer, avoid making any kind of mess and tread more lightly by changing the way we travel and camp. We can sign petitions and take to the streets too. Everything we do matters. Our voices also matter, and it's up to us to use them and, if we can, to help others use theirs.

As I have said before, we can fall in love with nature and encourage others to do the same, because it is only by falling in love with nature that we will find the fight to defend it.

I don't know about you, but I want to wake up in green spaces that are natural and wild. I want to see native forests thrive, engorged with epiphytes sucking up the clean, pure air. I want to hear the call of the birds and the crash of the rut. I want to be able to camp in places that are teeming with insects, bats and birds, with red squirrels and pine martens bending branches, mesmerised by the evening murmuration. I want to dive into rivers where fish tickle my feet and kingfishers flash brilliant blue as I swim. I want to surf in clean, unpolluted seas, where cetaceans glide tangle-free and long strands of kelp pump pure oxygen into the air for me to breathe.

I want salt on my skin, dirt on my feet and joy in my heart. And I don't mind working for it. How about you?

We need to talk about nature
(In a different way)

I have long been incensed by the surfing media and the way it describes the sport it represents. The language, often based on the notion of domination and aggression, uses words that are testosterone-filled and full of destruction, most likely to attract a younger, largely male audience. When surfers make turns on a wave they are described as slashing or slaying the waves. Good surfers rip and tear it up. As hell-men hell-bent on dominating the surf, they charge down the waves like rhinos. Boards that are used for larger waves are even described as rhino-chasers. As far as I am concerned this is macho bullshit. I have surfed for almost 40 years and have never once felt that I dominated the surf. Every single time I have entered the water to surf it is nature who has the upper hand.

Outdoors writing can be the same. Peaks are conquered, as if they have bent to the will of the climber. They are scalps to be claimed as trophies. In both cases nothing could be further from the truth. Nature wins every time and those who succeed in extreme places and in extreme conditions are merely dancing at the edge of possibility. Surfers are only able to ride huge waves because of the jetskis that tow them in. Climbers are only able to climb the tallest peaks because of the technology that puts them there. It's clever, but it's not necessarily smart. When that technology fails, disaster follows.

We need to forget the Billy Big Bollocks stuff and learn to accept that we need to work alongside nature if we are to succeed. Contrary to popular religious beliefs, we do not have dominion over the Earth.

The problem with domination is that it reduces the person or thing being dominated to second-class status and implies that it is OK to abuse it, use it up or exploit it. It demeans it to the point where we don't care if we destroy it. In the same way that aggressors aim to dehumanise their enemies, if we demote nature, it enables us to destroy it for personal gain or profit without conscience. If we reduce it to being nothing more than a resource, it becomes something we can take without care.

We are part of nature and must not forget it. We cannot bend it to our will. The mountain doesn't cower to man once it has been climbed. The storms don't stop because we slayed the waves, and to think it is any other way is nonsense.

The sooner we realise that nature isn't ours to use up, the better. If that means changing the language we use to describe it, then so be it. We can climb mountains, not conquer them. We can ride waves instead of ripping them to pieces. A simple shift in how we talk about nature and our experiences within it could be one way to develop a new relationship with it.

↓ It is well documented that those with the smallest carbon footprints will be those worst affected by the climate crisis. It is the stupid, selfish, rich white men who run the fossil fuel companies, water companies, and agriculture, pharmaceutical and chemical corporations who are doing the real damage to our society, not the gay couple doing a beach clean, the Asian kid riding his bike in the Peak District or the physically challenged girl who just wants to go camping.

↑ 'The lack of diversity that is a reality of green spaces in the UK is thrown into stark contrast when we consider figures from 2020 which showed that just 1% of visitors to UK National Parks were people of Black, Asian or ethnic minority backgrounds.'
SHELL ROBSHAW-BRYAN

Camping as a person of colour

By Shell Robshaw-Bryan, camper, writer, marketeer and all-round superwoman, who bounced back from a serious spinal injury in 2014 to start a blog about camping and all things outdoorsy.

Feeling at ease in predominantly white environments is a direct result of my upbringing in the 1970s (the only non-white child in my primary school for many years), and choosing as an adult to remain living rurally, so I'm acutely aware of the lack of diversity I'm exposed to on any given day. So much so, I'm always delighted and often surprised when I see someone else with dark skin close to where I live!

For people of colour who are more used to a multicultural environment, I can fully understand how daunting venturing into the countryside or visiting one of the UK's 15 National Parks might feel to them. The lack of diversity that is a reality of green spaces in the UK is thrown into stark contrast when we consider figures from 2020, which showed that just 1% of visitors to UK National Parks were people of Black, Asian or ethnic minority backgrounds.

The reality is that heading outdoors can be extremely daunting and the lack of diversity and representation means that it is easy for people with darker skin to conclude that hiking, camping and outdoor pursuits aren't for people who look like them.

This is one of the reasons why I believe camping has such an important role to play. For me, it was the activity that got me into the outdoors and eventually led to me walking up mountains and swimming in lakes for fun. Camping was my gateway to realising how big a role nature plays in my well-being and how much I love and benefit from being outdoors, and I think camping can play a crucial role for others who might not think of themselves as being outdoorsy or nature lovers.

Camping can provide a really gentle introduction to enjoying a very different way of life. Slow living is gaining in popularity as we become increasingly overloaded with the expectation to be connected 24/7, and sitting in a tent with a good book or around a campfire with friends, or simply lying on your back with your kids cloud- or star-gazing can provide a deep joy because it slows us down, anchors us in the now and grounds us.

Regardless of ethnicity, camping is an activity I strongly believe can lead to the discovery of a love of nature and the natural world, which may have remained forever unknown had that first accessible step of spending an extended period of time outdoors not occurred.

Part of what I do aims to normalise people who look like me doing things outdoors. I also document a lot of my solo micro-adventures as a way of demonstrating that safety in the outdoors in the UK has never been something I've worried about, either as a woman or as a woman of colour. Similarly, I have never once been on the receiving end of any overt hostility while camping or doing any of the multitude of activities I love to do outside.

I spent a few nights away on my own recently, cycling, swimming and camping. When I'm going solo, I choose to stay at a campsite rather than wild camp, which is down to personal preference, and the campsite I chose was, predominantly, caravanners.

After putting my little tent up and having a walk around the campsite to explore, I was acutely aware that I'd not seen any other person of colour. It can feel so daunting, and even more so to those who don't already feel confident in an environment with little or no ethnic diversity.

As usual, however, my experience was a positive one. Everyone was incredibly friendly and when I forgot the car park barrier code and went running up to a couple of older gents stood chatting between their caravans, they were quick to help me.

It's a sad reality that as someone who's brown, I can't just assume that people will be kind or helpful when approached with courtesy and good manners. Unfortunately, though, given the politics of the UK and the less-than-tolerant stance on race and immigration of some, it's usually somewhere in the back of my mind that anyone I encounter could respond to me with hostility.

This can create a huge barrier and stop people wanting to travel and socialise outside of the multicultural areas that may be familiar and safe to them. This is especially so when they might have seen something in the media that reinforces the belief that the countryside is predominantly for white people, and it's understandable that the fear of potentially being made to feel unwelcome and out of place can put people of a Black, Asian or ethnic minority background off discovering the outdoors in the first place.

That's such a shame because the myriad benefits offered by the outdoors are really easy to access. Even those in cities can benefit from spending time mindfully exploring green spaces like parks, and the mental health benefits can have such a positive impact. I feel like I'm on a mission to share the joy I experience when I'm outdoors, which is a driving force behind my blog and what I do on social media.

From my very first 'proper' walk in the Lake District a little over a decade ago, I have felt nothing but acceptance in the outdoors here in the UK and it makes me so happy to see the valuable work that people like Zahrah, the Hillwalking Hijabi, and wild swimmer Winnie Poaty are doing to promote diversity, which even just ten years ago was something that you didn't see.

People like them, and the brands that work with them, are flying the flag for racial diversity in the great outdoors and, anecdotally at least, I'm gradually seeing an increase in the number of people from Black, Asian and ethnic minority backgrounds who are accessing the countryside, coastal regions and our National Parks.

We've come a long way in the last decade alone, but we still have some way to go. I'm by no means wanting to be wrapped up in cotton wool or demanding safeguarding rights different to anyone else's, but I do like the notion of being an ally. I'd love to see something like a universal 'no space for hate'-type campaign or even a voluntary programme that could be adopted by campsites, glamping sites, outdoor businesses and retailers to help make it clear that they stand against discrimination, and that the outdoors is a safe space for everyone to access, regardless of race, gender or any other differences.

At the same time, I feel like people like me have a duty to not only represent people of different ethnicities but to educate them too. In my experience, fellow outdoor lovers will welcome anyone who treats the great outdoors with the respect it deserves.

For those who grew up in the countryside or were taken on hill walks as kids, how to behave in green spaces will, of course, be second nature, but that's not the case for all. While much of it is down to common sense, not all aspects of the countryside code or camping etiquette will be apparent to those who are unfamiliar. This ongoing education not only ensures that the great outdoors can continue to be enjoyed by all, with as little negative impact as possible, but it can help give people the confidence they need to venture outdoors and discover it.

When people are unfamiliar and disconnected from nature, it stands to reason that they will place less value on the natural world. That's bad news as far as conserving our countryside goes. Encouraging and welcoming a more diverse range of people into the great outdoors means they are much more likely to place value on it and help advocate for it. That means more people potentially supporting green initiatives designed to help maintain and enhance our beautiful woodland, National Parks and green spaces, which can only be a good thing in terms of sustainability.

Green camping with a disability

By Karla Baker, a full-time powerchair user with the genetic condition spinal muscular atrophy (SMA). She loves nothing more than immersing herself in nature and exploring new places, and travels across Europe in an adapted caravan with her partner, Stephen. She is a multi-award-winning writer and is passionate about sharing her adventures to prove that travel and nature isn't off-limits to people with disabilities and chronic illnesses – especially those who use a wheelchair full time. When she's not writing for magazines or creating content for her accessible travel brand, Adventure Wheels, you'll find her in the mountains, forest or by the sea!

By now we are all becoming more and more aware of the importance of being green. We've moved on from hypothetical possibilities to scientific evidence, with headlines painting a stark picture of what the Earth could look like in the not-too-distant future if we don't all ACT NOW! But how easy is it to make a

↑ 'People with disabilities are often left reliant on having their own car, but when you take into account the limited options for electric WAVs (wheelchair-accessible vehicles), it's easy to understand that there is no solution that satisfies both accessibility and eco-friendliness. I would have to say that being green to the extent I would like to be is certainly an able-bodied privilege. At present, it is often a matter of doing the accessible thing or doing the green thing. Never both.' KARLA BAKER

difference when you have a disability?

Although society as a whole is gradually waking up to the changes that need to be made, I feel like the world of disability has some catching up to do. For many of us, the choice is simply out of our hands.

You won't be surprised to hear that disabled people, on average, spend more time in the hospital environment than anyone else. We are no strangers to single-use gloves, syringes, tubing, and more. Of course it's important to remain sanitary under hospital conditions where cross-contamination is an issue, but for many of us, the difficulty of being green extends into our home lives too.

I personally need an electric wheelchair to get around, a ventilator to breathe overnight, and receive my nutrition via a tube in my stomach. All of these are obviously vital, but you can imagine how many disposable medical supplies I go through each month, many of which come individually wrapped in single-use, non-recyclable plastic.

It's not just people with medical needs that struggle to be green though. Simply getting around as a wheelchair user can create a larger carbon footprint (treadprint?) than our able-bodied counterparts. In an ideal world, we would wheel from one location to the other 'on foot', but bumpy, uneven pavements littered with more wheelie bins than dropped curbs, prevent us from doing so. The next best thing would be to travel by bus, but again this isn't always an option due to inaccessible public transport, and more often than you'd think, grumpy bus drivers who just can't be bothered to stop and let the ramp down.

People with disabilities are often reliant on having their own car to travel from A to B, but when you take into account the limited options for electric WAVs (wheelchair-accessible vehicles), it's easy to understand that there is no solution that satisfies both accessibility and eco-friendliness.

Thankfully, small changes are being made, but they're not nearly enough, and not happening half as quickly as they should be. Therefore, I have to say that being green to the extent I would like to be is an able-bodied privilege. At present, it is often a matter of doing the accessible thing or doing the green thing. Never both.

However, it's important to remember that being green is not black or white. It's fluid, with varying levels that everyone can achieve. While there are many things beyond my control, there are plenty of ways that I can make a difference…

It's well documented that camping/caravanning is one of the most environmentally friendly ways to travel – it also happens to be one of the few things that I, as a disabled person, am not naturally at a disadvantage for when it comes to being green, as my carbon footprint is not significantly greater than campers who don't have a disability.

And, in many ways, green camping and disability go hand in hand. Environmental impact aside, I would not choose to travel by plane anyway, because it's a horribly inaccessible mode of transport. And having a solar panel fitted to my caravan was initially a safety net that would allow me to continue running my ventilator and charge my powerchair in the event of a power outage, but is has since become a renewable source of energy that allows me to camp completely off-grid.

Another reason that green camping and disability go hand in hand is because, statistically, people who modify a caravan, camper van or motorhome to suit their access needs will keep their vehicle for longer than average. Not only does it cost a lot to have these modifications made but, generally, if we find something that works, we stick with it (I write this from the comfort of my 14-year-old wheelchair, because if it ain't broke, why fix it?!). Keeping vehicles for longer saves your pennies, keeps the comfort of continuity, and reduces waste. Everyone's a winner! (Except for the manufacturers who put sales above environmental impact.)

Like a lot of people who enjoy camping, one of my favourite aspects of this pastime is that it allows me to fully immerse myself in nature – sandy beaches, luscious woodland, waterfalls and mountains will never fail to feed my soul. I feel like this has only made me more aware of the importance of being green. After all, how can you enjoy escaping into the natural wonders of the world, and not want to protect it for future generations?

Luckily, my wheelchair is robust enough to withstand my adventures. It's not specifically designed for off-roading (it's more of a Rolls-Royce than a Land Rover), but I certainly put it through its paces, regularly taking it through grass, gravel, mud and even hard-packed sand. Through all of this it has been reliable and can go at least 16km (10 miles) on a single charge, meaning that I only need to recharge it every few days, which can easily be done through the solar panel when needed.

Of course, there are still improvements to be made, and it could be easier for disabled people to be green, but whether you have a disability or not, it's always important to do what you can.

Why camping is the greener choice for me

It enables me to fully immerse myself nature.

It suits my access needs.

More environmentally friendly than travelling by aeroplane.

The solar panel creates a renewable source of energy and allows me to camp completely off-grid.

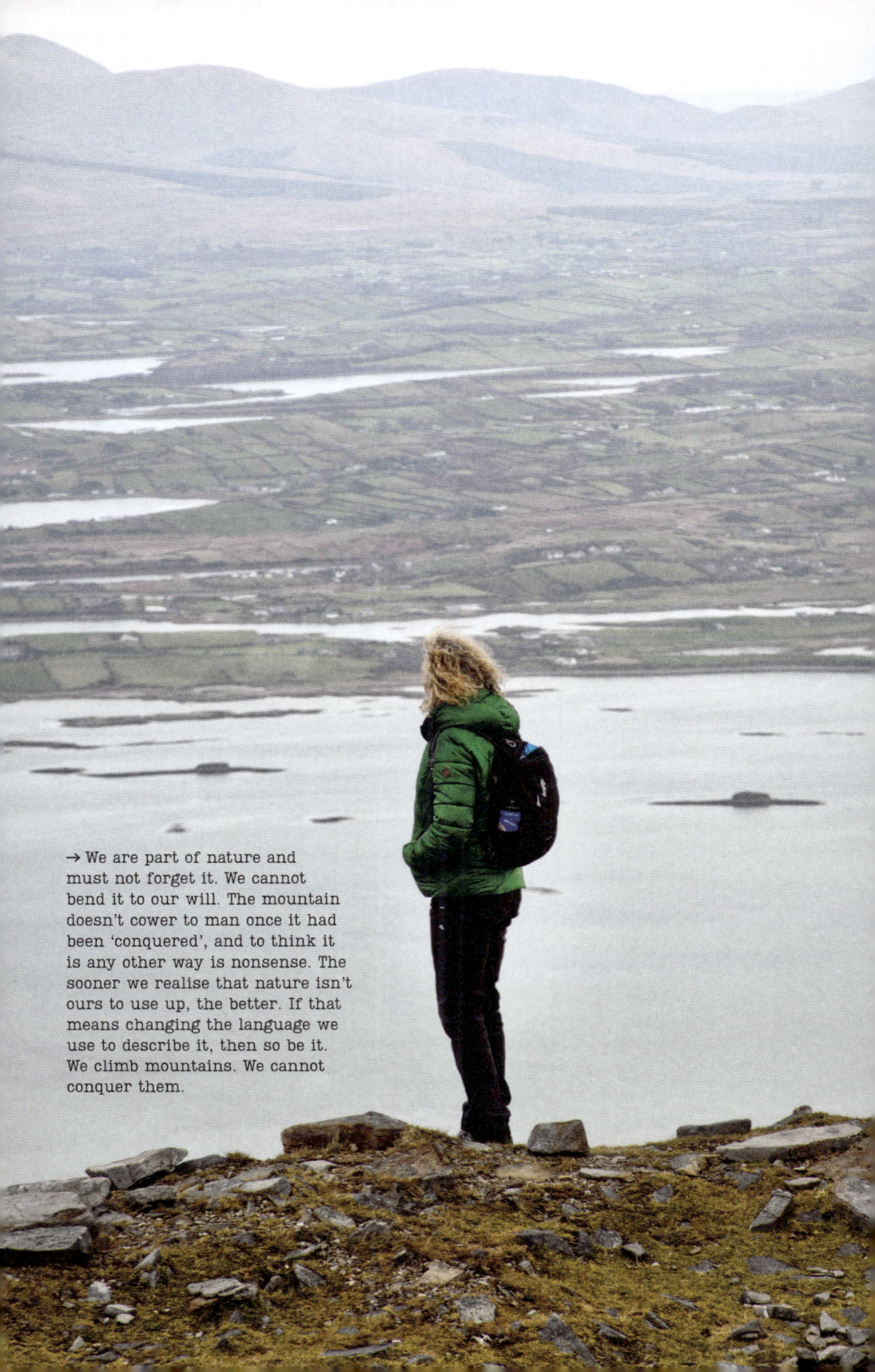

→ We are part of nature and must not forget it. We cannot bend it to our will. The mountain doesn't cower to man once it had been 'conquered', and to think it is any other way is nonsense. The sooner we realise that nature isn't ours to use up, the better. If that means changing the language we use to describe it, then so be it. We climb mountains. We cannot conquer them.

Accessibility for all

Jeantique Hommel (she/her) is a passionate outdoor enthusiast and nature lover from London. She is also disabled, autistic, queer and Jewish, and passionate about breaking down systemic barriers and challenging the status quo. She is part of team United We Climb, who help people facing systemic barriers such as racism and ableism to access climbing and the outdoors. Along with friends, she recently set up the UK Paraclimbing Collective for people with any disability, neurodivergence, mental health difficulty, sensory difference, and more. She is also an occupational therapy student, and enjoys writing and public speaking when not scaling a wall!

Unfortunately, as a disabled outdoor enthusiast, camping is not the most accessible activity! My disabilities get in the way of camping before I have even stepped foot on a campsite. I don't drive for health-related reasons, so a major obstacle is figuring out if and how I can actually get somewhere. Chronic pain, joint and cardiac issues dictate that hiking, hills and heavy rucksacks are not something I can do much of. I might need a trolley when others have a backpack, and mobility aids can be a nightmare when combined with muddy, wet and uneven surfaces.

Disabled life often necessitates planning for unique medical needs and unexpected events, so having clear, user-friendly information before any trip is invaluable. It is simple to make virtual information and booking accessible, but these considerations are often overlooked. Some form of national accessibility directory for campsites (remembering that accessibility does not look the same for everyone) would prove very beneficial.

The actual activity of camping is also very tricky to navigate. I need access to sanitary toilet facilities to attend to my medical needs safely, and I need to be able to take and use my medical supplies, and dispose of them appropriately, without feeling guilty that so much of this involves single-use plastic. Providing a way to move around in uneven terrain no matter what the weather, light levels or type of mobility aid I might be using is essential for being able to get around safely. Most campsites don't have electricity, which is essential for some of my medical needs, but something few non-disabled people are aware of. Not every corner of a campsite needs to have all these features, but at least part of it should be set up to cater for anyone who wants to camp.

However, activities that are promoted as being more accessible (such as glamping) are often also significantly more expensive. Disabled folk deserve access to the outdoors without having to pay extra, especially as many of us face additional financial impacts as a direct consequence of being disabled.

As much as I love going off-grid, it isn't always safe. Signposting to the nearest medical services and the option for mobile connection would provide reassurance in case of emergency and the need to seek medical help. Shuttle buses, flat pathways and local grants, or working alongside disabled charities for ongoing consultancy and adventure planning, could open up shared relationships and new opportunities. Options to rent equipment such as tents and air mattresses could also serve multiple purposes – not just financial and practical, but also environmental, by encouraging campers to not rely on their cars to get there.

When I go on adventures, I am usually dependent on my partner and friends, many of whom are also disabled, which means I often end up staying in a nearby hostel, or simply not going. This is costly and inconvenient, and doesn't help feelings of social isolation, but it is often the only option given the circumstances.

I would love to go camping more, but currently this is rarely possible. A lot of camping practices inadvertently exclude disabled people because being green is a privilege that many of us don't have. Investing in creative ways to improve sustainability, without sacrificing accessibility, is essential to ensure the camping industry is truly disability inclusive!

→ 'I would love to go camping more, but currently this is rarely possible. A lot of the practices promoted within camping inadvertently exclude disabled people because being green is a privilege that many of us don't have. Investing in creative ways to improve sustainability, without sacrificing accessibility, is essential to ensure the camping industry is truly disability inclusive!'
JEANTIQUE HOMMEL

9

How are you getting there?

Take a deep breath
(And fill your lungs with joy)
Why how you get there matters

This chapter is about transport, and how you can make your transport greener. This is relevant in a number of ways:

1. You'll be reducing your impact (see below) by travelling in a greener way.
2. You can benefit personally from choosing greener options in terms of your contact with nature, health and well-being, never mind saving money and avoiding pollution, congestion and stress. Fill your lungs with joy!
3. Your actions will influence others. By choosing the greenest transport options available, you'll send out a message to those running it – councils, government, operators – that you want more of it. It's very simple: if you want to cycle more, call for more cycle lanes. If you want better trains, use them, and call for better services. If you want to walk more, call for the right to roam and for more footpaths. Your power, as a consumer, is the power to reward success.

In the same way, if you fly or drive more it's a clear message to the fossil fuel and aeronautical industries that you approve of what they are doing – they knew about the effect on the climate of burning fossil fuels as early as 1977 – and want them to do more of it.

← Your actions can influence others. By choosing the greenest transport options you send out a message to those running it – councils, government, operators – that you want more of it. It's very simple: if you want to cycle more, call for more cycle lanes. If you want better trains, use them and call for better services. If you want to walk more, call for the right to roam and for more footpaths.

Your carbon footprint
(and why it's not your fault)

In the early 2000s, Big Oil psychopaths British Petroleum (BP) hired a global advertising giant, Ogilvy & Mather (O&M), to slant the use of fossil fuels on to the end user. O&M came up with the idea of the personal carbon footprint, based on a previous idea of an 'ecological footprint', which had been in use for some time.

What the carbon footprint does is put the blame for climate change firmly at your door. It is up to you to reduce your carbon consumption by your everyday actions. In doing that, Big Oil gets itself off the hook, when really it's Big Oil that is responsible for suppressing technology and casting doubt on the notion of climate change.

It is much like the Keep America Beautiful organisation, which was launched in 1953. The main funders were, and still are today, Coca-Cola and Pepsi. The campaign allowed them to blame the public for littering in order to take the focus away from the fact it was *they* who were producing the litter. As with BP, the only interest was financial.

What do we do about this? We need to keep our eyes on a brighter, safer, cleaner future. Imagine a world with more of nature protected by law and better access to it. Think about what it would be like to live in a world where meadows are buzzing with insects, the oceans are teeming with fish and there are more places we can camp, more bees to pollinate crops, more opportunities for enjoying nature and cleaner rivers to swim in, with better access for all. We have to act accordingly.

Having just rubbished the notion of a personal carbon footprint, I have to say it is now a universally accepted measure of the impact transport and other activities have on the climate. That just shows you the power that Big Oil's gaslighting has had upon us. Since it is designed to make you feel guilty, I think we should look at it with a certain amount of cynicism, in that it shouldn't be the only impact we look at, even though it is still relevant.

While it is important to look at impact in a negative way so we can avoid it, and understand why we should avoid it, I believe that we should also look at the positive impacts of the way we travel. Instead of thinking about the damage you do when you fly, let's think about the joy you might feel when you look at less impactful ways of getting there!

→ What do you want from a camping trip? Congestion, pollution, noise and aggravation? Do you want to sit in traffic? Do you want to be near barking dogs or rumbling traffic? Do you want to be sitting on a motorway for hours, queuing to get into a beach car park or fighting hordes to get a snack, ice cream or into an attraction?

The best way to travel
(And how it makes you feel)

There are lots of questions to answer here. What is the greenest choice? How can it fit into your camping trips? Is it possible to travel 'lightly' when camping? How can we make it better? How can you mitigate using less environmentally friendly travel methods if you have no choice?

I have to admit that driving means freedom to me. I totally get it and have based a large part of my career on driving camper vans and motorhomes as the 'greener choice' (compared with flying). As time has moved on and the situation has become more critical, however, I am beginning to realise that, actually, it isn't that much of a greener choice any more. I have also realised that there is more to it than being fixated by my carbon footprint: there are other ways in which my favourite form of transport affects the places I go.

And that's led me to rethink how I camp and travel in some profound but also tiny, yet effective, ways.

Why do you go camping?
(In case you forgot)

Back to basics for a minute – because that could affect how you get there.

There are lots of reasons for going camping. I go because I love it. I love being outdoors and waking up in beautiful, wild places. I like roughing it a little. I like silence at night, seeing the stars and hearing the birds twittering in the morning. I like being close to places that are interesting or attractive or that offer me the chance to surf, swim or hike. I also like that it's cheaper than staying in a hotel and offers me more flexibility. I like being able to leave if I want to and I like the opportunity to see new places. I also like the ability to switch off and do something different – eating outside, stargazing, walking, exploring; all those things are important to me.

What I don't want from camping is the kind of stuff I can get at home: congestion, pollution, noise and aggravation. I don't want barking dogs or rumbling traffic. I don't want to sit in traffic on a motorway for hours, queuing to get into a beach car park or fighting hordes to get a snack, ice cream or into an attraction. I want peace and quiet, calm and serenity. And I guess that begins with me, right?

Some people camp because it is the cheapest choice. But I'll bet that many of them will also go for the solitude, the peace, being in nature, unwinding and getting away from normal life.

And I would argue, again, that how you get there – and set the tone for your trip – matters.

↓ What would be the greenest camping trip? You walk out of your front door, with a pack you've had for years, containing a tent you've had for years, in clothes that you've had for years, with food you've prepared yourself, from ingredients you bought at a plastic-free shop. Impossible dream? Not really.

↓ There are 20,500km (12,739 miles) of National Cycle Network in the UK. Between 2019 and 2020 it is estimated that 4.9 million people used the network, saving £21.5 million in costs to the NHS because of the positive impact on people's health. That's amazing.

The greenest camping holiday ever?
(Just walk out of the door)

I have been trying to imagine how to go camping in the greenest way possible. That's a holiday that consumes the least resources, creates no waste, and has the least impact on the planet. You'd also want it to be fun though, wouldn't you?

It's an easy one really. You would walk out of your front door, with a pack you've had for years, containing a tent you've had for years, in clothes that you've had for years, with food you've prepared yourself, from ingredients you bought at a plastic-free shop. You'll walk from one eco campsite to another and then walk home again, buying local produce from local producers to eat.

OK, so this might not be right for everyone, but it isn't so far away from being a possibility.

There is beauty here
(And it might be closer than you think)

Wherever you are in the UK you are never more than 16–32km (10–20 miles) from a campsite. Failing that, if you live in central London or one of the UK's cities, the chances are that you can go camping within an hour or a couple of hours' ride on public transport.

Getting access to the UK's National Parks, however, isn't so easy, especially if you come from a disadvantaged background or live in some of the poorer parts of the country. A government report published in 2018 discovered that over half of the most deprived areas in the UK are more than 24km (15 miles) from a National Park or Area of Outstanding National Beauty (AONB). A lack of public transport or even private transport makes it difficult for people living in those areas to access and benefit from them.

Walking is the greenest way
(Do I really need to tell you?)

Walking really is the greenest way to get there. And it comes with extra benefits, too, like fitness and well-being, mental health and positivity. Walking isn't for everyone – of course walking isn't something everyone is capable of – but for those who can, it can be a joyful, visceral, cathartic experience, just like any other amazing outdoor experience.

England and Wales have over 20,500km (140,000 miles) of public rights of way, which include footpaths, bridleways and byways that anyone can use.

Among these are hundreds of Long Distance Paths, including the Thames Path, the South West Coast Path and the Coast to Coast Path. Scotland has 29 Great Trails – long-distance trails that are 'people powered', which means you can walk, cycle or kayak them, as they include the Great Glen Canoe Trail.

Walking and hiking: happy camping

- Taking all your kit in a backpack makes you nimble.
- Wild camping gets you into nature.
- Walking is peaceful and quiet.
- Walking gets you truly off the beaten track.
- Walk closer to home to avoid long car journeys.
- Stay on sites that are eco-conscious.
- Leave the car at the campsite.
- Take day hikes and forget the congestion and fumes.
- Book campsites close to beaches or facilities.
- Travel by public transport to get to out-of-the-way places.

What if...
(You could go anywhere)

The Right to Roam campaign is working hard towards getting greater access to England's countryside. Around 92% of it is currently off limits to all but a few wealthy landowners. With a right to roam (and good public transport infrastructure) we could walk out of our front doors, catch a bus or jump on the Tube and head into the countryside or into a National Park and pitch a tent, so helping to reduce congestion and pollution and also *dare I say it* reduce our own carbon footprint (or reliance on fossil fuels) and send a message to Big Oil that we rather like walking, ta very much, and that it's time to reshape our country.

On your bike
(And how bloody marvellous it is to pedal)

I absolutely love cycling and always have, although my obsession with camper vans has rather got in the way sometimes. Part of that was the difficulty of carrying surfboards on a bike and wanting to explore far from home. But forgetting about surfing for a moment, cycling is a low-carbon, high-fitness, high-fun way to get around.

There are 20,500km (12,739 miles) of National Cycle Network in the UK. Between 2019 and 2020 it is estimated that 4.9 million people used the network, saving £21.5 million in costs to the NHS because of the positive impact on people's health. That's amazing!

→ Cycling from the coast to coast with an overnight on Dartmoor, taking the train from Barnstaple to Plymouth and then cycling back to Barnstaple, was one of the most wonderful adventures of my life. I absolutely loved it. It's up to us to push the cycling agenda by using our bikes more — and going bikepacking, cycle touring or just by using our bikes more when we get to the campsite. © Elizabeth Kay

Bikepacking and cycle touring: happy camping

- Cycling produces zero harmful emissions or pollution.
- Cycling gets you to places that cars and camper vans can't go.
- It keeps you fit, healthy and strong.
- Being self-sufficient is really empowering.
- You can stay on campsites that are eco-conscious.
- You can leave the car at home or at the campsite.
- You can book campsites close to beaches or facilities.
- Cycling can keep you out of hospital for longer!

Why bikes are brilliant
(And keep you fit)

In 2020, during the first Covid-19 lockdown, my bike saw more action than ever before. I was able to cycle to the beach near my home and go surfing. It was therapy during a scary time. I wasn't alone: in 2020, bike sales went up by 22% according to Mintel.

In 2021, I cycled from coast to coast with an overnight on Dartmoor, taking the train from Barnstaple to Plymouth and then cycling back to Barnstaple. It was one of the most wonderful adventures of my life and I absolutely loved it. Fortunately, we were able to travel on an almost exclusively off-road route, which is what made it safe and fun. At the time of writing, I am planning a similar adventure that, I hope, will take me across Europe.

However, let's face it, cyclists are still second-class citizens on the UK's roads. The roads have been built around motorised transport, making it dangerous at times to cycle. For unknown reasons, too, the average motorist seems to have a big problem with cycling, either because they don't understand how to respect bikes, they just don't care, or because they resent them because … grrrr … road tax! (etc). Either way, it's up to us to push the cycling agenda by using our bikes more – and going bikepacking (a mix between backpacking and cycling, usually on gravel or mountain bikes and done on bridleways) or cycle touring, or just by using our bikes more when we get to the campsite.

← You'd think that taking bikes on public transport should be easy, wouldn't you? But since the guard's van ceased being a thing it is frustrating and difficult to book bikes on to train spaces, especially as demand increases.

Taking bikes on public transport
(Easy if you fold)

You'd think that taking bikes on public transport would be easy, wouldn't you? However, it's not: it's fraught with difficulty. Folding bikes are welcome on almost all public transport, including national rail without a reservation, whereas non-folding bikes can only be booked on some trains, subject to available space, and may not be welcome on most buses (unless they are special bike buses), and are only welcome on some inner-city transit systems during off-peak times. Tricycles and tandems, from what I can gather, are not allowed.

The more we use our bikes and the more we demand bike-carrying services, the better this will become in time. So don't forget to make your voice heard!

Which is greener?
(Analogue bicycle or e-bike)

Are you ready to go down a rabbit hole? Well, let's indulge ourselves for just a moment with this: e-bikes are, allegedly, better for the environment than analogue bikes, from a carbon point of view, even considering manufacture, materials and disposal, because of the food you consume to replace the calories when you put in more effort on a normal bike.

'Yeah, but that's bullshit,' said Lizzy, when I read the bits of an article from BikeRadar[1], 'because it depends where your food comes from. If you bought it locally or made it yourself from stuff in your garden, then it's got virtually no food miles and no carbon.'

I have to admit, it was a good point. I wondered how far we have to go down the carbon-footprint rabbit hole? We can't feel guilty for eating, surely, and it can't be healthy to feel so uptight about being green that we'd weigh in at every checkpoint in our effort to be green? Or do we take reasonable steps to live how we want to, make noises in favour of improvement, and forget about the rest of it? Tough call. How desperate is our plight? I'd prefer to be positive: bikes are fantastic!

The first campers
(On their analogue bikes)

It is interesting that the first camping club, The Camping and Caravanning Club, should be an evolution of the Association of Cycle Campers, a group that was founded in the late 19th century by Thomas Hiram Holding. In 1901, a small campout in Surrey led to the formation of the club and the club's first site. Holding also formed the Bicycle Touring Club in 1878, which went on to become the Cyclists' Touring Club and is now the world's longest-running tourism organisation.

↓ Campsites and camper van or motorhome parking are often on the edges of towns — a bike will enable you to visit without the stress of parking or paying congestion charges.

Why take a bike (When you go camping)

• Campsites and camper van or motorhome parking are often on the edges of towns – a bike will enable you to visit without the stress of parking or paying congestion charges.
• Jumping on your bike to get provisions is much easier than packing up the van to go to the shops, and faster than walking.
• Leaving the camper van or car at the campsite means less congestion and pollution and saves money.
• Bikes can get you places that cars can't go, such as along bridleways or forest tracks.
• If you have lights and wear a helmet, it's a lot less hassle to take your bike if you go into the local town for food. Just don't drink alcohol!

↓ Camper vans and motorhomes are FANTASTIC for seeing places because you get to take all your stuff with you in your own little house on wheels. And it is better than travelling on short-haul flights but the cumulative effect of thousands of them taking to the road all at once is a big problem.

Cycling has always been at the heart of camping and, as we search for a better way, is evolving constantly.

You don't have to go cycle touring to benefit from a bike when camping. Taking a bike when camping has all kinds of advantages and is a really useful tool, especially if you travel by motorhome or camper van.

Electric bikes
(It's not cheating, OK)

Electric bikes are already having an impact on the market. According to the Bicycle Association (the national trade association for the UK cycle industry), in Europe by 2030, there are projected to be 30 million bike sales per year with around half of those being electric bikes.

In my experience, electric bikes are fantastic for reluctant riders because they take all the excuses out of cycling but still offer exercise. They flatten the hills and shorten the flats and make cycling enjoyable rather than a slog. Of course, if you carry kit then you can expect to shorten the range and you'll need somewhere to charge up, which means campsites or cheeky cafe stops at lunchtime, if your bike has fast charging. Boost batteries (spares that fit in a drink's cage) can also improve range on lots of models.

Touring by electric bike takes a little bit of planning because you need to find electric points and places to charge up. Having removable batteries can make this easier (and could be very useful if you don't mind asking a cafe to plug it in during a lunch stop).

Travelling by camper van or motorhome
(Stop haring about)

Having travelled by camper van for most of my adult life, I am very sorry to say that travelling by camper van or motorhome is not what I thought it was. From an emissions point of view, it's not great – vans (and by that I mean *all* vans), make up 16% of all UK transport emissions – but there are also issues with overcrowding, visual impact, pollution from waste, and congestion on popular driving routes like the North Coast 500 in Scotland.

Camper vans and motorhomes are fantastic for seeing places because you get to take all your stuff with you in your own little house on wheels. And it is better than travelling on short-haul flights (only just though – a large diesel car weighs in at 209gppk (grams of carbon per passenger kilometre), versus 255gppk for domestic flights) but the cumulative effect of thousands of them taking to the road all at once is a big problem.

That said, according to research from 2020, a motorhome or car pulling a caravan creates fewer harmful emissions (CO_2) than flying and staying in a hotel. Even though it still causes congestions and pollution, it is a better choice.

Camper vans and motorhomes: happy touring

- Don't drive every day.
- Stay on sites for three nights minimum.
- Stay on sites that are eco-conscious.
- Use less water and power.
- Stay in places where attractions are close enough to walk or cycle.
- Never drive off-road without permission.
- Only use approved toilet emptying points.
- Don't 'do' routes or places. Try to really see them by staying longer.
- When not touring, leave the van at home (to save up for your big trip).
- 'Offset' your travel by getting involved in community projects.

Travelling with a caravan

Cars pulling caravans use more fuel than cars on their own. They travel more slowly and take up more space. Some detractors say they cause congestion and irritation on the roads. That said, caravans can be left at sites on seasonal pitches (the Freedom Camping Club allows this on its small sites), so reducing emissions if you are 'weekending' or going regularly to the same place.

The advantage of a caravan over a camper van is that you can leave it on a site and still be mobile, unlike with a motorhome. However, that's not really the point, is it? The point is to be able to camp without contributing to pollution, noise, congestion and CO_2, when you are on the way there and when you are there.

Caravans allow you to take lots of extra kit – bikes, boards, SUPs, etc – which means that finding a good site with easy access to the kind of activities you like is vital if you want to avoid driving every day when you are there. The idea is to switch off, so enjoy the peace and quiet and walk or cycle.

Caravans: pitch up, feet up

- Don't drive every day.
- Stay on sites for three nights minimum.
- Stay on sites with good green credentials.
- Use less water and power.
- Stay in places where attractions are close enough to walk or cycle.
- Consider leasing a seasonal pitch to avoid hauling the van back and forwards from home.
- 'Offset' your travel by getting involved in community projects.

↑ 'Cycling can boost your mood, improving the symptoms of some mental health conditions like depression and anxiety. Cycling can also help you maintain a healthy weight. Cycling is a low-impact exercise, meaning it's easier on your joints compared to high-impact aerobics activities like running.' NHS WEBSITE 2023

Travelling by car
(Is easier, it's true)

There is no doubt that travelling by car is easier than most other forms of transport, as long as you don't hit jams or accidents, especially when you have kit to carry. It is far more 'convenient' than travelling by public transport and our society is set up for it, thanks to years and years of grooming from the car and fossil fuels industries.

From a carbon point of view though, large petrol cars are the big bad boys of the bunch, generating 283gppk (grams of carbon per passenger kilometre), with domestic air travel notching up just 255gppk in comparison.

Aaargh! But you can carry all your kit and have freedom when you get there, and not worry about trains or buses or having to rely on anyone else! And where I want to go is really hard to access on public transport... Sadly, it's all true.

Cars also produce noise and pollution that contribute to poor air quality and a decline in mental and physical health in towns and cities. They take up far more space per passenger than a train and cause congestion, which, in turn, causes more pollution.

So, what can you do?

You've no doubt heard it all before about driving carefully and slowly, choosing your time to drive so as not to contribute to congestion, and piling the car up with people, so I won't go on about it. However, when it comes to camping, you can mitigate.

Cars: happy camping

- Always carshare.
- Travel at off-peak times to avoid congestion.
- Take vacations closer to home.
- Stay on sites that are eco-conscious.
- Leave the car at the campsite and take bikes
- 'Offset' your travel by getting involved in community projects.
- Walk or cycle when you get there.
- Book campsites close to beaches or facilities.
- Change how you use the car at home and 'save up' for your long trips.
- Think about how you could do it differently.

Why transport matters
(And it isn't just carbon)

ROAD AND TRAFFIC NOISE: The UK government says on its website that: 'It is estimated that the annual social cost of urban road noise in England is £7–£10 billion.' Noise affects mental health, causes stress and sleeplessness, and can lead to depression and anxiety, heart attacks, tinnitus and learning disabilities, according to the World Health Organization (WHO). Noise is what we escape from when we go camping, right?

CONGESTION: Being stuck in a traffic jam is stressful. It can cause anxiety, poor health and makes us late, depressed and unhealthy. Jams also cause excessive pollution and use more fuel, hold communities back and affect the economic viability of the area. Ultimately, congestion can ruin the thing we want most of all from our camping trips – peace and quiet, a lack of stress and a healthy environment.

> Ultimately, congestion can ruin the thing we want most of all from our camping trips...

AIR POLLUTION: The types of pollution spewed out by road transport have, according to the UK government, no safe lower levels and make up around 28% of the amount of nitrous dioxide and 26% of the particulates created from manmade sources in the UK.

Effects of air pollutants include a worsening of conditions like asthma and COPD, cardiovascular disease, heart attacks and strokes, dementia and cognitive decline, type 2 diabetes, infertility and some cancers, as well as a worsening of Covid-19 symptoms.

Something else to consider here is the social injustice of air pollution, which tends to happen in poorer areas. While it might not seem relevant to your camping trip, every drive contributes to the problem. Leaving cities in queues of traffic in the summer months does nothing for this. Time for a rethink?[2]

Camping and transport emissions
(How you get there matters)

16% of
Global emissions are from transport

11.9% are from **road** transport

24% of UK emissions come from transport

contribute **56%** of emissions

vans account for **16%**

Van travel **increased** by **40%** between 1990 & 2020

Carbon dioxide per passenger Kilometer

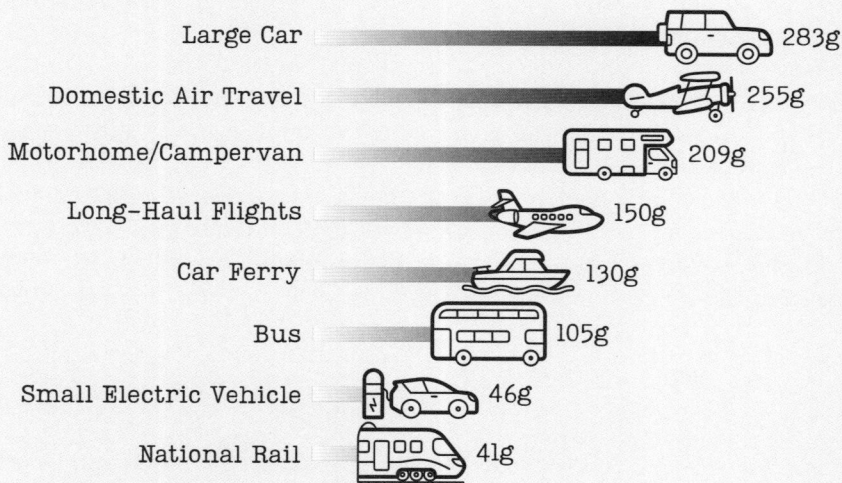

Large Car	283g
Domestic Air Travel	255g
Motorhome/Campervan	209g
Long–Haul Flights	150g
Car Ferry	130g
Bus	105g
Small Electric Vehicle	46g
National Rail	41g

→ The good news is that there are worse things you could do than go camping. Even going camping in a motorhome has the thumbs up when compared with a fly/drive/hotel kind of a trip, on the basis that hotels have high energy usage and that flying is, overall, worse than driving if there are two or more people travelling. © Elizabeth Kay

Final thoughts on transport
(No one is special)

Given what we now know – that global carbon emissions are causing changes in our weather, pushing up temperatures, melting ice caps, causing sea level rises, habitat destruction and a crisis in nature – it's time we accepted that none of us are special, that having money doesn't make you any more deserving than anyone else, and that we all need to pull together to avert our own extinction.

And we need to shout about it. You do what you can, when you can, and you make sure you reward success. You make the world that you want to see. As they say, 'be the change'.

And some good news
(Finally)

The good news is that there are worse things you could do than go camping. Even going camping in a motorhome has the thumbs up when compared with a fly/drive/hotel kind of a trip, on the basis that hotels have high energy usage and that flying is, overall, worse than driving if there are two or more people travelling.

But walking or cycling? Amazing! Dumping the car at the campsite for the week? Go you! Putting the caravan on a seasonal pitch and taking the train? Genius! The more I read, the more I realise that camping may well be the answer to everything.

10

What are you taking?

This chapter is about the stuff you take with you – the essentials – plus maybe some other stuff that you might need that I haven't covered in other chapters. This is sleeping bags, mats, coolers and all the other essentials that you don't sleep in, wear, or eat with.

The trouble is, though, fossil fuels – and the products they produce – are just so useful. That Ziplock bag, the waterproof coat, the fibre-filled sleeping bag, the rucksack, the lightweight lamp – sometimes it's like a festival of oil out on the trail. At least, now that I have seen it and spent far too long thinking about it, that's how I view it these days. It's just so hard to avoid.

But what if you can't? What then? Well then surely, as ever, it's a question of buying stuff that lasts, stuff that will perform as you need it to, that you can pass on to someone else when you have finished with it. Or maybe it's a case of buying second-hand or even renting kit.

Companies that rent kit for outdoor adventures

- Outdoor Hire: www.outdoorhire.co.uk
- Camping Gear Hire: www.campinggearhire.co.uk
- Contented Camping: www.contentedcamping.co.uk
- Decathlon/Quechua: www.quechua.com/take-the-hire-road
- Rab: www.rab.equipment/uk/rental
- Trek Hire UK: www.trekhireuk.com

← When buying kit, it's worth researching environmentally-friendly products. This rucksack is made from recycled 600 Denier yarn.

Sleep tight
(Don't let the bed bugs bite)

Sleeping bags come in lots of different shapes and sizes – all of which have their time and place – but they are generally made with two types of insulation: synthetic filling made from petrochemicals or natural insulation from duck or goose down.

Where do we stand on this? Of course, the 'natural' choice would be to go for the down filling because it's not manmade, right? But that's where the difficulties lie. Down is the soft layer of feathers on a duck or goose's chest and belly. It has to be harvested either when the bird is alive or when it is dead. Birds can be 'harvested' when they are alive and in moult, which is legal in the EU, but only under strict handling conditions. Even then there are doubts about the process, even though it is strictly controlled. Live plucking, when birds are not necessarily in moult, is not only condemned by the EU but also by the China Feather & Down Industrial Association (China is where the majority of down is produced). Birds that are plucked live are highly likely to suffer unnecessary physical distress, bruising, skin injuries and wounds.

The only 'ethical' way of getting down from birds without risking harm to them is to use the feathers that are a by-product of farming ducks and geese for meat, liver and eggs. However, the idea of rearing any animal for its meat – or feathers – is not considered ethical by many.

If you are OK with wearing or sleeping under down, then there are a few things you can do to ensure it is as 'cruelty-free' as possible and that it is ethically obtained and certified down.

- Look for Responsible Down Standard (RDS) certification, a scheme that promotes and rewards best practice from the feather and down industry to ensure that ducks and geese are treated humanely throughout the whole production chain.
- Look for other down tracing and welfare accreditation.
- Patagonia has a Traceable Down Standard that is accredited under the Advanced Global Traceable Down Standard (Advanced Global TDS). www.patagonia.com

Mountain Equipment developed its DOWN CODEX scheme, which places animal welfare, quality and sustainability at the heart of its down insulated products. The company's Down Cycle project keeps down out of landfill, as well as reducing the carbon footprint of sleeping bags and jackets. The range it has produced from this is called Earthrise. www.mountain-equipment.co.uk

↓ If you object to using down, even 'ethical' down, then the one solution is to choose recycled synthetic filling. Even then you will need to consider how you dispose of it when you have finished with it. Donating it can help others.

Sleeping mats to consider

- **NEMO** sleeping mats are made using recycled nylon and are guaranteed for life. Bluesign-approved partner. PFC free. They also include repair kits with the mats. Check with each product's details. www.nemoequipment.com
- **EXPED** produces all its products in a carbon-neutral way (through offsetting) and uses bluesign-certified textiles. It uses recycled polyester for a lot of its materials and includes recycled pumpbags with its air mats. PFOA free. No single-use plastic packaging. Check with each product for its exact spec. www.expeduk.com
- **BIG AGNES** mats are PFC free and manufactured using recycled materials. www.bigagnes.com
- **THERMAREST** is one of the leading manufacturers of sleeping mats. It manufactures them in Ireland and runs a programme in the USA to make camping more inclusive, taking young, disinvested people camping. www.thermarest.com

Don't forget that if you can't buy you can always rent:
www.outdoorhire.co.uk/sleeping-mats

Other things to consider include:

- Look for recycled down content in your sleeping bags and jackets.
- Rab collects down sleeping bags, pillows and jackets to be recycled.
  www.rab.equipment/uk
- Nordisk has its own range of traceable, free range, EU-sourced down it
  calls Crystal Down, which it uses in its bags. www.nordisk.co.uk
- Down is lighter than synthetic fill so is more useful for lightweight camping.
- Down can last longer than synthetic fill as long as it is looked after properly.

If you decide that synthetic fill is the only option, then don't forget to look for all the other green credentials:

- Recycled insulation.
- Recycled shell and lining.
- PFC free.

Sleeping mats
(Most important accessory?)

It's the same with sleeping mats as it is with a lot of camping gear. It will most likely be made from oil, although some do contain down. Sleeping mats have to be comfortable and lightweight and have insulating properties, but it's often a compromise between the three. The more foam and insulation, the heavier they tend to be. The colder the ground is likely to be, the heavier weight pad you'll need.

As with all equipment, it's a question of finding the brands that use post-consumer recycled content, are bluesign certified or that have sustainability at their heart. Look for B Corp companies and those donating 1% for the Planet (www.onepercentfortheplanet.org).

Longevity is also important. Guarantees for life are useful, too. If a company is willing to guarantee a product for life it must believe in it, right?

There are lots of brands available; in fact it's mind-boggling really what is available. It's easy to cut corners and go for cheap, but at what cost?

← Lightweight sleeping mats and pads are just like any other technical product that require fossil fuel enabled materials to keep you warm and comfortable. Choose carefully. Some brands use post-consumer recycled content, are bluesign certified or have sustainability at their heart. Look for B Corp companies and those donating 1% for the planet.

← On a basic level, it's fair to say that solar-powered lights and rechargeable lights are less wasteful than those that use batteries. Some lights can also be used to charge and power phones. Wind-up lanterns are useful if there isn't much sun and you don't have a power source to charge up batteries.

→ Is it better to have one recycled coolbox that you live with for ever and take with you wherever you go but have to, eventually, dispose of it, or to have a selection of diposables that you compost as you go along?

Torches and lights
(Light up my life)

Goodness me, there are a lot of options on the market for camping lights these days. When I was a lad (it was some time ago) we used storm lanterns or gas-powered lights on our camping trips. Today, there is so much choice that it's hard to know where to begin.

On a basic level, it's fair to say that solar-powered lights and rechargeable lights are less wasteful than those that use batteries. Some lights can also be used to charge and power phones. Wind-up lanterns are useful if there isn't much sun, and you don't have a power source to charge up batteries. If they are well made, and they are treated well, they should last for years.

As usual, buy from people who are proven to care. Better still, rent.

Cool it
(With a cardboard cooler!)

Cool boxes are generally made from plastic, which means, as usual, that they won't biodegrade or decompose. Occasionally, they are made from recycled plastic.

↓ Should sustainability be at the heart of every camping supplier's marketing and advertising? I think so, because it's what I look for when I buy products. So why don't more companies make more of it?

Igloo is a company that has been making coolers out of recycled plastic since 2019. It has developed insulation that well exceeds US standards. It has also launched a biodegradable cool box that is fully compostable and made from a kind of cardboard.

This raises interesting questions. Is it better to have one recycled cool box that you live with for ever and take with you wherever you go but have to, eventually, dispose of it, or to have a selection of disposables that you compost as you go along?

I'm not sure, to be honest. It seems to me that it encourages a throwaway culture. Or it might just be bringing a neat, sustainable answer to a throwaway culture that can't change easily. Discuss. www.igloocoolers.co.uk

Extra rooms
(More stuff)

Awnings are just like any other piece of camping equipment in that they have a footprint from their manufacturing, distribution, use and eventual disposal. Few are made with recycled materials, although there are some, notably one of Dometic's range of air beam drive-away awnings for vans (www.dometic.com/en-gb).

It's a drop in the ocean really and leaves me feeling a little flat, even though it's progress and could lead to bigger things. When I go searching and look at the company's sustainability report I see that it is doing more than I imagined to reduce its carbon footprint, work from renewables and be good employers. It's impressive. So why isn't this something that's front and centre – with concrete examples – of the company's consumer-facing offering? It's almost as if we won't believe the good work it is doing? Or that it doesn't believe the market wants to read about it. Or that it's not true and the awning is just a nod to sustainability in its otherwise vast repertoire of products made with virgin material.

Maybe sustainability isn't sexy enough to put on the front of your website. It is for a lot of companies. In fact, it's the thing some businesses lead on, because it is sexy. Why not for giants like Dometic?

Thoughts on mass market
(And sustainability)

I find it a little disappointing that I feel I can't write more about the big players in the industry because I firmly believe that, given the climate crisis is the biggest issue of our times, everyone should be talking about it. As a writer I have learned to look at everything from a consumer's point of view, and therefore see it at face value. Like consumers, I don't often have the will or the time to deep-dive into sustainability reports. So, I feel that sustainability should be a natural part of marketing and PR, and be a reason to invest in companies and a brand. Even if the mass market isn't ready for sustainability, I feel the job of the mass market, in these times, is to make people ready. They have huge audiences, make a huge amount of money and, as a result, have a huge footprint. Therefore, they also have a huge responsibility. With one brave and honest bit of copy they could do more to turn people on to making things better than I could ever do with this book. And even if they believe that sustainability is 'in their DNA' as a company and is therefore obvious, it doesn't come across to me. Pictures of people fly fishing or surfing don't say sustainability unless you tell me *why* it means sustainability. Otherwise it's just more plastic out there in the environment.

So, Dometic. We love your awning and we love your ambition and sustainability goals. But please, talk to your customers about it and do more of it. Don't hide your sustainability under a bushel. Thanks for coming to my TED talk about awnings.

Somewhere to park
(Your sorry arse)

Finding somewhere comfortable to sit is all part of the camping experience, right? As with everything else there is so much choice. Cheap camping chairs tend to break easily and end up in campsite or beach bins, so helping no one. Then there are those who can't be bothered to take cheap stuff home. It is estimated that UK festivals create around 23,000 tonnes of waste each year, with only about 50% of that going to landfill. Frankly, this isn't good enough. Any kind of camping chair is not a single-use item, even if it's cheap.

So, what's the answer, apart from buying something that is repairable, recyclable, made from recycled materials, from people who can repair it? Here are a few ideas:

VANGO's Earth Collection features chairs that are made from recycled PET plastic and with recyclable metal frames. Vango carries spares and can repair most items. www.vango.co.uk

HELINOX has committed to making 90% of its material recycled from 2023. It uses bluesign materials and guarantee its chairs for five years. It also uses PFC-free coatings. Helinox created a camping chair with **Finisterre** in 2023 that is made from 100% recycled material. www.helinox.eu and www.finisterre.com

KAMPA's Tub Chair is an inexpensive camping chair made from recycled nylon. www.kampaoutdoors.com/en-gb/uk

NORDISK makes fabulous wood and linen camping chairs and has a good reputation for sustainability, but they are a bit costly, so definitely for glamping. www.nordisk.co.uk

SNOWPEAK makes bamboo and cotton canvas chairs, as do lots of other companies. https://uk.snowpeak.com

↑ Cheaply made camping chairs
that break easily get dumped at
festivals, campsites and beaches
by the thousand every year.
Chairs aren't single-use items so
we shouldn't treat them as such.

ZEMPIRE has a wooden 'built to last' series of chairs and furniture that is made from either German beech or bamboo. Tables have metal legs and so are entirely recyclable. www.zempire.co.uk

ALPKIT makes aluminium camping tables for both car camping and lightweight camping. Aluminium is infinitely recyclable, so its end of life is assured. www.us.alpkit.com

Campfires and firepits
(What it's all about)

Having a real fire is what camping is all about. You sit there in the evening, staring into the embers, contemplating all the wonders of life and all that. It's basic stuff, and what life's all about. Once you've made fire you can marvel in your ability to survive out in the wild – after all, to get this far as a human you and your ancestors have had to get through some tough times.

The question is: how do we make fire without destroying the planet or burning everything else down to the ground?

First, let's think about the rules of lighting fires in the wild. Here are a few basics:

- If you can, take a firepit that will contain your fire and help you avoid burning grass or plants. Even campsites that allow fires will insist you do not light fires on the ground.
- DO NOT light your fire anywhere near flammable items such as dry grass, fences, trees or peaty soil.
- Always keep a bucket of water handy in case your fire gets out of hand.
- If you are thinking of lighting a fire on grass, don't, as it will kill it. If you must, at least dig out a sod of turf, light the fire in the hole and replace the sod afterwards, once the fire is fully out.
- Beware lighting fires on stones or flint that may chip and explode with heat.
- NEVER LEAVE YOUR FIRE to burn out. If you must leave, make sure the fire is put out completely and that the environment is put back exactly as it was. Do not leave mess, nails from old wood or litter.
- NEVER LIGHT A FIRE OR TAKE A STOVE INTO YOUR TENT. They produce a lot of carbon monoxide.

← Small firepits that won't damage habitats, can be carried in and out again and can be used time and time again are a serious option if you can't camp without a fire to warm your hands.

Green firepits (recycle reuse remake)

Old washing machine drums make excellent firepits! They have long been used in the VW world (I first saw one about 15 years ago) as they offer good containment, draw really well, are lightweight, and allow you to make use of something that might otherwise get melted down and used for scrap. Taking drums out of washing machines isn't easy, I'm told, but it is worth it.

If you don't want the hassle of doing it yourself, you can get them from Fire Drums. www.angusfiredrums.co.uk

UCO GEAR makes firepits that can be cooked upon, stand off the ground and can fold flat. www.ucogear.com

ALPKIT's wood stove also packs flat and is lightweight and easy to carry. www.us.alpkit.com

LIFE UNDER CANVAS sells a similar firepit that folds and stands above ground. www.lifeundercanvas.co.uk

GENTLEMEN'S HARDWARE sells a collapsible firepit that's small enough to pack in a rucksack and looks kinda groovy. It also sells a collapsible BBQ.

Lighting the fire
(Eco stuff you need)

TRADITIONAL FIRELIGHTERS are made from kerosene, which is an oil-derived fuel. It burns with smoke and smells, and can affect food tastes if you cook while it is still burning.

GREEN FIRELIGHTERS are available all over the place. They are usually made from compressed wood shavings and may be coated in paraffin for extra burn.

FIRE STEELS will add a spark to your dry kindling and make no waste.

MAGNESIUM FIRELIGHTERS will burn very hot for a few minutes and will ignite damp wood if necessary. Shave off lumps of magnesium then use the fire steel to ignite them.

ROCKET STOVES are popular and burn very hot and efficiently, in the same way a Kelly Kettle will burn. They are both reusable and recyclable, as they are made from metal.

→ The drums from old washing machines make great firepits and, if you make sure they are off the ground, won't damage habitats. It's a great way to recycle your old washer and turn it into something useful.

11

What are you staying in?

Wherever you lay your hat or sleeping mat

'Sharing our stuff is not a compromise.'
Rebecca Heaps, Tentshare

This chapter is about ways of going camping. That means it's about tents, camper vans, motorhomes and, to some extent, caravans. The idea is to give you some thoughts on doing this more sustainably. What's the best tent? What's the best motorhome? What's the best caravan? It's as simple as that.

However, of course, there are politics behind it because, as we know, camping and caravanning is a multimillion-pound business in the UK alone, and therefore it has to commit to making profits. That said, the more people I talk to, the more I realise that it is an industry that, especially at the less mainstream end of the market, is committed to sustainability and best practice.

You will have to forgive me, though, while I head off into the kind of territory one might call 'a hippy rant about possessions and consumerism'. That's right. I am going Neil on your ass. Man. Here goes.

As time goes on and the climate and nature emergencies become ever more urgent, we scratch our heads to find ways of treading more lightly while governments and corporations do absolutely nothing. That's right, I am talking about all the greedy, selfish politicians and every other self-serving and fossil fuel-funded, trough-faced snuffler who hasn't acted for the benefit of wider society in the last 40 years.

So, it's up to us to do what we can, where we can, and hope that popular movements towards environmentalism and – let's face it, saving our own sorry arses – can shame governments to do the right thing, finally, before it's too late.

For us to make a big difference, we will have to look at some of the ways we see the world. One of these ways is our current ideas of ownership.

The constant manufacturing and consuming of new stuff, followed by the subsequent disposal of said stuff, is the root of climate change nightmares. The whole process uses oil and precious metals, and scars and rapes the Earth in the process. It consumes energy, creates greenhouse gases through transportation and production, and eventually produces or turns into waste, whether that's the item itself or the packaging it comes in.

On a finite planet, let's call this wee beastie Earth, it simply isn't sustainable – and by that, I mean it cannot continue – to keep producing goods indefinitely, unless we change rapidly to a circular economy where creating waste is a very last resort. Constant growth, which is our current measure of success, simply isn't possible. From a greenhouse gas point of view, we can't keep churning out carbon dioxide either, and from a pollution point of view, we can't keep letting plastic and other noxious chemicals, nitrates and insecticides from industrial production and agriculture screw up our precious environment. Besides, we have enough stuff. I have a houseful; I bet you do too.

Not long ago we used to share resources as communities. People were, generally, poorer, so we'd share our labour, machinery and tools for the greater good. Remember the old phrase 'It takes a village to raise a child'? That's what I am talking about.

Today, now that we have had half a century or more of throwaway culture, a century of mass production, together with rising personal wealth and standards of living, the individualistic ideals of neo-liberalism in the 1980s have given us a more self-centred world view than that of our forefathers, and it isn't working. We value possessions as signs of wealth over community or happiness and prefer to live in isolated family units or as individuals, gathering the things we think we need – or that will impress others – over the course of our lives. Corporations, who love selling their soon-to-be-obsolescent washing machines, cordless drills and other sorts of stuff, are raking it in. They pay vast sums to advertisers to tell us that our lives are worthless without their products. We must have the latest must-have. And so it goes on.

So, it's up to us to do what we can, where we can...

However, even though we like the convenience and the cash, it isn't working. We have seas full of sewage, our atmosphere is changing, rivers are dying, the air is killing our kids, and nature is more depleted than it's ever been.

In view of that, what's wrong with sharing? Of course, some things that we use all the time are not ideal for sharing, like phones or laptops. But other things, like camping kit, motorhomes and caravans are perfect for sharing. Why wouldn't you? Or, put the other way, why would you spend hundreds of pounds

↓ The answer to the question of 'What is the most sustainable tent?' is simple. The most sustainable tent is the one you already own. Or that somebody else already owns.

↓ 'As a non-driver and solo festival traveller the option to rent a tent and equipment was such a brilliant solution, meaning I was able to travel with just the minimum needed for the festival. Having the ability to book at the time of getting your ticket and the choice of tents and extras made this such an easy process. This is such a brilliant idea, good for campers and good for the environment.' TENTSHARE CUSTOMER © Tentshare

on camping kit if you only use it once or twice a year? If you don't have money to burn and infinite storage space, sharing could well be the very best answer to having it all without blowing it all. Think about it.

The camping industry, although a lot more forward thinking than many industries – by a long, long way – is still an industry and needs to sell stuff to survive, keep its shareholders happy and pay its workers. The planet, on the other hand, needs less stuff. Nature, though nurturing us, needs some love back too. Sharing is one way to do it.

And if you can't share, for whatever reason, then the next best thing is to choose very carefully what you buy. Buy really good-quality stuff that can be repaired if it breaks and that will last a long time, from decent people and companies who do good things for the planet as part of their MO.

Tents

The most sustainable tent (and how to get it)

The answer to the question of 'What is the most sustainable tent?' is simple. The most sustainable tent is the one you already own. Or that somebody else already owns.

Tents are just like any other manmade object: it takes resources to make them, ship them, sell them, and dispose of them. In the case of most tents, especially those made from nylon (even recycled nylon), the materials they are made from will not rot down or biodegrade into nothing and will, eventually, end up in landfill or be burned for energy recovery (which sounds great but isn't). Even the lucky ones that get made into other things, like beach-cleaning bags, will eventually have to end their days somehow. Let's hope it's in landfill or energy recovery because the alternatives – including being abandoned in the natural environment – aren't worth considering.

Tents that are well made, used repeatedly over many years, repaired when they break, stored properly and loved by their owners are the very best kind of any tent. A tent that you borrow or rent is the next best thing. A borrowed tent has stories to tell. Yes, so it may have been around the block a few times, but it's been well used and has had a good life. And if it's fit for purpose, it'll do you proud because it's been tried and tested.

Go to the library (of things)

Have you ever heard of a Library of Things? It's an idea that has been gathering pace in the UK whereby anyone can borrow items as they would books from a normal library instead of buying them. Rental is very cheap and the time you can borrow those things for varies. The idea helps people who cannot afford to buy expensive items but also reduces waste and consumerism. Why buy when you could borrow?

According to a report from Bude Climate Partnership, tents and camping equipment are among the top ten items requested by people when they were engaging with a Library of Things in Totnes called Share Shed.

Borrowing items from your local Library of Things is generally a lot cheaper than hiring from specialists, although you may find there is less choice when it comes to tent style and sleeping capacity. It's still worth a look for a one-off weekend or holiday.

Why buy a tent (when you could rent it?)

I have enjoyed speaking with lots of people while writing this book. One of the most enjoyable was the half hour or so I spent talking to Rebecca Heaps of Tentshare, a tent-sharing platform that could well transform the way you and I camp. It came about when Rebecca rented her bell tent to families in her neighbourhood who wanted to go glamping but didn't want the expense of having to buy or store a tent. Thereafter the idea was born.

Given that over 250,000 tents end up in landfill each year, for whatever reason, Tentshare is one answer to a growing waste (and overproduction) problem. It is a sharing platform, like Airbnb or Quirky Campers, where people who have tents rent them out to people who don't have tents. It couldn't be simpler really. It's beneficial to the tent owners because they can make their tent work for them and earn some money from it. They can also get access to a community of likeminded tent owners and gain knowledge on making repairs or how to do things better. That kind of sharing is important.

The benefits to the hirer are many, too. You can choose a tent that's right for the trip you are doing, which means you don't have to buy another one if the tent you have isn't right. You can also hire other items of camping gear like sleeping mats and cookers, which saves even more hassle, storage and money. In some cases, you may not even have to pitch it yourself. Some hirers will offer a pitching service. For first-timers who might not be too sure about pitching or getting set up, that's fantastic! You tap into the camping knowledge of those who rent their tent to you.

Finally, and best of all, Tentshare is much more sustainable than buying tents, storing them and then, finally, sending them to landfill or to be converted into beach-clean bags, or whatever. Keeping them as tents for as long as possible is the best way for them to live their very best lives fulfilling their camping destiny. www.tentshare.co.uk

As well as having the community's tents for rent, Tentshare also rent out tents from Olpro. This company runs its own 'Loan and Go' scheme to help campers save money: www.olproshop.com

'As a family business, our deep-held values of honesty and courtesy are essential to the decisions we make. We're a business rooted in the great outdoors, and therefore we take our responsibility for our communities very seriously, at all levels of the organisation and in all business decisions.'

Regatta Great Outdoors, 2022 Sustainability Report

Is it fit for purpose: wind and rain

HYDROSTATIC HEAD: This is a measurement of how much water a fabric will take before it leaks, taken from the way material is tested. Typically, this involves clamping material over one end of a clear tube then filling the tube with water. Roughly speaking, the height of the water in the tube at the point it leaks is the hydrostatic head. A hydrostatic head rating of 2,000mm, for example, means that the column of water was 2 metres (2,000mm) tall before the material leaked. The higher the hydrostatic head, the more waterproof the material.

WIND RATING IN TENTS: Some tent manufacturers give wind ratings for their tents. This will give you a rough idea of the maximum wind strength it is designed to withstand, an important consideration if you intend to camp in difficult weather.

The best tents (and who sells them)

From a green point of view, the best tents are those that are both fit for purpose and have the smallest impact. It's that simple, and only you can decide.

A pop-up tent that you buy from a gigantic sports retailer might be fit for what you want to use it for, sure, if it's a couple of nights at a festival, for example. It may be repairable and it may be possible for it to be repaired by the retailer, and that's great. It may even be made from recycled material. And, of course, you could pass it on when you have finished with it.

But how about the company itself? It might be 'on the road to sustainability' but is that good enough? What about its human rights records? What about where it manufactures? What about the materials it uses? Is it listed as 'good' or better on websites like Good on You (www.goodonyou.eco) or Ethical Consumer (www.ethicalconsumer.org), who can give you an extra insight you might not get from a consumer-facing, glossy website that promises but may not deliver?

How do they rate on bluesign, an organisation that examines the entire textile manufacturing chain, so reducing harmful effects on the environment and people? (www.bluesign.com/en) Brands that are signed up to bluesign include Helly Hansen, Haglöfs, Burton, Mammut, Jack Wolfskin and Thule.

↑ Who makes the best tents? Check out the company and what they say about sustainability. It might be 'on the road to sustainability' but is that good enough? What about their human right records? What about where they manufacture? What about the materials they use?

All these questions are perfectly reasonable and legitimate and the more we ask them, the closer we'll get to the answer. The market changes all the time and every tent manufacturer is on its own sustainability journey, but here are a few highlights:

VANGO sells tents made from recycled materials, as well as refurbished tents that would otherwise go to landfill. It offers repair services. For disabled access or for parents with buggies and pushchairs, search for tents with low thresholds. www.vango.co.uk

OLPRO is a B Corp company. It also rents its tents through Tentshare. www.olproshop.com

CRAGHOPPERS has a strong sustainability policy, and makes some of its tents from a mix of cotton and recycled plastic bottles. It also provides free repairs. www.craghoppers.com

ALPKIT is a B Corp company, part of 1% for the Planet, a living wage employer and runs a foundation to distribute unwanted outdoor gear. www.us.alpkit.com

TERRA NOVA has announced that the majority of its tents from 2023 onwards will be PFC free and use its DWR coatings (waterproofing). It also offers a trade-in service and repairs. www.terra-nova.co.uk

KHYAM plants a tree with every tent order, among other green initiatives. www.khyam.co.uk

REGATTA OUTDOORS' excellent 2022 sustainability report claims the company is a member of the Ethical Trade Initiative, uses bluesign-approved fabrics, sends returns to charity, is PFC free and uses recycled fabrics whenever possible. www.regatta.com

BIG AGNES is a US company with good green credentials and a range of sustainable tents and camping equipment. Its range is made using PFC- and chemical-free fire-retardant materials, as well as materials made with drastically reduced water and chemical consumption. www.bigagnes.com

NEMO EQUIPMENT has introduced a range of 'Endless Promise' products that are recycled, recyclable and repairable to keep them out of landfill, among other strong initiatives to do with corporate governance, reduction in CO_2 and sustainability. www.nemoequipment.com

MSR makes long-lasting, repairable mountaineering tents and equipment in the USA. It is a bluesign company and is committed to limiting the use of harmful chemicals. www.msrgear.com/ie

What to look for when buying a tent (if buying is what you need)

Do your research: Look into the green credentials of the company online.

Look for recycled: If buying nylon or polyester, look for recycled content.

Look for chemicals: Make sure the tent is free from PFCs, PFASs and fire-retardant chemicals.

Think end of life: Does the brand offer trade-ins or the chance to donate your tent? Is your tent recyclable or repairable?

Is it fit for purpose: Will it last you? Will it withstand rain and wind?

If access is an issue, does it have easy access and low thresholds.

Don't trash it, repair it

When your tent breaks, mend it. Repair is a radical act. It defies the status quo that wants you to buy more and more stuff, use it until it breaks and then buy more stuff. If you mend something, you break that cycle and the stranglehold that big businesses have on you. In the world of fast fashion and wanton consumption, that's profound, and pokes a stick into the spokes of consumerism.

↑ Repair is a radical act. It defies the status quo that wants you to buy more and more stuff, use it until it breaks, which it surely will, and then buy more stuff. If you mend something you break that cycle and you break the stranglehold that big businesses have on you.

It's easy to get a kit to mend a tent, or get spare poles or parts, patch up a mattress or stitch a rip in a sleeping bag. Lots of manufacturers offer kits, while others will do repairs for you. Even Decathlon, the Titanic purveyors of cheap tents and outdoor gear, will repair a tent for you. The company can mend poles, elastic and even replace the integral poles on pop-ups. And it's not that expensive.

Repair is a simple thing that has the power to connect you better to the things you own because you are invested in them. Lots of companies like Alpkit, Patagonia, The North Face and others will repair your items for you. Some see it as a loss leader while others see it as an essential part of building community. At Alpkit, the company sees repair as an essential part of the selling process because the repair brings you into the store, creates interactions between the staff and customers and, ultimately, builds a community around the store.

This modern reiteration of the age-old idea that we need to look after our kit has led, in part, to the renaissance of 'visible mending', where patches and mends are clearly visible, like scars or marks of achievement or honour. You could call it virtue signalling if you wanted to throw shade on it because you like the idea of box-fresh being cool – like it's cool to throw stuff away – but actually, it means not buying new all the time, and that breaks the cycle that consumerism has on you. And that is awesome and could well save you a small fortune, too.

Tent and gear repairs

There are a lot of companies offering repairs all around the UK. Some of the most notable are:

DECATHLON: Big boys getting in on the repair action. www.decathlon.co.uk
SCOTTISH MOUNTAIN GEAR: Repairing tents since 1983. www.scottishmountaingear.com
TERRA NOVA: British-designed and -made tents, plus repairs. www.terra-nova.co.uk
LANCASHIRE SPORTS REPAIRS: For Go Outdoors and Colemans tents, among others. www.lancashiresportsrepairs.co.uk
CIT CAMPING: Tent repairs in the South East of the UK. www.citcamping.co.uk
TAUNTON LEISURE: Equipment to repair your tent on the high street. www.tauntonleisure.com
VANGO: Runs a spares service, as well as repairs. Any material or poles from beyond-repair tents go into spares for future repairs. www.campingspares.co.uk. Vango also sells returned, end-of-line or last season's stock cheaply to avoid them going to landfill. www.campingrecycled.co.uk

Keeping your tent in tip-top condition

It's obvious really, but the longer you keep your tent in good condition, the better it is for the environment. And if you pass it on, it's better that it's useable to others.

REPROOFING: After several uses in rain or sunshine your tent's water-repellent coating may wear off. This will cause your tent material to 'wet out' (absorb water) instead of it beading up and rolling off. If you experience any 'wetting out' you will most likely have to reproof your tent. This can be done with reproofing sprays, which are available at outdoor shops. Ensure you use PFC-free products. Use it according to the manufacturer's instructions, with the tent pitched (probably easier) or not. Spray the reproofing product on the material, wipe off any drips or runs and leave to dry.

REPAIRING YOUR TENT: If you end up with a small tear in your tent then you can either send it away to be repaired or have a go yourself. Most tents come with patches of material that can be used to patch, so if you are on a trip, it may be easier to effect a repair yourself. To do this:

- Cut the swatch of material to cover the hole.
- Ensure the tear is clean and dry.
- Place the swatch over the tear.
- Use Tear-Aid (clear self-adhesive patches) to stick the patch to the material.
- Repeat this process with the other side of the material.
- Optional: Use seam sealant to ensure the patch is watertight.

CLEANING YOUR TENT AND TREATING MOULD: Cleaning an inner tent can be done with a sponge when pitched. Flysheets can be cleaned by spreading them out on the ground and cleaning affected areas with warm water, natural soap or mild detergent and a sponge. It will need reproofing afterwards.

To treat mould, use Milton's sterilising fluid. Dilute it well and sponge down the affected area. This may not remove the mould, but it will stop it from spreading and smelling.

To prevent mould, keep your tent as dry as possible. Dry your tent prior to folding it and putting it away. If necessary, put it up when you get home and leave it to air and dry thoroughly.

To keep your tent in tip-top condition, consider using a footprint, which is easier to clean than a tent, and always dry and clean your tent before storing. Other tips include:

- Do not wash your tent in a washing machine.
- Do not pitch your tent into the wind.
- Avoid pitching under trees.
- Keep your fire away from your tent.
- Avoid direct, strong sunlight for long periods as it will weaken the fabric.

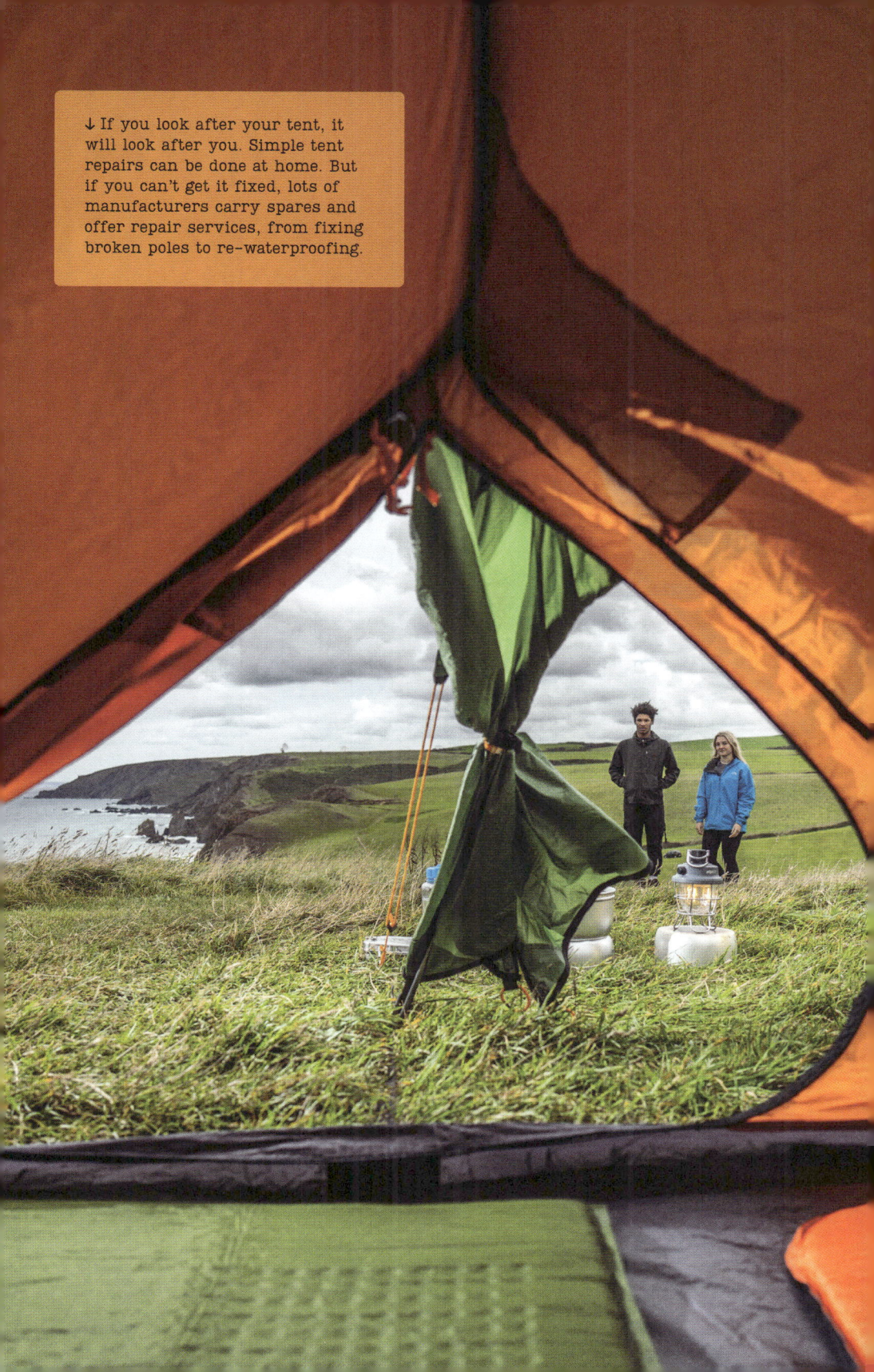

↓ If you look after your tent, it will look after you. Simple tent repairs can be done at home. But if you can't get it fixed, lots of manufacturers carry spares and offer repair services, from fixing broken poles to re-waterproofing.

↑ Platforms like Quirky Campers are serving a real and tangible need and benefit everybody: camper van and motorhome owners can earn a little cash to help them fund their motorhomes and camper vans while people who want to holiday in a van can save many thousands in ownership costs.

- Avoid pitching where sharp objects may puncture groundsheets.
- Don't force zips. If stuck or stiff, clean them with an old toothbrush.
- Keep your tent ventilated to avoid condensation.

The very last resort (turn it into something cool)

The very last resort for any tent is to turn it into something else. When I was running the #2minutebeachclean campaign we took tents that had been abandoned at a local festival and turned them into beach-cleaning bags for our 1,000 or more beach-cleaning stations. If you have a tent that is beyond repair, you can do the same. Get in touch with Rooted Ocean in Bude. www.rootedocean.com

Camper vans and motorhomes

I have already talked about camper vans and motorhomes and how we can make small changes to the way we use them to make our travels more sustainable. So, I won't say too much more about it.

Camper vans and motorhomes are great ways to travel, and it would be hypocritical of me to diss them because I have made a career out of loving them. I still do. Some of the best times of my life have been had thanks to the humble camper.

However, the time comes when even the best ideas need reassessing, and that's fine. I have a camper van because I use it all the time, spending months on end in it to write my books. So, it makes sense for me to own one and to own one that works for me. Even then, when you look at the 'cost per night' of ownership, and then think about the environmental cost of ownership – including 'embedded carbon', fuel costs, manufacturing cost, the impact of conversion – does it really make sense to have one? I'm not sure.

Cost of ownership (wow is it that much?!)

Shall we have a little fun right now? OK. I paid around £50k for my camper van, if you include the trade-ins on old vans. I have owned it for two years so far and spent around eight months of that two years – that's 240 nights, a third of the time – in it, and it still works out at £208 per night (even if you don't include road tax, insurance and fuel, as well as camping fees). A similar rental on Quirky Campers would cost me around £150 per night.

Of course, I will have that van for years to come and do a lot more camping in it before it is done, so it will get cheaper, but it does show that you need to do *a lot* of camping to make it cheaper than staying in a hotel.

I am even less sure about owning one that might cost upwards of £50k and leaving it sitting on the drive or in storage for 40 weeks of the year. I totally get the 'freedom' thing about taking your own home with you wherever you go, but when there are so many of us, we may have to look again. Hence the stuff in Chapter 2.

Sharing a ride (is caring)

Sharing camper vans isn't such a mad idea as you might think. In fact, renting one would be my best recommendation for those of you who are thinking about buying one but aren't yet sure if it's the right thing to do. Rent first. Ask questions later.

Camper and motorhome sharing platforms

Quirky Campers:
  www.quirkycampers.com
Goboony: www.goboony.co.uk
Camplify: www.camplify.co.uk
PaulCamper:
  www.paulcamper.co.uk
Spaceships Rentals:
  www.spaceshipsrentals.co.uk

Companies like **Quirky Campers** have been doing it for years now, connecting motorhome owners with hirers and making dreams come true for people who would love to own a camper but haven't got the money to buy and maintain one.

Campers are expensive and, at the time of writing, very few new vehicles are available from the manufacturers due, in part, to war, Brexit and global supply problems following the Covid-19 pandemic. Some manufacturers are no longer taking future orders, and some are offering vehicles for delivery in 18 months' time! This is putting the price of second-hand campers up too, as people clamour to buy something – anything!

Platforms like Quirky Campers are serving a real and tangible need and benefit everybody: camper van and motorhome owners can earn a little cash to help them fund their motorhomes and camper vans while people who want to holiday in a van can save many thousands in ownership costs. When you look at the cost of ownership in cost per night, it makes sense to hire if you don't camp that much.

The other great advantage of renting is that you can change the type of van you rent as your needs change. For example, if the kids refused to come with you or the kids wanted to bring friends. Renting would leave you open to many options and allow you to book smaller or larger vans depending on your immediate need.

On top of that, you don't have to worry about maintenance, storage, road tax or insurance.

And, as one final bonus, you can rent a van in the place where you are visiting, which means you can travel by train or bus and cut down on your impact.

From a sustainability point of view, it makes a lot of sense, too: one camper, with just one set of stuff like plates and cups, used many times, is way better in terms of carbon, resources and impact than many campers used less often.

Caravans

The caravan press, and associated bloggers and experts, have been creaming their pants in recent years, with some claiming that towing a caravan is actually good for the environment (take a bow Allens Caravans, 2014). The reality of it is that it isn't. As with all motorised transport, even when towing an old caravan using an EV (electric vehicle), there is always some kind of environmental damage done, whether that's through the design and build of the caravan, the environmental footprint of the vehicle and the energy used to power it, or the fossil fuel or electricity created with fossil fuels.

That said, towing a caravan is among the least damaging, carbon dioxide-wise, ways of holidaying when compared with flying, especially if you travel with two or more people. So don't park it in a Cornish field to rot just yet. But compared with a holiday where you take your bike on a train and then cycle to a pre-pitched tent, it doesn't look great.

That said, I am not here to berate you for your caravan, because caravans and caravan holidays have all kinds of wonderful benefits that you may not even have considered besides giving you good memories and a chance to commune with nature. My job, as someone who is trying to inspire a shift in behaviour to reduce our collective impact, is to help you make your caravan holiday even greener.

↓ If you are looking for a caravan then it is perfectly reasonable to buy second hand, especially from a reputable dealer. They are like motorhomes in that they will need to be inspected properly to make sure that the habitation is intact and, above all, safe.

You, as someone who loves their caravan, and camping in general, are going to have to make some changes if you want to carry on camping at all. Just like the tented campers, wild campers, campervanners and motorhomers. That's kind of the stark reality. If we don't act fast there will be nothing left of anything, never mind camping.

Buy carefully (or second hand)

If you are looking for a caravan then it is perfectly reasonable to buy second hand, especially from a reputable dealer. They are like motorhomes in that they will need to be inspected properly to make sure that the habitation is intact and, above all, safe. There are lots of books about buying second-hand caravans and, unfortunately, this isn't one. However, buying second hand is still better than buying new from a planetary point of view because the carbon emitted during its construction has already been emitted. Giving it more life and more adventures is kinder than breaking in a new one, too.

If you can, get a warranty and gas safe certificates.

Buying new (if you have to)

As with all things in this book, my recommendation is to do some digging before buying anything new. Why? The reason is that your buying decisions matter when it comes to sustainability. Who you buy from, how they behave and what their eco credentials are is important. It is your choice as to whether you give your money to someone who is doing the right thing or who isn't. I know what I'd prefer.

Consider an EV (clean and green)

Electric vehicles (EVs) have a much smaller carbon footprint than large petrol or diesel cars, produce zero pollution (apart from during their manufacture) and have been proven, time and again, to make really good tow cars. That said, they are still cars and still the product of the car industry – an industry that is desperately trying to see its future too. EVs won't save the planet, but they will surely save the car industry.

However, EVs are the lesser evil, for sure. Many newer EVs can be used as power stations for caravans, which means you can live completely off-grid for as long as the power source in the EV lasts. In a test, by caravan specialist (and my good mate) Andrew Ditton in 2021, heating and cooking used up around 20% of the car's battery capacity in one night. I was surprised by this as I assumed it would chew through the lot in a few hours. This feature is good for short stays, but it isn't quite perfect yet for long-term off-grid caravanning. However, it does mean you can, in theory, get rid of the gas and run an all-electric caravan. This will save weight and offer further fuel savings when towing. Plus you can get rid of gas when prices are rocketing and the LPG network appears to be disintegrating.

↓ Electric vehicles have a much smaller carbon footprint than large petrol or diesel cars, produce zero pollution (apart from during their manufacture) and have been proven, time and time again, to make really good tow cars.

There is much to be written about EVs as tow cars and not space enough here, but it does seem that the common arguments against them are based on 'dislike of change' rather than anything else. The UK government's website has a page devoted to debunking myths about EVs in the run-up to 2035 when all new diesel and petrol car sales will be banned.[1] If you are serious about making caravanning greener, open your mind to something different. An EV might just be the way to continue with 'business as usual' for a little while yet.

As EVs become more popular, the clubs are planning for the future, installing EV-charging points at some sites and offering slow charging, through the unit, on all sites, for a cost. The principle is that the EV can be topped up overnight by plugging it into the unit, not the EHU bollard, using a standard 220V plug.

Book a seasonal pitch (and save the chugging and the community)

If you tend to go away for a few weeks at a time during the camping season, it can pay to book a seasonal pitch at a campsite. This guarantees you a pitch and means that you can come and go as if it were your own holiday home. Then you only have to tow the caravan once at the start of the season and then at the end. If you can leave your car at the site, or even better, bicycles, then you could even take public transport and save yourself the driving, plus fuel, plus carbon dioxide.

Lots of sites offer seasonal pitches. The Freedom Camping Club is the first Certified Location/Certified Campsite (CL/CS) club to offer seasonal pitches on smaller five-unit sites.

Caravans can also have a positive effect on coastal, rural and island communities because they offer a viable alternative to holiday homes. There is a huge housing shortage in many places in the UK, especially in popular holiday areas like Cornwall, Norfolk or the Lake District, where the housing market has been decimated by people owning holiday homes. People who want the prestige of owning a second home, but who don't care for the communities they choose to buy in, push up prices and force locals out. The locals, usually on lower wages, find themselves with absolutely no hope of buying a home for themselves in the place where they were born. Holiday homes wreck communities, cause tensions and create division.

In places like the Outer Hebrides, holiday homes are also decimating the local housing market and literally forcing people off the island, all for the sake of some people wanting to spend a few weeks of the year somewhere else. On a personal note, I live next door to a holiday home. The owners turn up occasionally for a

← If you tend to go away for a few weeks at a time over the period of the camping season, it can really pay to book a seasonal pitch at a campsite. This guarantees you a pitch and means that you can come and go as if it were your own holiday home. Then you only have to tow the caravan once at the start of the season and then at the end.

week or so then disappear. In the last 12 months I have seen them for about four weeks in total. They might visit for 24 hours every month (presumably to keep their insurance valid), which in itself is a lot of carbon, but for a lot of the time we just don't see them.

So how do caravans fit in? Booking a seasonal pitch, especially in places like the Outer Hebrides, will still enable you to enjoy the benefit of being there for extended periods – because that's what's most important – but without contributing to the demise of the local community by taking housing stock from locals.

How to be a greener caravanner

Consider booking a seasonal pitch and commute to it from home – leave a tow car and commute by bus or train.

Leave the car at the pitch as much as possible.

Stay on sites with eco credentials.

Pitch up close to attractions you can walk or cycle to.

Reduce energy use.

Don't change your caravan too often – love the one you have.

Use bikes to get around when you have pitched up.

Consider an EV for your next tow car.

Support local businesses by shopping, eating and drinking local.

Stay on pitches for longer – don't move every day.

Reduce water use.

Consider salvage parts if you need to make repairs – there are salvage specialists all over the UK.

↓ Booking a seasonal pitch, especially in places like the Outer Hebrides, will still enable you to enjoy the benefit of being there for extended periods — because that's what's most important — but without contributing to the demise of the local community by taking housing stock from locals.

↑ We can educate ourselves about the impact of our clothing and outdoor gear. We can find out where our gear comes from, how it gets transported, who is making it, where it's being made, what it's made from and what chemicals are used in its production. We can also get clued up on the impact the clothes make while we wear them, when we wash them and when we dispose of them.

12

What are you wearing?

Outdoor clothing and fast fashion

He was right, Alfred Wainwright, wasn't he? He was the geezer who originally said: 'There's no such thing as bad weather, only unsuitable clothing.' He might have been more famously paraphrased by Billy Connolly, but he was right. We have all the world's technologies at our disposal today when it comes to outdoor apparel so there is never an excuse to be cold or wet, even in the harshest of climates.

Money aside, we can dress ourselves for anything. I like that. I like that, today, I can buy a wetsuit that I know will keep me warm in the middle of the winter. Forty years ago it wasn't so easy. I often wore two wetsuits and then took days to warm up afterwards.

We've made a huge amount of progress in the last 50 years and it's been truly excellent for our lives, for our outdoor pursuits and for our personal well-being. But. And there always has to be a but. What has been the cost?

Technical outdoor fabrics like Gore-Tex and polar fleece (as well as almost every other fabric since the Industrial Revolution) have made many people rich – and kept people dry and warm – but have also come at an environmental cost. Everything we do has an impact, whether it's to raise a sheep to knit a woolly jumper or dig up oil to make a polyester base layer. What we need to work out is what is going to keep us warm, dry and happy without causing lasting damage to the planet. We also have to ask ourselves how far we are prepared to go to protect it. And if it means a little personal discomfort, would we mind?

I am not interested in pointing the finger at just the outdoor industry here, because every item of clothing we wear has some impact. However, this book isn't about the rest of our lives (although, let's face it, I hope that it might influence your life beyond your camping experiences) so this chapter is about the choices you can make when you walk into an outdoor store, look online or think about kitting up for that next adventure (if you aren't able to use the stuff you already own, that is).

We have to be honest and face up to the fact that producing apparel – from growing the crops or digging up oil to weaving, dyeing, making, transporting and selling – is having a profound effect on the planet. If we are to continue being able to enjoy the outdoors, and for our children to enjoy it the same way, things have to change.

According to the European Parliamentary Research Service (EPRS) half a million tonnes of microfibres are washed into the oceans each year from washing synthetic fabrics, which accounts for 35% of the primary sources of microplastics released into the environment. In addition, 10% of global greenhouse gas emissions are caused by clothing and footwear production. That's more than all maritime shipping and international flights combined.

According to the EPRS, around 79 billion cubic metres (2,790 billion cubic feet) of water was used by the textile and clothing industry in 2015. They make it a little easier to fathom the scale by stating that it takes around 2,700 litres (713 gallons) of water to make one T-shirt, which is the equivalent to around 2.5 years of drinking water for one person.[1]

We also have to think about the working conditions of the people who make your clothes. At its very worst, people die making your clothes, like at the Rana Plaza factory in Bangladesh when a building housing garment workers collapsed, killing over 1,100 people. This is a very extreme example, but it shows the scale of the issue.

We have to be honest and face up to the fact that producing apparel [...] is having a profound effect on the planet.

So, what do we do?

First, we can educate ourselves about the impact of our clothing and outdoor gear. We can find out where our gear comes from, how it gets transported, who is making it, where it's being made, what it's made from and what chemicals are used in its production. We can also get clued up on the impact the clothes make while we wear them, when we wash them and when we dispose of them.

We can buy from companies who take part in initiatives like, for example, B Corp and 1% for the Planet. We can buy second hand.

Honestly, it's a mind fuck to consider it all. There is so much to think about. At some point you're going to have to make a decision. You can turn a blind eye to all of it if you want to. Many do because it's easy. Much of it is out of sight anyway. But please don't.

Then again, don't beat yourself up about it if you fail in your lofty green ambitions. Perfection is pretty much unattainable but making one good choice

↘ Visible mending is cool! Patches and repairs are like battle scars and memories to treasure on clothes that are fit for purpose and somehow you just can't let go of just yet.

↓ The end of life is an important consideration when trying to buy outdoor kit ethically. If you know the answer to 'what will happen to it at the end of its life?' and it isn't landfill or incineration then you're starting to win. Throwing stuff away just isn't sustainable.

Any full price purchase >> when you donate your old kit here >>

15% Off

Gift Your Gear

is better than making one bad choice. Making two is better. Three is amazing, and so on.

While I am not one to happily deal in clichés, there are some that are just perfect. The one that says 'We don't need a handful of people doing zero waste perfectly. We need millions of people doing zero waste imperfectly,' says it all for me. It applies to all kinds of environmentalism and means that you don't need to be perfect. All those small, positive changes can add up to make a big difference.

Changes that will make a difference

- Lose the fast fashion mentality. Buy only clothes you need. The average American throws away around 37kg (82lb) of clothing each year.
- Buy clothes and kit that will last. The longer you love it, the better it is for the planet. If it's good to start with it'll last the course.
- See repair as a radical act. Fast fashion relies on us thinking of fashion as throwaway. It isn't. Repairing clothes to make them last is an act of rebellion against waste and wantonness.
- Look for honesty in the brands you buy from. Are they prepared to be honest about what they do. Or are they schmoozing you with green sleaze that lacks any real substance? Time to switch on your greendar!
- Consider the end of life of your clothes. Where will they go after you have finished with them? Could you donate them? Fix them? Love them for another year?
- Look for second-hand gear. Keep it going for a little longer and love it as if it was new!

Buying online
(How wardrobing kills us)

Have you ever heard of the term 'wardrobing'? I hadn't until I started this book. But I had a feeling that there was something difficult about internet shopping. All those vans driving up and down your road every day when there used to be just one, once a day (your lovely pre-privatisation postie) are contributing to climate change because of the emissions involved in transporting all those deliveries.

According to government sources, vans make up 16% of all road transport emissions in the UK[2]. Some of this will be camper vans and motorhomes but the majority will undoubtedly be delivery vans. They criss-cross the country every minute of every day, carrying your internet shopping on their daily rounds. Yesterday I had three deliveries. They came via three different delivery companies. So much for deregulation.

What's the solution? Buying from local shops maybe, if it's available? Finding delivery companies that use electric vehicles? That really depends on who you buy from I guess as they will choose their courier. Ironically though, the Royal Mail scores well on CO_2 per delivery, with an electric fleet and an army of posties still delivering on foot. If I was an outdoor retailer, I'd be looking at this for the future and challenging the fleets to do better to lower the footprint of each delivery.

Wardrobing is the act of buying multiple items on the internet, then wearing them once and returning them. It is a kind of fraud against the retailers and a kind of fraud against the planet. While some brands repackage and return unsoiled items to sale, many do not. Some of what gets returned to internet retailers gets sent to landfill, so wasting all that energy and the resources to manufacture it, transport it, sell it, return it, and send it to a hole in the ground, or even to a developing nation like Chile (where a lot of fast fashion ends up). It is estimated that 2.6 million tonnes of returned clothes end up in landfill each year in the USA.

Bracketing is just as bad. Bracketing is the process whereby you buy one item in several sizes to make sure you get the one that fits. The result of this is that you invariably end up sending one or more items back because some of them don't fit. Again, this is OK if you can guarantee that the company you buy from has a zero to landfill policy, but if you can't, the chances are that your clothes will end up in a hole in the ground. That, frankly, is shit. We can do better.

Given that this is usual practice for retailers, what can we do to avoid returns going to landfill?

- Buy less!
- Buy only what we genuinely need and, if possible, buy it locally.
- Don't 'wardrobe' clothes ever. Be honest.
- Instead of bracketing, try it on in a shop!
- Search online, then ask your local retailer if they can get it for you
  = fewer deliveries.
- Buy from internet retailers who use green couriers.
- Get your internet shopping delivered to a drop-off point, then pick it up when you have multiple items.

Good news! **Reskinned** is a company that takes returns from manufacturers like Finisterre, cleans and repairs them and sells them on microsites, instead of sending the items to landfill.
www.reskinned.clothing/finisterre

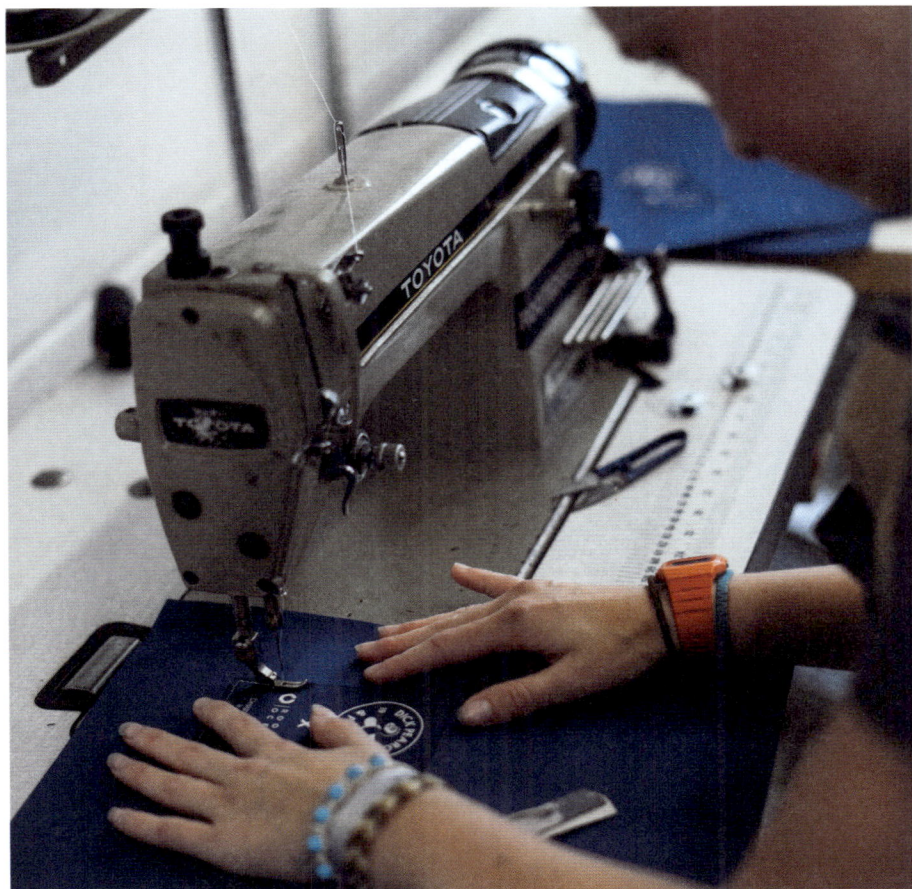

↑ Repair is a radical act. Loving your best stuff for longer connects you with makers and craftspeople, helps to keep your clothes out of landfill and helps you to stop consuming new stuff. Plus it'll save you money. It's a win–win!

Kit that's dead to you
(What you can do with it)

You might have a garage full of old outdoor clothing that's no good to you but, with a little love and care, could be priceless to someone who wants to go camping but can't because they haven't got the kit. So donate or sell it!

There are lots of ways you can donate your old kit so that it doesn't clutter up your shed. You could start with Vinted and eBay but you can also make it work for others by donating it to charities and Community Interest Companies (CICs), which use old kit to help people get into the outdoors who otherwise might not be able to.

The item's end of life is an important consideration when trying to buy outdoor kit ethically. If you know the answer to 'what will happen to it at the end of its life?' and it isn't landfill or incineration, then you're starting to win. Throwing stuff away just isn't sustainable. So, it's important to know where it will go. Here are some. companies who will help you:

KitSquad is a charity that gifts used outdoor gear to people with low incomes. Simple. Brilliant. www.kitsquad.co.uk

Rohan runs a Gift Your Gear scheme that donates kit to charities that get people outside who might not otherwise be able to. According to the Rohan website, the company has gifted almost 200,000 pieces of kit since 2012. Brilliant. www.rohan.co.uk/giftyourgear

Alpkit's Continuum initiative gifts gear to those who need it. At the time of writing, the company was sending unwanted kit to Ukraine, while still supporting its usual charities. Nothing goes to landfill, and you can send it to Alpkit free of charge. www.alpkit.com/pages/continuum

The reGain app allows you to recycle or donate your old kit to charity in exchange for discounts at some retailers. www.regain-app.com

Outdoor Gear For Good takes excess inventory from retailers and manufacturers and donates it to charities, recycles it or sells it for profits that then go to outdoor charities, so reducing landfill and enabling others to get into the outdoors. www.outdoorgearforgood.com

Ellis Brigham collects unwanted outdoor kit and clothing and donates it to the homeless. www.ellis-brigham.com/giving-outdoor-gear-a-2nd-life

Cotswold Outdoor, Runner's Need and Snow+Rock accept old textiles as part of their 2nd Life project. Drop off your stuff at their stores in the UK. The textiles are then either donated or recycled. www.cotswoldoutdoor.com/recycle-my-gear.html

Mend it!

All kinds of places will mend your kit for you these days, including Alpkit, Rab, Lowe Alpine, Patagonia, Mountain Equipment, Cotswold Outdoor, and many others. Contact them for details. There are also a host of independent repairers dotted around the place. My favourite, Rooted Ocean, is based in Bude. www.rootedocean.com

Chemicals and your outdoor gear
(Good, bad and ugly)

Perfluorochemicals (PFCs) are chemicals that are used to make coatings and products that resist heat, oil, stains, grease and water. These coatings can be used for all kinds of applications but for the benefit of this book, we are talking

↑ PFAS, PFOS and PFOA are fluorinated chemicals that have similar properties to PFCs in that they are persistent in the environment, some of them are of concern to animal and human healthy, and they are present in some outdoor clothing and equipment. They are particularly present in DWRs (Durable Water Repellent) coatings.

about waterproof coatings for outdoor clothing, although they include furniture, adhesives, food packaging and heat-resistant, non-stick cooking surfaces. Many PFCs are a concern because they do not break down in the environment and can bioaccumulate in wildlife. PFCs have been found in rivers, lakes and many types of animals on land and in water. They have been proven to cause harm to animals in lab tests, reducing their immune function and affecting organs. PFCs can be released from waterproof clothing at all stages of manufacture and during their lifetime.

In 2016, in a report entitled 'Leaving a Trace', Greenpeace tested a range of outdoor equipment, including tents, trousers, coats, backpacks and sleeping bags, from brands across the outdoor sector, and found that, of 40 products tested, only four were PFC free[3]. PFCs have been found in pristine environments all over the world.

PFAS, PFOS and PFOA are fluorinated chemicals that have similar properties to PFCs in that they are persistent in the environment, some of them are of concern to animal and human health, and they are present in some outdoor clothing and equipment. They are particularly present in DWRs (durable water repellent) coatings. While your waterproof coat might not be of significant concern, it is the accumulation of PFAs in the environment that is a problem, whether that's from manufacture, washing or disposal of products that use them.

What can you do?
(Make better choices)

Since Greenpeace's multiple campaigns against PFCs, lots of outdoor brands have made commitments to remove them from their products and supply chains. This is great. However, don't be complacent when making a purchase. Most suppliers who sell outdoor clothing will declare their items PFC free or PFA free if they are. Look for it, and ask questions, before you make a purchase. If enough of us ask questions, those questions will go up the supply chain to the people who make decisions – buyers, CEOs, designers and product developers.

Technical fabrics
(And the issues with them)

Humans are clever. Perhaps not as clever as an octopus or a dog at times, but they are bright enough to create all kinds of fabrics and textiles that do all kinds of amazing things. They can keep us dry in the rain, keep us toasty warm while we are sitting around the campfire, stretch while we do yoga, bend while we run and hike, and support us when we bounce. What a time to be alive!

Technical fabrics have all kinds of fancy names that sound like innovation and the future but really are just manmade, synthetic fabrics, often made from fossil fuels. They include acrylic, nylon, polyester and polypropylene.

The trouble with this stuff is that it's basically just different types of plastic, often using all kinds of chemicals and coatings to give it different properties. These properties may well save your life, so I am not going to diss any of them – and it's hard to avoid them if I am honest.

The trouble comes when these textiles and fabrics shed fibres (and chemicals), whether it's when they are washed or when they are worn, get caught on brambles or grazed against rocky outcrops, and also when it comes to disposing of them.

Plastics, as you already know, do not biodegrade in the environment. They degrade, sure, but that's just into smaller and smaller pieces. Microfibres that are shed from clothes like fleeces and jackets are tiny – already too tiny to be caught up in sewage treatment filters and wash straight down the drain and into rivers and the sea. They do not break down and are ingested by everything, including us, when they are airborne.

As they are plastic, microfibres attract persistent organic pollutants that can bioaccumulate up the food chain, so making our food, if we eat seafood, potentially toxic to us.

A report from the University of Gothenburg in 2017[4] aimed to quantify the number of fibres shedding

Evidence of microfibres (and microplastics) have now been found on the Antarctic seabed, in the fish we consume and even in our own bodies.

from different types of material while washing in a washing machine. PET fleece was found to shed as many as 110,000 per garment per wash. The report found that all fibres shed but that PET, nylon and acrylic knits shed about the same (according to the report there were 7,360 fibres for each 10 x 10cm/4 x 4in piece of polyester fleece fabric, versus around 87 for polyester fabric textiles).

Evidence of microfibres (and microplastics) have now been found on the Antarctic seabed, in the fish we consume and even in our own bodies. We know that plastic in seawater attracts POPs (persistent organic pollutants) and the occurrence of microfibres in the guts of fish has been well documented. In a study by the University of Plymouth, every sample of mussels in UK waters, including those for sale in supermarkets, had microfibres in them. What do we make of that?

Oh, the irony of your cosy fleece changing robe! You wear it to the beach to keep you warm after a cold-water dip, and yet all the time it's shedding fibres that will never go away or break down.

Microfibres and industry
(Working hard enough?)

The Microfibre 2030 Commitment is a project from The Microfibre Consortium Limited (TMC), a British-registered company, which brings together both specialist and mainstream clothing manufacturers, universities, retailers, supermarkets and electronics manufacturers to 'work towards zero impact from fibre fragmentation to the natural environment by 2030'. This involves research, knowledge sharing and will, eventually, lead to a better understanding of how fibres are shed and what measures can be taken to mitigate it, with a commitment by all signatories to achieving a goal of zero impact.

One of the benefits of this is not just who is signing up to the commitment but the global rating system for fabrics that TMC promises by 2025, which will, in their words, enable mitigation action at scale, 'equipping brands and manufacturers with a tool for assessing and comparing material impacts'. If this is available for consumers it could become a standard and a way for us, as wearers, of knowing the harm our clothes are doing to the environment. Given this knowledge, it could guide us to make better decisions.

How to stop microfibres
(From contaminating the oceans)

- Wash your synthetic clothes less often.
- Use shorter washing cycles.
- Wash cold, as it damages clothes less.
- Dry spin at lower speeds to avoid damaging the clothes.
- Buy a Guppy Bag to wash your manmade fibres in. In tests, the Guppy Bag captured 99% of fibres released in the washing process.
- Install an inline washing filter for your washing machine. Available from www.cleaner-seas.com

Natural fibres
(Naturally great)

You might think that natural fibres are the answer to the microfibre problem – and they are because they biodegrade – but they all come with problems of their own. Natural fibres include cotton, wool, hemp, leather and silk and break down naturally in the environment. However, each has its issues, whether that's down to water use in the case of cotton or animal welfare in the case of leather and furs.

Making careful choices about your outdoor gear – whether it's PFC free or organic – matters as much as it matters what the technical performance capabilities of those garments are. Usually there will be a natural alternative to manmade fibres, whether that's a wool jumper, alpaca socks, soft bamboo base layers or a waxed cotton hat.

The benefits of natural fibres are:

- They are sustainable and renewable.
- They have a smaller carbon footprint than oil-based textiles.
- Hemp grows really quickly and requires far less water than cotton, as well as having antibacterial properties.
- Wool, merino and cotton are breathable.
- They will biodegrade in a matter of weeks.
- People who produce natural fibres are often ethical in their business practices.
- They are durable and can work out great value in cost-per-wear.

Polar fleece
(Problems and alternatives)

You could say that fleece is a wonder material. It's been a mainstay of the outdoor world since it was developed in the late 1970s by Patagonia, with the help of Malden Mills (they have since become Polartec), from virgin polyester. Intended to be lighter and with better wicking qualities than wool, polar fleece became huge in the 1980s. It is still worn by many as a lightweight mid-layer.

The problem with fleece, however, is that it's made from plastic, namely polyester, and that is made from fossil fuels, which have to be dug up, processed and spun. So, it's not good from any angle. Patagonia, ever the innovators, started to use recycled fibres in the 1990s to avoid using virgin plastics and the inevitable carbon footprint they bring.

The hidden menace with fleece is that it sheds microfibres each time you wear, wash or even just agitate it, which makes it a hazard to the environment if you don't take care of it properly.

What's the alternative?
(And is it ethical?)

Wool fleece has been around since forever but can get heavy when wet, even though it has magical properties, which is why fleece became so popular. Some outdoor companies are now blending recycled wool with recycled polyester to make fleeces (Finisterre and Patagonia).

Merino wool has become the industry favourite in recent times because it has a lot of the same properties as regular wool – antibacterial, temperature

regulating, moisture wicking and light – as well as being sustainable and not made from fossil fuels. If fibres fragment, the microfibres that are shed will biodegrade eventually, unlike with polyester.

However, there are some concerns about merino that are to do with all the usual ethical issues associated with animal products and the garment industry. Animal welfare is an important consideration, particularly as merino sheep can be subjected to a process called mulesing, which is where the farmer cuts away the sheep's skin from around its anus. The scar tissue that grows back doesn't produce wool, so keeping parasites, urine and faeces away from the fleece. PETA, the animal charity, says that sheep are beaten, punched and kicked by shearers – a process itself that may cause harm – and may be transported live, causing them great distress.

Then there are the working conditions for the people making the clothes, the carbon of transporting wool from farm to garment factory, dyes and processes used to make the fabric, and the impact of overgrazing from large sheep flocks. All these considerations make decisions even harder for the consumer. However, there are some markers that you can use to decide:

- Mulesing-free merino is the basic benchmark.
- Look where the merino comes from. Some manufacturers use British wool. New Zealand merino is subject to stringent animal welfare regulations.
- Look for its organic certification. Seek certification like the Nordic Swan Ecolabel (the Swan), the sustainability and ethical standard for the Nordic countries.
- Look at the supply chain of the merino: where is it coming from, where is it spun, cut and sewn?

Dirty laundry
(A handy tip)

All clothes shed fibres in the wash. That's a given. They go straight to the ocean because they are too small to be trapped by filters in sewage treatment plants. This is fine if the clothes you are washing are made from natural fibres because they will biodegrade. But when they are manmade fibres they will not. They will be ingested by fish and shellfish and eventually make their way up the food chain into us. Along the way, they will attract persistent organic pollutants that will bioaccumulate up the food chain. It's grim.

A Guppy Bag will stop it at source by trapping the microfibres in your wash before they leak into the sewerage system. Plus, the bag can be used to store your dirty stuff while it waits for a washing machine to become free.

← Some companies are now producing wool fleece as a more sustainable alternative to polyester fleece. It has similar qualities but can be heavy when wet, unlike polyester. That said, it's fabulously warm and cosy.

↓ Cover up. You don't have to stay in the shade but if you do use sun creams and blocks, ensure they are reef safe and don't harm aquatic life when you swim.

13

How are you accessorising?

Accessories are the icing on the camping cake. They can make life easier and more efficient, keep you warm, safe and your phone topped up.

Staying sun safe
(And reef safe)

It's important to stay safe from the sun. As someone who has had skin cancer and who also has lost friends to skin cancer, I can safely say it's no joke. But there are concerns over what chemical sunscreens do to the ocean when you swim in it. Sunscreens contain chemicals – commonly oxybenzone, octinoxate and octocrylene – that wash off when you swim and have been proven to cause coral bleaching in areas of high 'human recreation'. They can also be toxic to fish, even in small concentrations. In many parts of the world, chemical sunscreens are now banned.

You can avoid causing damage with your sunscreen by using reef-friendly types, which you might consider to be sun blocks that use minerals to block the sun's effects rather than use chemicals to do the same job. Zinc oxide is one such ingredient. However, according to the Surfrider Foundation, the size of the minerals used is just as important as the minerals themselves. If the minerals are 'nano'-sized then they can be harmful in high concentrations. So, the key is to look out for sun blocks that use microparticles, not nano particles! Confusing? Well, yes. And because there is no regulation that determines if products are actually reef safe, it is easy to buy something that isn't safe. And while you might argue that you don't swim when wearing sunscreen, think about the chemicals washing off your body when you shower back at the campsite. They go straight down the drain.

Tips for staying safe in the sun (and being kind to the coral, too) include:

- Avoid microbeads as they are plastic.
- Avoid 'nano particles', instead look for labelling that says 'microparticles' or 'non-nano'.
- Avoid chemical sunscreens that include oxybenzone, octinoxate, octocrylene, 4-methylbenzylidene camphor, PABA, parabens and triclosan.
- If you swim, wear a rash vest instead of plastering yourself with sunscreen.
- Wear a hat.
- Stay out of the sun in the heat of the day.

Wetsuits: warmth in the water
(At what cost?)

The wetsuit has been a boon for the outdoor industry. It enables us to swim, surf, SUP and dive in water that might otherwise kill us. In plenty of cases it has helped make a British summer holiday bearable for kids who want to spend all day in a rock pool. The price of wetsuits can range from as little as £10 to as much as £500 for a top-of-the-range, tailor-made surf 'steamer' winter suit.

Wetsuits are either natural rubber (Yulex) or neoprene, insulating fabrics that work by trapping a thin layer of water next to the skin, which is warmed by the body. The snugger the fit, the warmer the suit. The same applies to thickness. The thicker the suit, the warmer the suit: 2mm is suitable for summer or warmer climates, 5mm is generally considered OK for a UK winter, 6mm for Scotland and 7 or 8mm for diving. Warmth is also determined by the construction – if a suit is stitched at its seams all the way through (overlock stitch) then the stitching holes will let in water and make it cooler. If the suit is stitched just part of the way through (blind stitching) and then glued it will let in less water and be warmer. If seams are taped it can also make the suit warmer.

Beware the supermarket (honestly just do)

While it is possible to buy wetsuits off the rack at supermarkets and even at motorway service stations, the warmth they offer makes for very poor economy. They are often badly fitting, use overlocking stitching, no taping and utilise cheaper, stiffer neoprene. These kinds of suits are pretty much destined for landfill and are very hard to recycle in large numbers. Avoid! They are shite!

Neoprene versus yulex

Neoprene was invented by DuPont in the 1920s as a synthetic rubber. Its main component is chloroprene, which is used to form a polymer through a chemical reaction.

According to the National Library of Medicine's website, chloroprene is a colourless, flammable, carcinogenic, chlorinated hydrocarbon with a pungent, ethereal odour. Chloroprene is used as a chemical intermediate in the

↓ It is possible to buy products that have a much smaller footprint than others. This rucksack is made from offcuts and parts that other manufacturers would otherwise have thrown away.

↑ Wetsuits have become ubiquitous these days as part of an outdoor experience. At the cheaper end of the market they can be made from materials that are harmful and can be badly cut or made with cheap, stiff materials, so rendering them not fit for purpose.

manufacture of neoprene rubber. Exposure to this substance causes damage to the skin, lungs, central nervous system, kidneys, liver and depression of the immune system. Chloroprene is a mutagen and carcinogen in animals and is reasonably anticipated to be a human carcinogen.

In 2022, a film by Patagonia exposed the issues with neoprene in Reserve, Louisiana, where the factory built by DuPont (now owned by Denka) that produces most of the world's oil-based neoprene is located. In the areas closest to the factory, the predominantly Black residents face a risk of cancer that is 50 times higher than the average.

In 2022, a licence for another plant to produce plastics in the area was revoked by the Environmental Protection Agency (EPA). Lawsuits against the EPA for failing to protect the residents of 'cancer alley' have been lodged. In short, neoprene might not be harmful in its form as a wetsuit, but it has a dirty history.

Limestone neoprene is a slightly greener, lighter, stretchier alternative but still uses chloroprene (made from non-renewable limestone) and is energy-intensive to produce.

Yulex is a wetsuit material that was originally developed by Yulex with Patagonia from guayule. Initially its performance was poorer than traditional neoprene until the company started to use *Hevea* trees. A part of this was securing crops that were grown to certified Forest Stewardship Council (FSC) standards (so helping to reduce deforestation). Yulex from *Hevea* is 100% natural and renewable, uses around 80% less energy to produce (and no fossil fuels) and is stretchier and more durable than neoprene, so lasts longer.

Patagonia, being the company it is, 'gave' Yulex to the surfing world in 2016. Today, more and more wetsuit manufacturers are making suits from Yulex and it remains the better environmental choice.

Wetsuit repairs (*keep 'em alive)

Rooted Ocean is a company that's run by two diehards, Matty and Lee, who love the planet they play on. They repair wetsuits and give them a new life. They mend all kinds of other gear too.
www.rootedocean.com

Powered by the sun
(Light up your life)

The days of powering camping trips with a chugging, smelly generator, or a bunch of batteries that you have to chuck away when the lights go out are over. If you are that type of camper you now have options for powering your campsite. Solar charging and lithium ion have superseded wind-up torches, diesel gennies and AA batteries. What this means is that, if we want it, we can now have power at the flick of a switch, wherever we go. Using a power bank that you charge with a solar panel can help save money while staying on campsites. With electric hook-up (with electricity that could come from non-renewable sources) costing around £5 a night it can add up. Solar charging means that, aside from the initial outlay, and as long as there is enough sun to power your needs, you can have free electricity. Depending on what kind of size power bank you go for, you can run fridges, strings of fairy lights, computers, tablets and TVs. It means off-grid camping is ever-more realistic and accessible if you can't let go of modern life.

Jackery power packs of 240W, with a 100W charger (which take about four hours to charge fully in full sun) cost about £500 and will power an electric compressor fridge plus phones and lights for a few days before it needs charging. It's good news. Or is it?

We have to work out how we can coexist with nature so we can both thrive, protect one another and heal each other.

Buying anything is just more stuff. And that stuff has to be dug up, manufactured, shipped and packaged, and the environmental impact of that considered. Lithium, cobalt and nickel are all required to make modern batteries and that has to be mined, often at great environmental – and sometimes human – cost. The batteries have an impact at the end of their life too, requiring careful recycling if they are to be useful again and not leach chemicals out of landfill. The same applies to solar panels: they require precious elements to make but aren't yet cost effective to recycle.

So where do we stand on this? While it's easy to dismiss solar and battery technology as being a Trojan horse of 'business as usual', I feel that the benefits may be felt more acutely in the longer term. If they help us to embrace change, make us realise that self-reliance is more relevant than ever and help us to imagine that living off-grid, away from societal pressure and the grasping, greedy power of the established power generators, might be possible, then it's a good thing.

With electricity to charge our phones, tablets, laptops, cameras, fridges and gadgets we can begin to imagine a different relationship with nature. I don't think it's about taming the wild like never before, but more about making camping more comfortable, more accessible and more enticing for those who might have struggled under candlelight. And that will mean more people can get out there, learn to love the countryside and become stewards of nature, giving it a voice, fighting to help save and restore it. A charged phone is a powerful weapon.

While those who deny there is an issue will claim they aren't yet ready to give up their cars and phones and go and live in a cave, I would argue that we don't have to unless we want to. We just have to work out how we can coexist with nature so we can both thrive, protect one another and heal each other.

The first step is to enjoy nature responsibly and encourage as many people as possible to be active in its survival. If we need to check our social media while we do it, so be it.

But of course, those precious experiences of life in the outdoors (when our phones are tucked away) are there to inspire us to have more precious experiences of life in the outdoors. For some, it'll be one step at a time, gently and slowly, without fossil fuels, without plastics, without chemicals and without causing havoc. For others, it'll be boots first, yomping into the backcountry without a care (or a gadget) in the world. And that's fine.

The most important thing about camping is that we go and do it. And when we go and do it, we fall head over heels in love with nature and the natural world. That's our safety net. And we can't afford to fuck it up.

↓ Solar charging means that, aside from the initial outlay, and as long as there is enough sun to power your needs, you can have free electricity. Depending on what kind of size powerbank you go for, you can run fridges, strings of fairy lights, computers, tablets and TVs. It means off-grid camping is ever more realistic and accessible if you can't let go of modern life.

↓ This chapter is about why our food choices matter and what you can do to make things better. It is also about cooking methods and the equipment you use to cook while you are camping because, when it comes to the environment, they matter too.

14

What are you eating?

'Ninety-six percent of the mass of all the mammals on Earth is made up of our bodies and those of the animals that we raise to eat.'

David Attenborough, *A Life on Our Planet: My Witness Statement and a Vision for the Future* (Ebury Press, 2020)

Eating under the stars
(The best meal ever)

Camping food is special. At least it should be, if only we could shed the old cliché of bangers on sticks or potatoes lobbed into the dying embers of a fire. And we must learn to live without disposable BBQs (more later). We can!

Thankfully, camping food has come on leaps and bounds since I last went to Scout camp. We, as a nation, appreciate good food more than ever so camping should be an opportunity to try new things, whether that's a way of cooking, recipes or ingredients.

Camping brings us closer than ever to local food – because it takes us out into the food-producing areas of our country – and gives us a challenge to ourselves to be better and do better. The more we do that – and love it – the more sustainable it can be.

Food is magic, alchemy, and a reflection of ourselves, if we allow it to be, and eating outside when camping brings it all together.

In this chapter I am going to talk about why our food choices matter and what you can do to make things better (if you feel you need to – I hope you do). I am also going to talk about cooking methods and the equipment you use to cook while you are camping because, when it comes to the environment, they matter too. Did you know, for example, that melamine, the popular choice for camping crockery, is made with formaldehyde? Or that disposable BBQs kill campers every year?

↓ Stainless-steel containers are robust and can be reused over many years without fear of them breaking down or leaching chemicals into your food like plastic or melamine can. They can also be recycled when you have finished with them.

In this chapter you'll also find a few useful recipes that I hope will enable you to do away with at least some of that kind of camping food that comes in a bag and is favoured by people with rucksacks on long hikes. A little advance preparation will enable you to cut out the waste, reduce food miles and impact, and enjoy on-the-trail snacks that you just can't buy over the counter at your local outdoor store. Trust me.

As someone who has tried all methods of cooking while camping – including cooking fresh mackerel in newspaper, smoking oysters and making seawater potatoes – I understand the importance that food has in the camping experience. It brings us together, brings us closer to the communities in which we travel and, if we have done it right, gives us everything we need to be bright eyed, bushy tailed and up with the larks. And all that.

Change is needed
(Change is good)

Now, as life becomes ever-more precarious, I realise that we have changes to make if we are to have a positive impact. Since my first book, *The Camper Van Cookbook*, came out in 2009 I have changed the way I eat. There are many reasons for it, but mostly it's about not wanting to support bad, planet-fucking practice, which means animal cruelty, unsustainable fishing, transporting food thousands of miles and not wanting to expect the world to deal with the pointless plastic packaging a lot of food comes in.

I'm not vegetarian but I eat meat less regularly now, and if I do, it is usually locally bred (and slaughtered). I avoid caffeine and gluten (wheat) if I can. When I buy fresh produce, I try to make sure that it comes from the UK or Europe and actively avoid fruit and veg that is grown further away (take a look next time you are in the supermarket – it is amazing how far some stuff travels). I haven't eaten beef in years and have given up lactose (dairy) for health reasons, but also because I don't think keeping cows in calf is that clever. I don't eat prawns because of the bycatch (90% in some fisheries). I don't eat fish unless I know it's sustainably caught because of what fishing is doing to our oceans. I don't eat lobster because the last time I put one in a pot it felt mind-numbingly barbaric.

You know what? I feel better for it, physically and mentally. That's important. After a while it becomes untenable to eat some things because of the way it's grown, harvested or killed. Sometimes you just know you need to do the decent thing. Food is a great way to start.

You are what you eat
(And so is the planet)

Food is vital in any story. And the food we eat defines us. As outdoor people it is vital that we get the right kind of nourishment for our activities, that we care about where our food comes from and what it does for us. Food has the power to bring us together and to nourish us and our environment. It can benefit communities too.

Conversely, eating rubbish, processed, factory-made food can make us feel shit. It can make us unhealthy, diabetic, obese, slovenly and, ultimately, very ill. Rubbish food can also contribute to damaging ecosystems or the demise of nature as agribusiness and the fishing industry ravage the land and seascapes of our precious planet. Food that is grown and eaten without a thought for its impact or provenance can do irreversible harm to us as well as to the planet. Food matters. It really does.

The politics of food
(And climate change)

Are you vegan? Or vegetarian? Or going that way? If you are, you won't be alone. There has been a lot of talk in recent times (and for a long time before that) that a plant-based diet is better for the planet than one that includes animal products. There are a lot of compelling arguments for this, not least of which is the fact that animal agriculture takes up far more space for the amount of food it creates (never mind killing animals) than growing plants, and is currently eating up virgin forest in the Amazon (reason enough to quit). Now that there are so many of us, we need to think about how we can feed ourselves without taking all the land for growing our food.

Globally, our food systems account for about one third of greenhouse gas emissions. So, reducing that impact is important, even if you don't go the whole courgette. Simply switching to fresh, local produce can make a difference because of the drastic drop in food miles and the impact to the local economy. Choosing growers who take care of their land properly, avoid pesticides and minimise the impact to water courses (not allowing slurry to pollute rivers, for example) will help to encourage best practice. Once again it comes down to making the good guys rich, not those who would sell their own Mother Earth for a profit!

As climate change begins to threaten our food security here in the UK – unseasonal weather can devastate crops, for example – it makes sense to start thinking about what we can do to make things better. We can support growers doing the right thing, shop to avoid packaging, stop wasting food (according to the WWF, around 6–8% of climate gases could be avoided if we stopped wasting food), think about a change of diet, give unsustainable seafood a miss or give up dairy.

→ Food is vital in any story. And the food we eat defines us. As outdoor people it is vital that we get the right kind of nourishment for our activities, that we care about where our food comes from and what it does for us. Food has the power to bring us together and to nourish us and our environment. It can benefit communities too.

↓ Travelling makes it possible to buy local produce from local producers or from local shops. You might not think it has much to do with being 'green' but it has everything to do with it. Buying local is not just a way of supporting local businesses, it also solves issues of food miles, and allows you an opportunity to understand how the food is grown and to cut down the impact the food you eat has on the world.

The joy of travel
(And eating well)

One of the greatest pleasures of travelling is getting to try dishes and ingredients that you may not find at home. And even if you can get it back home, it's always, always going to be better when it's sampled where it belongs. Foods that have PDO (Protected Designation of Origin) status are designated because there is something special about the area where they were grown that makes them unique, whether that's history, technique or, in the case of Champagne, terroir (the lay of the land, roughly speaking). Think Cornish pasties and the Waterford blaa (a kind of bread roll).

While you can get pasties almost anywhere these days, they cannot be called Cornish if they weren't made in Cornwall. And I can tell you that they do not taste the same when you eat them east of the Tamar, if only because they won't be as fresh.

Travelling makes it possible to buy local produce from local producers or from local shops. You might not think it has much to do with being 'green', but it has everything to do with it. Buying local is not just a way of supporting local businesses, it also solves issues of food miles, and allows you an opportunity to understand how the food is grown and to cut down the impact the food you eat has on the world.

It's quite simple really. Local produce that is in season and grown without pesticides or harmful chemicals, which doesn't have to be transported for thousands of miles, is way better for you – because of its nutritional content – and for the planet. Buying direct from the producer cuts out the middleman and means you get better value and the producer gets paid better. For you, it can be cheaper too, especially if you make your meals from scratch.

Buy it when you get there
(Not when you leave home)

As I have just said, one of the best things you can do for the communities in which you travel is to buy local. That means getting it from local shops when you get there instead of stocking up from your local supermarket before you leave. Buying food from supermarkets does nothing for the places you go because, more than likely, most of the profits will go to the shareholders rather than the people making the food. Supermarkets are notorious for demanding lower and lower prices from their producers, so forcing them to up their yields in a way that is unsustainable. They also make it difficult to buy food without packaging. Buying direct breaks that cycle. And I can guarantee, the food will be better.

What you eat with
(Beware the greenwash)

This section is about what you eat off, serve up in or cook with. It's an area that seems to have exploded of late, with all kinds of options to look at. Lots of foodware gets labelled 'eco' these days, especially camping foodware, when really it's only just marginally better than plastic.

There are pitfalls and traps to avoid when it comes to choosing dinnerware and I would ask you to make careful choices because, as with all things, just because it says 'eco' on the box, doesn't mean it's 'eco' on the inside. This is when you need your greenwash radar working hard for you. When green sells, there will always be someone who is keen to exploit it.

Ask yourself questions (Why is it 'eco')

The EU, at the time of writing, is drawing up laws to require that companies that claim products are 'eco-friendly' are able to back up any claims they make, owing to the fact that consumer confidence in sustainable businesses is low. The laws will aim to ensure that any sustainability claims can be properly verified. On the European Commission's website it is claimed that 53% of green claims give vague, misleading or unfounded information. Until then, and until the UK adopts a similar policy (doubtful because Brexit means we don't have to comply with these kinds of sensible, unelected, plutocratic rules), we will have to be vigilant about what is genuinely green and what isn't.

→ It is possible to save waste even when washing up. Bars are lighter, easier to store and can make less mess than bottles of liquid. Plus, no waste packaging.

We need to educate ourselves about what is and isn't believable and what actually matters. While 'recycled' packaging is important and does matter, making something 'recyclable' isn't of any real merit unless it actually gets recycled. And if the facilities (or technology) for recycling that product are not available to the user – if your local authority will take it – it's worse than useless as a claim.

Likewise with products that are made of recycled materials. Plastic can only be downcycled because it degrades as it is recycled. This may lead to more toxins leaching from recycled plastics than from virgin plastic. There is a lot to say about recycled plastics – as expected – but the fact remains that we should simply stop using plastic because it will, inevitably, end up in landfill, will always leach toxins and will never 'go away'. Which is why choosing dinnerware, water bottles and on-the-go coffee cups is really important, even though it might seem like a drop in the ocean.

However, putting post-consumer plastic to good use is important as it uses up, and secures, a resource that would otherwise go to landfill or the ocean or the environment. It also creates a demand for recycled material, so increasing the demand for recycling and giving it a value.

Quick thought

Imagine you have two takeaway coffees a day every working day for ten years. If you use a reusable cup you will save around 460 cups.
If you persuade ten colleagues to do the same, it will save 5,060 cups.
And if you persuade 100 people, it will be 46,460 cups.

Compostable products

'Compostable' is a term that crops up time and time again. Compostability is the ability for something to biodegrade and decompose without releasing harmful chemicals into the environment. However, the difficulties occur when it comes to commercial claims about compostability as the characteristics depend on many factors, including, time, heat, light, pH and enzymes present.

If a product is described as 'home compostable' then it is assumed that the product will break down under normal composting conditions – a garden compost bin, for example. However, products will often only break down under 'industrial composting' conditions (like you'd find at your local recycling centre) where heat, oxygen and agitation are present, and without the use of solvents or chemicals. In the UK, there are currently no universal 'home compostable' standards for packaging products.

Bamboo

Lots of bamboo products are made with bamboo fibre mixed with polymers (plastics). This might make it more 'eco-friendly' because it uses some natural fibres, but it also makes it difficult to recycle, which makes biodegradability impossible and its ability to compost laughable.

In Germany, the German Institute for Risk Assessment has deemed some 'bambooware' plates made using melamine-formaldehyde-resin (MFR) to be unsafe for using with hot liquids and food, owing to the danger of melamine and formaldehyde migrating from the tableware to the food.

Spun bamboo, a product that has been made for over 900 years, also uses glue to hold the fibres together, making it difficult to dispose of.

Only bamboo products made from 100% natural fibre are genuinely compostable. Some 'disposable' tableware is made from bamboo. It may compost in about six to nine months under the right conditions.

Melamine

Melamine is another product that's been popular with campers and picnickers for decades because it's light, strong and durable. But beware, there have been concerns about its make-up and disposability. Melamine is an advanced polymer made with formaldehyde, which can leach when it is heated. For that reason, it is best to avoid using it in a microwave or oven – it is not heat-safe. Similarly, melamine cannot be recycled like normal plastics.

Stainless steel

Stainless steel is a good choice for dinnerware because it won't corrode, doesn't leach chemicals (as long as it's not lined) and can be relatively light. It can also be recycled at the end of its life and the material can be recycled indefinitely.

Plastic

Plastic has a bad rep. And rightly so. It's made from oil and is toxic, so is not great on any level, although there is no denying that it has transformed our world, often for the better: plastic is in everything. The trouble with plastic is that it doesn't biodegrade, rarely gets recycled (only about 30%), attracts natural toxins in seawater, and has helped us to develop a 'throwaway' culture that has filled our seas and hedgerows with it. We must wean ourselves off it, somehow.

Chemical additives in some plastics are what makes them toxic and have been proven to cause health problems. BPA (Bisphenol A), a known endocrine disruptor and synthetic oestrogen, which has been linked with 'adverse perinatal, childhood, and adult health outcomes, including reproductive and developmental effects, metabolic disease, and other health effects',[1] is one such additive. It is now being phased out on a lot of products after global health scares. You'll see the term 'BPA free' on a lot of plastic food products, showing that the plastic is 'safe'.

↑ When you buy anything, it's worth considering what will happen to it once you have finished with it. Where will it go? Can it be sold on? Can it be repurposed? Can it be reused? Can it be rehomed, hired or lent? Can it be composted? Will it biodegrade? And, finally, can it be recycled?

Choosing plastic that is BPA free is a wise choice in any case. However, there are suggestions that chemicals used in place of BPA, namely BPS, BPF, BPAF and diphenyl sulfone, may also have potentially harmful effects.

The verdict? Avoid plastic! If you do use it, throw it away once it gets scratched or damaged and don't put it in microwaves or dishwashers as it may leach chemicals more when the integrity of the material is compromised.

Bioplastics

Bioplastics are products that are made from more sustainable materials than oil-based plastics. In that respect they are better for the planet because they do not use oil and do not have all the associated issues with oil-based plastics (drilling, processing, etc). Bioplastics are often dishwasher safe and BPA free.

However, plastic is still plastic, even if it's bioplastic, no matter what the source material is. If it behaves like plastic then it may not rot or degrade in a reasonable timeframe, under normal conditions. In many cases bioplastics cannot be recycled because the infrastructure to do it isn't in place and they cannot be put into normal plastics recycling as they do not behave in the same way as normal plastics. In the case of coffee cups, starch-based versions will contaminate waste streams if they enter them. So generally, unless the producer has clear guidelines of disposal or a takeback scheme, they may well end up in landfill.

Bioplastics are difficult because they are such new technology. Generally, they can and do claim to be more eco-friendly than plastic, but their disposal is ultimately what matters. Some bioplastics claim to break down in five or ten years. But what use is that if it's been eaten by a whale in the meantime? And therein lies the issue – bioplastics, in some ways, encourage us to continue with business as usual when what we really need is not something that mimics what we have already but instead performs the same function but without any kind of impact.

What happens to it
(When you go home)

Every product we use will die eventually when it is no longer serviceable and cannot be repaired or reused. This is the point at which its make-up becomes important (see above, bioplastics). Ultimately, recycling should be the last resort for anything rather than landfill.

So, when you buy anything, it's worth considering what will happen to it once you have finished with it. Where will it go? Can it be sold on? Can it be repurposed? Can it be reused? Can it be rehomed, hired or lent? Can it be composted? Will it biodegrade? And, finally, can it be recycled?

What you cook with
(And why it matters)

Camping stoves

What is the most eco camping stove? It's a good question and one that I have been trying to find the answer to. One simple answer is 'the one that you already own', but somehow that doesn't really go far enough, even though making do with what you have got instead of buying new is a good start.

What you cook on depends on who you are with and what you plan to do, so it's always a moveable feast. It doesn't mean you have to be wasteful though. Stoves can be borrowed or begged and even hired from Outdoor

Hire (www.outdoorhire.co.uk), a company based in Sussex that will courier any gear to you. Hiring cooking gear works out at a fraction of the cost of buying in many cases. You can also hire portable stoves from Contented Camping (www.contentedcamping.co.uk).

How green your stove is will depend on what fuel it uses, where it is manufactured and whether it creates waste in the form of packaging or single-use plastic. All stoves that use a flame to cook will, of course, produce carbon dioxide plus, in some cases, other gases.

Unless you use solar cookers or solar panels with batteries and an electric hob of some kind then it's hard to avoid producing gases. Conversely, solar panels, lithium-ion batteries and induction hobs aren't without impact – a lot more than wood gathered at your campsite!

Non-stick pans (and the plastic in them)

There are a few concerns over using pans with PTFE (plastic) Teflon non-stick coatings. First heating a pan with non-stick coatings up to high temperatures (above 260°C/500°F) has been known to cause 'Teflon flu', when fumes are released from the pan. This can cause headaches and flu-like symptoms and, in severe cases of long-term exposure, lung damage.

Second, non-stick coatings are made from types of plastics that can wear away from the pan and end up in the food or washing-up bowl. Nothing about that is nice, although it is unknown how it will affect you. However, microplastics in the environment are a concern simply because there are so many of them. Allowing frying pan coatings to wash into the environment is not a good look.

If you do use Teflon or coated pans, use wooden or soft plastic (silicon) utensils to stir and serve as they are less likely to chip away at the surface than metal spoons or forks. If your Teflon-coated pan is excessively scratched, replace it.

While PFOAs have been eliminated from most non-stick coatings since about 2013, non-stick coatings may still contain PFAs. The amount given off by your frying pan may be minimal; however, do consider the cumulative effect on the environment. Nature is under enough pressure as it is.

Alpkit's camp cookware includes a range of pans with non-stick coatings that are PFOA free.

The disposable BBQ (and why I hate them)

Earlier in this chapter I posed the question of the greenest camping cooker. That will come in a bit. First, I would like to start with the *worst* way to cook while camping. While the disposable BBQ might appear to be convenient and cheap, you still pay a price for them in the long run. Some campers have paid the ultimate price for using them and have died as a result of the massive amount of carbon monoxide they produce. Aside from their killing abilities, these wasteful death trays use up valuable resources that could be used

↓ The telltale sign of a disposable BBQ. While they might appear to be convenient and cheap, you still pay a price for them in the long run. Some have paid the ultimate price and have died as a result of the MASSIVE amount of carbon monoxide the produce. Aside from their killing abilities, these wasteful death trays use up valuable resources, are often produced in the Far East, contain charcoal that may not have come from sustainable sources and are laced with accelerants that are noxious.

elsewhere. They are often produced in the Far East, contain charcoal that may not have come from sustainable sources, and are laced with accelerants that are noxious. On top of that they are packaged in plastic and paper – more wastefulness. Then there's the bin fires I see every year from people dumping them, the burnt feet from people walking on the sand where they have been, the cuts and grazes from people stepping on them and, finally, the wildfires caused by them. Please, just don't.

Cooking fuels
(And where they come from)

The sun

The sun is the ultimate in renewable energy sources. So why not use it to cook with? Solar cooking is nothing new but it could offer us a glimpse of something different if we are to face a brand new future without fossil fuels. There are numerous solar cookers on the market that cook either in vacuum tubes or using parabolic mirrors to reflect heat and light on to a cooking vessel.

Solar cookers are either expensive or difficult to get hold of, especially in the UK. There are a lot of people experimenting with using parabolic mirrors to cook food in a pot, and it really does work. One company investing in solar is Slick Solar (www.slicksolarstove.com). If you are prepared to invest a little time and energy into cooking without fuel costs, give it a try.

The good old BBQ

While I am anti disposable BBQs for the reasons noted previously, there are arguments for using locally produced charcoal from sustainable sources. After all, wood is a renewable source. At the very least it is carbon neutral and may support local businesses too, which is something that does matter. It also doesn't get shipped halfway across the planet to get to you and produces little waste. If you use a BBQ time and time again then it's not wasteful.

Beware, however, briquettes that are impregnated with accelerants and which come from hardwood sources abroad.

The fossil fuel lobby (gas, petrol and diesel)

BUTANE AND PROPANE: Butane is a form of liquid petroleum gas, a fossil fuel. Propane is also a form of liquid petroleum gas. Both have become a little harder to get hold of lately as supply, no doubt exacerbated by greed and excused by war and Brexit, becomes unsteady and unreliable. This isn't great for campers but, when you can get it, both provide a reliable source of energy for cooking, produce good, hot flames and will cook quickly.

LPG PROPANE: LPG propane is available in bottles that can be refilled at service stations or in refillables that can be swapped. In Europe, where it is used as a cooking fuel in many homes, you may need an address to swap LPG bottles. In camper vans with refillable gas tanks, LPG can be used to power heating and cooking. LPG is a popular choice for gas BBQs and refillable bottles. Gaslow (www.gaslowdirect.com) now has an app that will give you a level indicator of your tank. Handy if you are heading into an area where there is no LPG available. Other bottle gas cylinders include Safefill (www.safefill.co.uk).

CAMPINGAZ: This is a mixture of both propane and butane and is used by campers globally. It will not burn in conditions below around 5°C (41°F) so

↓ Solar cookers are the ultimate in low-impact cooking, producing zero emissions and using no fuel. That said, they do take some sun and can take a little time to cook. This one, a portable from GoSun, cooked a really beautiful meal of fresh tomatoes in around 30 minutes.

isn't much use in winter. However, the larger refillable bottles are available universally in Europe so they remain a popular choice. Campingaz is available in single-use bottles – down to tiny, lightweight backpacking sizes – as well as in refillable bottles that can be swapped at most camping shops and service stations.

REFILLABLES: These are by far the better alternative but are not always practical for lightweight camping. In this instance, it may be wise to consider a solid fuel or liquid fuel stove.

Beware the single use

Single-use Campingaz canisters and bottles can be recycled but they must be empty and marked as empty before you recycle them, so that the recyclers know they are empty and not pressurised or full of explosive gas. Burn off the last of the gas before recycling with your local recycling centre. Local authorities aren't keen on them in your home recycling.

→ Some outdoor retailers and campsites will recycle single-use gas canisters. Check before you buy. If you recycle them they must be empty – check with your local authority that they are willing to take them.

← Campingaz is a mix of butane and propane and can be refilled universally, making it a better choice as there is no waste associated with them. However the refillable bottles are heavy and not much use for lightweight camping.

MULTI-FUEL BURNERS: These can also burn petrol, diesel or kerosene. They are stalwarts of the expedition world and will work in extreme low temperatures. Fuel is also available globally, which is an advantage if you are going far from Western civilisation. They can be heavy and dangerous if not handled properly.

THE PRIMUS STOVE: The Primus was invented in 1892 in Sweden. Its design was based on a blowtorch and used pressure and heat to produce a very hot and efficient burning flame. The Primus was extremely successful and was used by expeditions and adventures the world over because of its ability to work in difficult conditions. It was used by Amundsen, Mallory and Hillary on their respective South Pole and Mount Everest expeditions.

The Primus had many iterations, including full kits in tins and lightweight versions for campers, and could be used with kerosene, petrol and even diesel in some instances.

Non-fossil fuels (and how they work)

LIQUID FUEL STOVES: These are lightweight and use methylated spirits or bioethanol. Methylated spirits is an industrial form of ethanol alcohol that is often distilled from raw sugar (but not always – it can also be a by-product of fossil fuels) and has been used in camping stoves for decades. It is often dyed purple and can smell when burning. It won't burn as hot as gas. That said, cooking with a Trangia methanol stove is actually very easy. They are lightweight, easy to use and, while taking a bit of getting used to, are about as simple as it gets.

> ...buy in bulk, decant for usage and easy transport, and dispose of the container responsibly.

An alternative is to use bio-ethanol, a similar fuel that is made with fermented sugar beet or grain. It is a sustainable material, although it comes in plastic bottles that will have to be recycled. The same applies to bio-ethanol that is burned in traditional Trangia stoves: they don't burn as hot as gas but are much greener as products. Trangia stoves are still made in Sweden (www.trangia.se/en).

Alcohol gel is also used in liquid fuel stoves, and favoured by many because it is quick and easy to ignite, lights when wet, is non-toxic, odourless and made from sustainable natural biofuel. Again, the only downside is the packaging it comes in, which is either a plastic pouch or a plastic bottle. As with all these things, buy in bulk, decant for usage and easy transport, and dispose of the container responsibly. Plastic pouches are more difficult to recycle than plastic bottles.

SOLID FUEL COOKERS: These use pelletised blocks a bit like firelighters made from hexamine, a substance made from formaldehyde and ammonia.

↑ Trangia stoves, which use methylated spirits or bio-ethanol, don't cook as hot as a gas stove so take longer, but are a good choice of lightweight stove if you want to avoid waste. Buy meths or bio-ethanol in bulk and decant into reusable bottles.

↑ Kelly Kettles are extremely efficient because they create a 'rocket' effect, drawing oxygen into the base to create a lot of heat out of not much at all. They will boil water really quickly, using just dry twigs.

They are small and lightweight and light easily but cannot be regulated aside from adding more pellets. They are highly toxic if ingested and produce noxious fumes. For outdoor-use only, and be aware they are affected by damp and wind.

WOOD BURNERS: These can burn extremely efficiently compared with a wood fire. They can use fuel found while you are out, which makes them possibly the greenest, although they can be difficult to light if your fuel is wet. They can be used with wood pellets and starting paper, which makes them a lot easier! These types of stoves include Kelly Kettles and Rocket Stoves, which also use wood and are extremely efficient. Kelly Kettles are very efficient at boiling water as the draft from the chimney effect heats water up directly in the jacket.

Haybox or wonderbag cooking (an old-fashioned miracle)

The principle of 'haybox cooking' was first used during and after the Second World War to save fuel. The idea is that a meal – usually a stew or soup – is brought to a simmering boil then taken off the heat and placed into a box filled with straw. The insulating properties of the straw meant that the stew would slow cook for several hours and be ready at the end of the day. It greatly reduced the use of fuel.

The Wonderbag was invented in South Africa as a way of saving money on fuel. It uses the same simple principles as the haybox with recycled foam insulation. If you are heading out for the day on a hike and can prepare your food in advance, this is a great way to save fuel and to slow cook a meal safely. Perfect for leaving at base camp while you go off to explore.

A wide-necked Thermos flask can also be used for the same principle, except it's more portable and could therefore be taken with you on a hike.

THERMOS VEGGIE CHILLI WITH CAULIFLOWER RICE

Makes 4 portions

Cauliflower rice is a really tasty and easy-to-use 'ingredient'. It's readily available, cheap and gluten free. It's also a vehicle for flavour so, when you use it, under-season it and then embellish with whatever herb or spice you have to give it a kick. It's an ingredient that travels well, as well as being nourishing and filling without being heavy on the stomach.

Make the rice by grating the cauliflower with a box grater, or blitzing in a food processor (before you leave home), so it resembles small rice-like pieces.

This recipe has lots of flavour and nutrition and can be easily embellished. It is also a good example of food that can be started in the morning on the stove and then transferred to a Thermos to finish cooking slowly, so it'll be ready by lunchtime.

INGREDIENTS

Good glug extra virgin olive oil

Large red onion, peeled and finely chopped

2 garlic cloves, finely chopped

½ fresh chilli, finely chopped

400g (14oz) veggie mince (or other alternatives – cubed smoked tofu, tempeh or mixed beans of choice – cannellini beans will make it more creamy. Lentils will also bring a heartier depth to the chilli

1 tsp hot smoked paprika (tweak to taste)

1 heaped tsp ground cumin

1 heaped tsp ground oregano

400g (14oz) tin chopped Italian tomatoes

1 tbsp tomato puree

1 tbsp organic cider vinegar

400g (14oz) aduki or black beans, drained and rinsed

1 tbsp miso paste or yeast flakes, which act as your stock cube

Large handful fresh chopped coriander

Lime wedges, kefir or Greek yoghurt to serve

METHOD

Heat the oil in a large pan, add the onion, garlic and chilli and fry over a medium heat for approximately 5 minutes until soft and lightly browned – don't burn the garlic.

Add the veggie mince or whatever protein you're using, and smoked paprika, cumin and oregano. Cook for a few minutes more, stirring. Add the tomatoes, tomato puree and cider vinegar – refill the empty can with water, then add this to the pan. Stir in the beans and miso paste or yeast flakes, or if without those, simply use a crumbled stock cube. Season well. Stir and bring to a gentle simmer.

Cook for approximately 10 minutes or until the sauce has reduced and thickened. Keep stirring to avoid sticking to the pan but gently so you avoid breaking down the beans. Taste, tweak the seasoning. Have ready to one side your cooked cauliflower rice (see page 265) or cooked grain of choice, then simply layer your Thermos flask with this and the veggie chilli mix. Leave space at the top for some chopped coriander and a fresh lime wedge. Remember to pack kefir or Greek yoghurt, which would also taste amazing on this too.

→ Thermos flasks allow you to cook your food with no fuel during a hike or while you do other things. Simply start the recipe on the stove, decant and let it keep cooking.

THERMOS VEGGIE CHILLI
WITH CAULIFLOWER RICE

MEXICAN QUINOA
& BEAN SALAD

Some simple recipes
(Waste free and good for ya)

My friend and neighbour, Ali Miglorni Stubbs, is a kitchen wizard who also happens to run a company that takes people hiking all over Europe. So, when it comes to food on the go, she knows her alliums. She worked with me to come up with some recipes that will enable you to ditch the packaging and make food on the go or in advance. Forget energy bars, lose the packet meals – you can save money and waste by making it yourself.

Breakfast

CARROT CAKE OVERNIGHT OATS

Makes 2 portions

The process of making overnight oats is easy, and doesn't involve cooking. For this recipe, prepare your food jars in advance (the day before) and put them into the fridge before eating.

Overnight oats can also be baked into bars or eaten warm. To do so, mix all ingredients together and bake for 20 minutes at 180°C (350°F). Once out of the oven, portion them off and put into food jars to keep warm or leave them to cool, then cut into bite-sized pieces and eat as baked 'oat cake'.

Soaked oats can also become the basis of a smoothie. Blend it all and add more milk or yoghurt to your desired consistency. Adding more fruit will embellish the flavour and nutrition, so will keep you feeling fuller for longer. It is also delicious with yoghurt, kefir or cream.

INGREDIENTS

80g (2.8oz) rolled oats	250ml (8.5fl oz) milk of choice
2 tbsp chia or flaxseeds	Small handful jumbo raisins
1 tsp ground cinnamon	
½ tsp ground ginger	*For the topping*
1 tbsp local honey (or maple syrup for vegans)	Greek yoghurt
	Runny honey
2 medium carrots (grated)	Handful of halved walnuts

METHOD

Add all the ingredients into a bowl and mix. Decant into food jars, add the topping mix, cover, and put in the fridge overnight.

SPICED ORANGE GRANOLA

Makes approx. 10 portions

This make-at-home recipe produces approximately 1kg (2lb 3oz) in cooked weight of granola, which will have a shelf life of around a month. It can be eaten on the go as trail mix or can be stuffed into Medjool dates for a high-fibre snack. Eat with milk, yoghurt or kefir at other times.

For a pudding option, grate apple or add berries to it and serve with cream. Alternatively, warm through apples in a pan and then top with the granola for an instant crumble. It could even become a rustic pancake: add a couple of bananas into it, some nut butter, and maybe even an egg! Pan fry.

Note: If you want to control your sugar and salt intake, only add coconut sugar *or* honey, not both. Or leave it completely unsweetened so individuals can add honey or maple syrup.

INGREDIENTS

700g (24.7oz) oats
135g (4.8oz) chopped almonds
100g (3.5oz) walnuts, roughly chopped
100g (3.5oz) pecans, roughly chopped
50g (1.8oz) Brazil nuts, chopped
50g (1.8oz) mixed omega seeds
100g (3.5oz) coconut sugar or honey
1½ tbsp ground ginger or grated fresh ginger

2½ tsp ground cinnamon powder
3 tbsp freshly grated orange zest, plus the juice of one very large orange
8 tbsp good local honey or maple syrup
8 tbsp rapeseed oil or coconut oil
3 tsp vanilla
Pinch sea salt
Sprinkle of cinnamon to serve

METHOD

Preheat the oven to 160°C (320°F).

Mix together the oats, nuts, seeds, sugar, ginger, cinnamon and orange zest. Add the remainder of the ingredients and mix well.

Transfer the mix on to two lined baking trays, spreading evenly, and bake for approximately 20 minutes. Stir occasionally to stop the nuts from over-browning.

After 20 minutes, stir well and bake for a further 15–20 minutes or until golden and crunchy. Allow to cool on the trays.

SPICED ORANGE
GRANOLA

LENTIL & CHICKPEA
HUMMUS

Snacks

LENTIL & CHICKPEA HUMMUS

Makes 2 portions

This easy make-at-home recipe is very versatile and will last a couple of days in a sealed container, although it's best in the fridge.

INGREDIENTS

3 garlic cloves, finely chopped
200g (7oz) chickpeas, cooked
200g (7oz) lentils, cooked
4 tbsp oat or nut milk
3 tbsp organic cider vinegar
3 tbsp tahini

5 tbsp extra virgin olive oil, plus
    extra to drizzle on top
1 heaped tbsp yeast flakes (optional)
Seasoning
Any other herbs or spices or
    seeds and nuts to top

METHOD

Put a handful of chickpeas and lentils to one side – bake or pan fry them to add as a nutty topping. Blend the remaining ingredients till smooth or leave chunky. If on the trail, crush them with a fork and mix well for a really rustic dip.

THINGS TO DO WITH HUMMUS!

- Load up in pittas or use white or red cabbage leaves or heavier green leaves like cavolo nero as alternative 'wraps' and load up with hummus and veggies.
- Layer hummus, sliced avocado and a handful of chopped seasonal greens, watercress or rocket plus lime juice and chilli flakes, or fresh sliced chillies, extra mixed seeds and crushed walnuts. Drizzle with extra virgin olive oil.
- Hummus can also be the foundation for a stuffing mixture that can be pan fried with oats, quinoa flakes or cooked grains.
- Add milk or water to it for a sauce to stir through pasta or stir-fried veggies.
- Shake it with a little more vinegar to make a creamy vegan salad dressing.
- Mix a couple of tablespoons of hummus with mashed butter beans, oats, grated veggies, seasoning and herbs to make falafels. Roll it into balls and pan fry.
- If you haven't got time to make hummus before leaving, simply pan fry chickpeas and eat them as snacks. They could even go into your nourish bowl. To do this, take two tins of chickpeas, rinse and add a little extra virgin olive oil, smoked paprika, dried herbs, sea salt, cracked pepper and a handful of cashews or pecans, plus a couple of tablespoons of organic cider vinegar. Mix well and pan fry until they start to brown off and become nutty.

BIG CHUNKS OF OATY BANANA!

Makes 12 portions

Another, packaging-free snacky dollop for you to customise. It can even be eaten raw with yoghurt or milk and berries for a speedy breakfast. Or pop it into a feed jar and layer it up with yoghurt, more fruits, nuts and seeds for a portable offering. This can be made the night before eating to allow the oats to soak, which makes them creamier and easier to digest. You can eat these bites straight away or leave them until you really need them – they will stay fresh for a while. If you batch cook for multiple adventures, they will freeze well.

INGREDIENTS

90g (3.2oz) pitted dates
60g (2.1oz) walnuts, halved
50g (1.8oz) chopped almonds
100g (3.5oz) rolled oats (use quinoa
   flakes for a gluten-free version)
50g (1.8oz) unsweetened coconut
   flakes
2 ripe bananas
1 grated apple or a good handful
   of fresh berries

1 tsp ground cinnamon
A pinch of sea salt

For extra yumminess

Add mixed seeds, milled chia seeds, raw cacao nibs, goji berries, extra cinnamon or nutmeg. Add a heaped tablespoon raw cacao powder for a richer chocolate flavour.

METHOD

Preheat the oven to 180°C (350°F).

Prepare a square baking tray (approximately 20cm/8in) or a silicon ovenproof ice cube tray (the bites will need less baking if smaller).

Whizz the dates in a food processor or chop finely by hand and put in a mixing bowl. Add the chopped nuts, oats or quinoa, coconut flakes, mashed bananas, apple, cinnamon, sea salt and any of the extra ingredients as above. Mix it all well using a fork to make a mushy mass, then place it either on the baking tray or in the ice cube tray. Spread evenly and place it in the oven to bake for approximately 30 minutes or until the edges brown. Leave to cool, then turn out, slice into chunks if necessary and store in an airtight container.

Lunch/dinner

YOU CAN'T BEAT A BUDDHA BOWL

Whatever you call them – Buddha bowl, nourish bowl or poke bowl – you just can't beat a jar of everything you need to nourish your mind and body on hikes, bike rides or camping trips. They don't take ages to make and yet can tick all the boxes for a delicious, life-affirming lunch. And when you make them in a see-through jar or pot they look like a great day out should – rich, tasty and full of everything you love.

Buddha bowls can be made ahead to save time when you are out in nature and, if refrigerated properly, will last a couple of days at least. They are healthy and infinitely adaptable too, although this recipe will give you a good head start. Best of all, they reduce your washing up if you eat them straight out of the jar.

The more you make these kinds of meals the more you'll come to realise that there are no rules. You can do whatever you like! Be bold with flavours and combinations, layer your greens with pulses, grains and proteins, and add fish or meat if you need it.

Aim for 25% of your jar to be made up of proteins such as chickpeas, and for another 25% to be made up of complex carbs like peas or beans. Add around 10% of healthy fats such as olives, hard-boiled egg, nuts or seed and make the rest out of veg and fruit with some leafy greens.

HOW TO BUILD YOUR JAR

Start with a good base: Make or use dressing at the base. For example, mix up something simple with honey, mustard, seasoning, vinegar and oil. Layer the dressing with leafy greens, such as lettuce, spinach, watercress, rocket, cavolo nero, cabbage leaves or chard, etc. For a little extra crunch, add sliced white cabbage, Romaine lettuce or little gems.

Next, layer it up! Add cubed cucumber and tomato or even sun-dried tomatoes for an extra-intense flavour. Carrots will add texture, flavour and nutrition. Grate or dice them finely. Roasted veggies work well here too, while sweetcorn adds sweetness. Radishes will also add a peppery crunch.

Top it off: Beans, chickpeas or prepared hummus will add extra protein to top it off. You could also add shredded meats, fish or olives or even a few finely chopped sprinkles of chilli, garlic or ginger.

MEXICAN QUINOA
& BEAN SALAD

CAULIFLOWER RICE

Makes 4–6 portions, depending on the size of the cauliflower

INGREDIENTS

1 large cauliflower, blitzed or grated to resemble rice
1 tbsp extra virgin olive oil
Seasoning to taste

METHOD

Grab a pan, heat up the oil and then add your cauliflower rice. Use a lid to cover the cauliflower so it steams and becomes tender. Cook for approximately 5 minutes, stirring occasionally. Season to taste. And that's it!

MEXICAN QUINOA & BEAN SALAD

Makes 4 portions

The recipe for this salad uses quinoa but it can be based on any kind of grain you can get your hands on, including brown rice or even assorted veggies. It is great cold but can also be warmed through in a stir-fry style.

INGREDIENTS

180g (6.3oz) quinoa
1 red pepper, cubed
1 yellow pepper, cubed
400g (14oz) tinned aduki or black-eyed beans, drained
200g (7oz) sweetcorn
4 spring onions, roughly chopped
Fresh herbs and wedges of fresh lime to serve

For the dressing

2 tbsp organic cider vinegar
1½ tbsp honey or maple syrup
2 tbsp lime juice
10g (0.3oz) fresh coriander, leaves only, finely chopped
1 fresh jalapeño chilli, deseeded and finely chopped
1 red chilli, deseeded and finely chopped
½ tsp English mustard
1 garlic clove, finely chopped

METHOD

Cook the quinoa as per packet instruction and leave to cool. Mix well with the other ingredients. Mix up the dressing in a jar. Serve the salad with dressing added as required.

ONE-POT SMOKED ALMOND & HERB COUSCOUS

Makes 6–8 portions

This is an easy base for lots of meal options. It's simple to make around the campfire and can be added to with all kinds of veg. If you cook too much it can be packed in jars or a lunchbox as it will travel well. Thereafter it can be reheated, thrown into a soup to bulk it out, added to eggs to make an omelette or even mashed with beans and stuffed into peppers to go on the BBQ.

INGREDIENTS

2 tbsp olive oil
4 garlic cloves, finely chopped
95g (3.3oz) almonds, lightly crushed
1 tsp smoked paprika

720ml (24.3fl oz) water
480g (17oz) couscous
1 tsp sea salt
15g (0.5oz) fresh parsley or herb
of choice

METHOD

Heat the oil over a medium heat in a large pan until shimmering, Add the garlic and almonds and sauté until the garlic is fragrant but not burnt and the nuts are lightly toasted – about 2 minutes. Add the paprika and sauté for few seconds more. Add the water, stir to combine and bring the mixture to the boil. Turn off the heat and immediately stir in the couscous and sea salt. Cover and let stand until all the liquid is absorbed, approximately 5 minutes. Uncover and fluff with a fork. Chop and mix in the fresh parsley (or other herbs) and serve.

VEGGIE RICE WRAPPERS & NORI

Makes 1 portion

These make tasty, speedy eats: little parcels of food without the need for bread. They are a great way to use up hummus and all the veggies you have prepped or leftover. Eat raw or pan fry for a completely different food experience.

INGREDIENTS

2 rice wrapper sheets (or 4 sheets
to double wrap each portion IF you
are pan frying or baking off in the
oven)
40g (1.4oz) carrot batons
40g (1.4oz) courgette batons
30g (1.1oz) cooked beetroot batons

2 spring onions, finely chopped
4–6 leaves fresh mint, finely chopped
4 stems fresh coriander, finely
chopped
¼ tsp wasabi paste (adjust to suit)
1 tbsp fresh lime juice
2 nori sheets

METHOD

Place the ingredients in the middle of a rice wrapper with a little lime juice, if desired. Roll up a little bit and then fold in either end before finishing rolling the wrapper. Roll in a nori sheet. Serve on platter but leave space in the centre for a bowl of homemade satay sauce (see page 271). Make an alternative dip with soy sauce, fish sauce, fresh lime juice and zest.

VEGGIE RICE
WRAPPERS & NORI

PASTA FOOD JARS

Makes 4–6 portions

These recipes are classic Italian pasta combos that use storecupboard staples and take less than 15 minutes to make. So they are really easy and don't use up too much fuel. These recipes make great lunch box offerings for hikes or for a shared supper if there are a few of you. Serve with salad for a greens fix.

INGREDIENTS: 500g (16oz) dried spaghetti (other pasta would work too)

Pasta with olive oil & garlic
8 tbsp extra virgin olive oil
10 garlic cloves, finely chopped
1 tbsp red chilli flakes
Handful of parsley, chopped

Fiery pasta
8 tbsp extra virgin olive oil
2 garlic cloves, finely chopped
600g (21oz) tinned chopped tomatoes
2 tbsp chilli flakes
Handful of parsley, chopped

Pasta with anchovies
5 tbsp extra virgin olive oil
2 garlic cloves, finely chopped
2 tbsp anchovies, finely chopped
1 tbsp red chilli flakes
Handful of parsley, chopped

Amatrice spaghetti
2 tbsp extra virgin olive oil
2 garlic cloves, finely chopped
½ onion, diced
400g (14oz) tinned chopped tomatoes
½ tsp chilli flakes
180g (6.3oz) cooked chopped bacon
  or bacon lardons

Pasta with fresh tomato & basil sauce
4 tbsp extra virgin olive oil
2 garlic cloves, finely chopped
800g (28.2 oz) fresh cherry tomatoes,
  halved
Handful of fresh basil, torn

Tomato spaghetti
5 tbsp olive oil
3 garlic cloves, finely chopped
1 onion, diced
800g (21oz) tinned chopped tomatoes
Handful of fresh basil leaves, torn

Spaghetti with olives & capers
8 tbsp extra virgin olive oil
2 garlic cloves, finely chopped
400g (14oz) tinned chopped tomatoes
½ tbsp red chilli flakes
100g (3.5oz) black olives, sliced
2 tbsp capers, chopped
Handful of parsley, chopped

Pasta & tuna
6 tbsp extra virgin olive oil
2 garlic cloves, finely chopped
½ onion, diced
400g (14oz) tinned chopped tomatoes
150g (5.3oz) dolphin-friendly tinned
  tuna (if in oil, use the oil), drained
Good handful of parsley or herb
  of choice, chopped

METHOD FOR ALL RECIPES

Cook 500g (16oz) dried spaghetti or your choice of pasta in a large pan of salted, boiling water. Stir the pasta once or twice while cooking. Prepare the sauce by mixing the ingredients in a bowl. When the pasta is ready, scoop out 1 cup of the cooking water before draining the pasta. Add the pasta to the sauce (use tongs if you have them to avoid using a colander) and ¾ of the cup of the pasta cooking water. Toss until the sauce thickens and sticks to the pasta. Use more water, if needed, to loosen. Season to taste.

TOMATO SPAGHETTI
PASTA FOOD JAR

TOMATO SPAGHETTI
PASTA FOOD JAR

SATAY SAUCE

Makes 400g (14oz)

This can be used as a dip to have with chopped veg but is equally delicious mashed into butter beans and eaten on bread or with rice wrappers. Add to pan-fried cauliflower florets or veggies for an easy veggie dish.

INGREDIENTS

200g (7oz) smooth peanut butter

1 tbsp sesame oil

150ml (5fl oz) water

2 garlic cloves, finely chopped

2 tsp coconut sugar or honey

1 tsp fish sauce

2½ tbsp soy sauce

2½ tbsp coconut milk

1–2 tbsp organic cider vinegar

Pinch chilli flakes or Tabasco
sauce to taste

METHOD: Blend everything together if you're making this before you leave or mix it up well with a fork if you're making it while at camp. Add more liquid for a thinner sauce.

VEGGIE RAMEN NOODLE JAR

Makes 1 portion

These are really versatile and can be layered in a food jar to create a tasty, wholesome lunch on the trail. Or prepared fresh and eaten straight away.

INGREDIENTS

100g (3.5oz) dried rice noodles
(or precooked grains)

230–250 ml (7.7–8.5fl oz) water

2–3 tsp soy sauce or 1 tbsp miso
paste

1 tsp toasted sesame oil

25g (0.9oz) mushrooms, thinly
sliced, or dried mushrooms

1 small carrot grated or cut into
thin strips

20g (0.7oz) leafy greens such as
spinach or chard, chopped

Handful of fresh herbs

2 spring onions, chopped

1 garlic clove, finely chopped

Chilli flakes or fresh chilli, finely
chopped

Handful of tofu, cubed

METHOD: Prepare the noodles (or grains) according to the instructions. Heat the water and then mix it well with all the other ingredients. Add the noodles (or grains). Leave for a few minutes to infuse.

Desserts

NO-BAKE DESSERT IDEAS

Food jars make these simple, easy pudding ideas possible to make on the go, at camp or before you leave. If you prep them beforehand then you can avoid having to carry out any packaging waste. These are just suggestions, and can be tailored to suit your tastes.

Trifle jars: Layer a food jar with sponge cake (you could use fruit loaf or breakfast muffin leftovers), jam or fruit compote and yoghurt or cream, then more compote and finally grated chocolate.

Apple crumble jars: Layer a food jar with grated apple, honey and yoghurt then more grated apple, cream, homemade granola and ground cinnamon.

Banoffee jar: Layer bananas, yoghurt or cream and granola (plus add dulce de leche if desired). Alternatively, use maple syrup or honey in between the layers.

APPLE CRUMBLE
NO-BAKE DESSERT

ALI'S SUPERFOOD FLAPJACKS

Makes 10-12 portions

These wee oaty chunks of heavenly energy and goodness make a cheap and packaging-free trail snack that will last a good week in a container, which means they are perfect for making ahead of time and for bringing out when spirits are low. They can be devoured whole or crumbed down into a bowl with yoghurt, kefir or milk for an on-the-go comfort bowl.

If you wanted to mix it up a bit you could add some mashed banana, an apple and an egg and then warm it up in a pan as an on-the-hoof pancake. Add yoghurt for a pud with a difference. If you really wanted to push the boat out you could roughly chop it and use it as a crumble topping. Here's how: grate apples, mash down banana and add a few berries (blackberries straight from the bush?) and then top with the crumbled flapjack leftovers.

The point of all this? Flapjack is a wonder snack, a superfood with potential way beyond an afternoon pick-me-up. Got some left? Chuck it on top of your Buddha bowl. Gone a little stale? Warm it through with a few slices of apple or some of those juicy foraged blackberries. Go on, I dare you.

INGREDIENTS

3 ripe bananas, chopped
250g (8.8oz) oats
20g (0.7oz) mixed omega seeds
2 tbsp coconut sugar
50g (1.8oz) chopped almonds
50g (1.8oz) walnut halves
5 tbsp peanut butter

4 tbsp butter (or coconut oil for vegans)
3-4 tbsp honey (or maple syrup for vegans)
2 tsp ground cinnamon
Pinch of sea salt
Large handful jumbo Chilean flame raisins

METHOD

Preheat the oven to 160°C (320°F).

Mix together the bananas, oats, seeds, sugar and nuts. On the hob, melt the peanut butter and butter. Add the honey, cinnamon and salt, and then add the oat and banana mix and combine well.

Pour into a lined baking tin.

Bake for approximately 30 minutes or until the flapjacks go a deep brown colour. Leave to cool before cutting into hungry camper-sized bites.

ALI'S SUPERFOOD
FLAPJACKS

15

Where is the bathroom?

This chapter is all about how your camping ablutions affect the environment and what you can do to limit your impact. It's all quite easy really but may require a bit of extra work to change habits or learn new ones.

Some of the ideas in this chapter will help you to minimise your environmental impact, keep your washbag extra tidy and may even help you when it comes to going to the shower block. The chapter will also cover the general rules when going in the wild, if you have to, and what you can do to avoid an environmental disaster if you get caught on the hop with no porcelain.

The first rule of bathroom club, however, is that you never, ever, ever use wet wipes. Even 'flushable' ones. These are evil things that clog up drains, don't biodegrade and make a mess in the countryside.

Why we need to talk about your ablutions

Washing and bathing are important, as you know. And going camping doesn't mean you should have to give up being clean and healthy (with the emphasis on healthy). However, in the world of cleaning and personal hygiene, there are a lot of players who care more about money than the planet. Thankfully, though, there are lots of other emerging brands who can make your ablutions non-toxic and waste free. If you need to work out why it's important, here are some thoughts.

← Keeping clean and healthy while camping isn't always easy, but there are ways to do it that won't damage the environment or create a huge amount of waste.

During 1 year in the UK, we use:

11,000M wet wipes
90% are plastic

200M plastic toothbrushes
They will never decompose

60M razors
They are here forever

Roughly 1.5–2B menstrual products
Most of them contain plastics

520M shampoo bottles
But only 45% of plastic waste is recycled

How does a camper shit in the woods

When I was a nipper and played out in the woods all day every day I got caught out regularly. I lived a little further away from the woods than an urgent poo would allow so either had to detect a motion prematurely and leave enough time to dash home or do it right there in the woods. Often, when I knew a dash would mean disaster, I did it right there, deep in the Chiltern Hundreds. It was great training for a life of camping and the off-the-map surfing that was to come and taught me not to fear the cool breeze on the bum that comes when nature calls (unexpectedly).

Of course, I never carried toilet paper with me on those jaunts so I had to make do with what nature had to offer. Deep in the beech woods of Buckinghamshire, where there was an understory of nettle, holly and laurel, the best and least painful thing I found to use for a wipe was the humble dock leaf. As we know, the dock grows in similar conditions to those loved by nettles. We used to use it on stings so why not on our bums? The procedure was simple and is exactly the same as advice given to campers today who go out in the wilds:

↗ The recommended depth to dig a latrine is 15cm (6in). If this is difficult because of the terrain, move to somewhere it will be possible (for example, if you are up a mountain, move down the slope). And make sure your hole is away from paths and at least 60m (200ft) from a stream or river. Don't bury the paper.

1 Get far away from the river (at least 60m/200ft).
2 Get off the path (away from other campers and campsites).
3 Gather some dock leaves (or equivalent: moss, leaves, etc.).
4 Dig a 'cathole' with a stick (or, if you are a well-prepared camper, a trowel) about 15cm (6in) deep.
5 Drop the load into the hole without dropping it on your strides (keep them at knee, not ankle, height).
6 Wipe, and drop the soiled leaf into the hole.
7 Cover over and carry on playing.

It's pretty similar for camping unless you are squeamish about leaves, in which case you will have loo paper with you. Sadly though, by the rules of 'leave no trace' you will have to carry the loo paper out with you and not bury it in the hole (because of it being a non-natural element), which means you'll also have to carry plastic bags or dog poo bags. I would never advocate that, sadly, as it means contributing to landfill, unless you are willing to wash and reuse the bag.

Some people recommend burning loo paper in the field, but I can't see this is good, unless you are having a roaring fire later, in which case you would still need a plastic bag.

Why bury it
(Do you have to ask?)

Burying your poo is important for a number of reasons. First, it's not nice to leave turds out in the open. They smell, attract animals and insects, and contain all the waste products your body doesn't need. That includes toxins, bacteria and viruses and consequently can be a serious health hazard to anyone else who happens to trot along.

Second, poo breaks down better when it is buried. It gives all the beasties, enzymes and bacteria a good chance to get into it, digest it and turn it from a toxic hazard into something that's benign and ready to create new life.

The recommended depth to dig is 15cm (6in). If this is difficult because of the terrain, move to somewhere it will be possible (for example, if you are up a mountain, move down the slope). And make sure your hole is away from paths and at least 60m (200ft) from a stream or river.

The camper van toilet
(How and why)

There are lots of types of loo that can be used with a camper van or motorhome. The most common is the cassette toilet, an inbuilt device that is a type of chemical loo, which draws water from the freshwater tank or a header tank to flush. The cassette can be removed from the toilet and emptied at any emptying

The wet wipe menace

While wet wipes are good for cleaning up and washing when there is
no running water or toilet paper or flannels, they are often made from
plastic (90% of them are plastic) and come in plastic wrappers. They do
not biodegrade in the environment and are well known for clogging up
sewer pipes and waterways. Even those that are 'flushable' and made of
viscose or any other 'natural' material will not break down easily in the
environment. Having travelled extensively in Europe, where they make
up a large proportion of litter, I can safely say they are a blight on many
a landscape.

Some companies sell wipes that are called 'Wilderness Wipes'. Even
though they are 'compostable' (not sure by which standard) and made
from viscose, the company still recommends taking them with you.
Thereafter, while I can't be sure, they probably need to be composted
under industrial conditions, which means putting them in with your
compostable food waste and not into landfill.

Avoid? I can see the advantage but, seeing as I wouldn't want to carry
around a bag full of shitty wet wipes, I'm not really sure why you would
want to use them.

point. Some have wheels and handles like cute little shopping trolleys! Handy if
they are a bit full as they can be heavy.

The cassette uses chemicals (usually blue or green) to neutralise smells. The
liquid in the cassette, which contains the poo, wee and chemicals, is known as
black waste. It should never be emptied anywhere but an approved emptying
station. In some cases, when chemicals containing formaldehyde are used,
pouring black waste into a septic tank can seriously affect the chemical balance
of the tank. Once emptied, some people use cleaners (often pink in colour) to
rinse out the cassette before returning to the van.

SOG FILTRATION: The SOG system is a ventilation system for cassette toilets
that eliminates the need for chemicals in the cassette. The system sucks out
odours from the cassette and expulses it to the outside, via a deodorising charcoal
filter. The manufacturers claim that the system aids decomposition of the waste
in the cassette and doesn't smell. However, there have been complaints against
these systems, especially when used near other vans in overcrowded aires.
However, if getting rid of chemicals is important, it could be a useful piece of kit.

PORTA POTTIS: These work on similar principles except they are self-contained
units with a header flush tank and a waste tank that slot together. They use
chemicals to neutralise 'nasty niffs' and should not be emptied anywhere except
an approved emptying point.

Using the right chemicals
(Formaldehyde-free)

There are lots of options for chemicals to use in your loo. Many of them will be formaldehyde-free, which is good. Formaldehyde is a toxic biocide that kills the bugs in your poo to stop it smelling. Unfortunately, formaldehyde also kills the bugs that work to treat poo in a sewage works or septic tank, so making it useless and damaging its make-up. Hence the rule about emptying.

There are lots of eco liquids on the market these days. Some are green and others are still blue (the standard colour). Check the bottle that it is formaldehyde-free.

Some people use laundry detergent or fabric softener in their cassette toilet. There is nothing wrong with this; however, it doesn't always work to mask the smell. Better to buy loo chemicals.

REDUCING WASTE: Some products, like Kampa and Solbio, come in pouches to avoid plastic waste and can be used as refills to use in old bottles. As yet, no one refills camping loo liquid like refill shops do with other liquids and detergents, but it could only be a matter of time. Caravan suppliers and campsites take note!

> **TIP:** Buy toilet fluid in large quantities (5 litres/5¼ US quarts) to reduce waste (and save money) and decant into smaller bottles to save weight and space on trips.

GEL TOILETS: There are some toilets that are a lot simpler than cassette or Porta Potti thunderboxes. These are the shit-in-a-bag-type loos that use a gelling agent to turn your excretions into gel and to stop the smell. You might describe these as 'bucket toilets'. Some are available that collapse, like the CarpLife Bivvy Loo (www.carplife.uk.com/product-page/bivvy-loo), while others are simply buckets.

The idea is that you line the bucket with a bag (either compostable or plastic), then do your business. After each evacuation you sprinkle gelling agent into the bag, which then turns it to gel. The bag, when full, or not so full that you can't carry it, can then be put into the rubbish, just like a nappy.

According to the manufacturer: 'The powder is a super absorbent polymer that has no harmful effects on the environment and in the quantities used per use in our toilets (under 10 grams per use) they can be disposed of in many ways. Customers should always check local regulations if unsure but disposing of the waste in general household waste (as you would with nappies or incontinence underwear) is fine in most cases. The waste could also be buried but should not be buried adjacent to a watercourse. Many customers also utilise dog waste bins.'

SEPARATING TOILETS: The gold standard in environmentalism for off-grid loo lovers is the separating toilet (some call it a composting toilet, although that

↑ Composting toilets are the ultimate in sustainability on campsites. But can they work in a van? Separating toilets are often called composting loos, but really all they do is separate the waste. You still have to dispose of the solids.

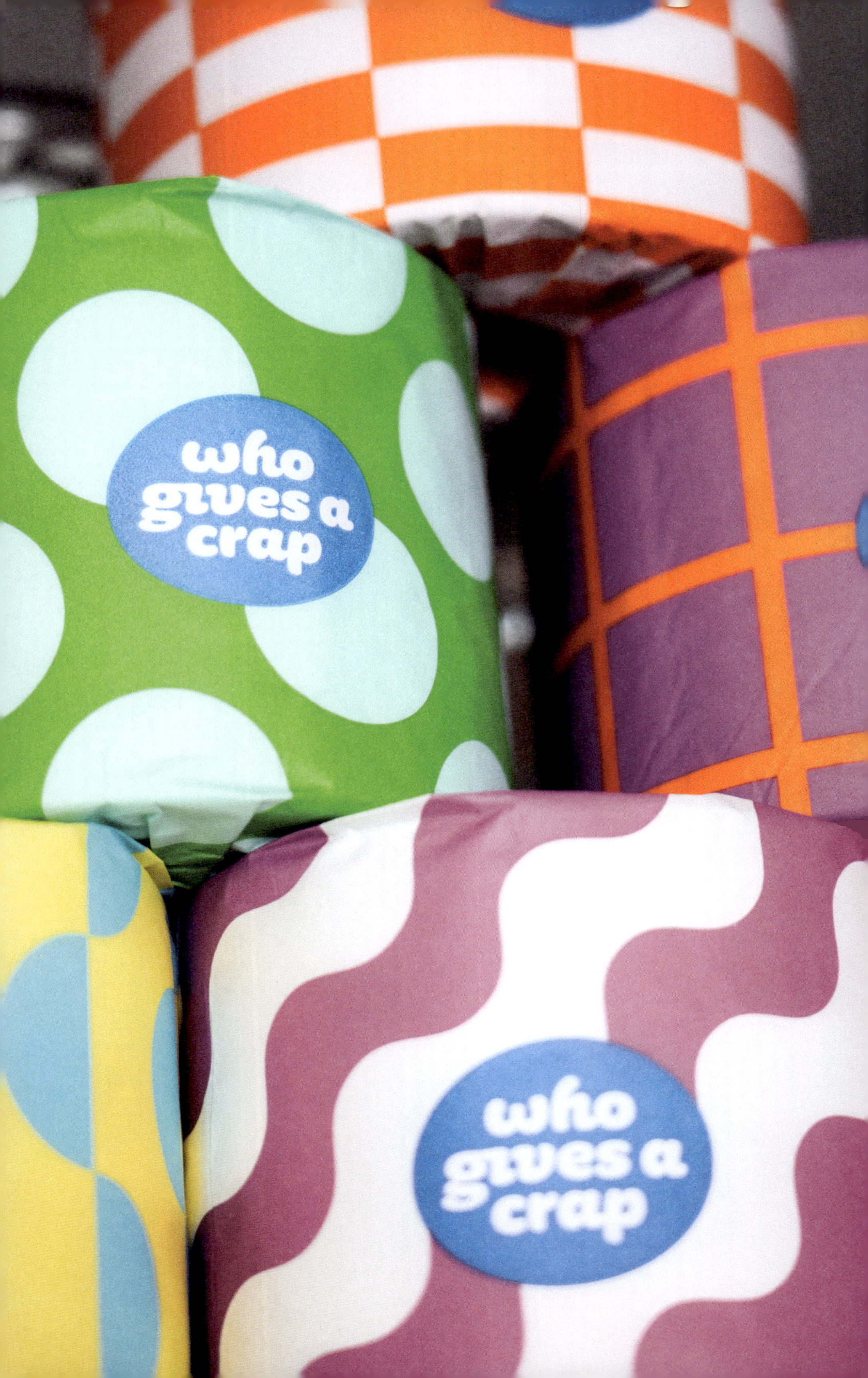
who gives a crap
who gives a crap

is a bit of a misnomer). Camping versions of these loos – like the Blue Diamond Nature Calls Composting Toilet (www.blue-diamond-products.co.uk/eco-friendly-composting-toilet.html) – have two compartments that allow you to pee in one and poo in the other. Once you have pooped you sprinkle sawdust or coffee grounds (or some other neutralising agent) on top, which will help to dry it out and cover the smell. The wee can be poured into the environment.

What happens to the poo is moot. The assumption is that you line the poo section with some kind of bag so that it can be bagged up and then put into the compost, hence why it's called a composting toilet. The question I have about this is this: whose compost? And if it can't go into the compost then where does it go? Into the general waste and then to landfill? And what happens to the paper? Do you bag that? Or do you put it in with the poo? If you do, does it break down?

I can see this being great for wild or off-grid camping where water is at a premium. However, putting solids into a bag and then putting it into landfill isn't ideal since landfill doesn't allow for composting or degrading in any normal way that you'd expect from a compost heap because there is no movement, air or microbes – most of the waste is inorganic.

However, if you are able to put the solids on to a compost heap, either at home or on a campsite, then it is truly a brilliant waste-, water- and chemical-free solution, even though nothing will actually compost while it's in the loo itself – it doesn't stay there long enough.

Loo paper
(Quit the quilts)

If you are a quilted loo roll kind of a person, it might be time to quit. Quilted, so-called luxury loo paper, is more resistant to breaking down in chemical loos and Porta Potties (and in the sewage system, too). This can clog up your cassette and make for a dangerous blockage and potential kickback situation. Loo roll usually comes wrapped in plastic, too, which often fails to get recycled.

Cheap toilet paper breaks down easier and saves money. If you shop at your local plastic-free shop you will be able to pick up a box of Who Gives a Crap (www.uk.whogivesacrap.org) or Naked Sprout (www.nakedsprout.uk) paper, or you can order it online. Their recycled and bamboo loo papers break down easily and are free of plastic packaging. So, it's a double win for camping and life in general.

← Quilted loo paper often comes in plastic and is so well made it won't break down in camper van toilets. Waste-free, recycled paper (and cheaper paper) breaks down easily and is plastic free. Win-win!

What's in your washbag
(Keep it plastic- and chemical-free)

Plastic-free, waste-free, cruelty-free, planet-friendly ablutions aren't so difficult to achieve even though the cosmetics industry makes it hard when it comes to chemicals!

Take a trip to your local waste-free shop to pick up all kinds of Earth-kind products, from toothpaste tablets to flannels and make-up removers. It should be possible to get hold of the basics for most washing stuff, for boys and girls.

While it's easy to focus on packaging – which makes up about 70% of the beauty industry's waste – it's just as important to think about what's in the products you use, especially if you are using them outdoors. What's interesting about waste-free products like shampoo bars or toothpaste tablets is that using them can also help save weight when lightweight camping.

Some people like to use waterless body wash and shampoo from places like Pits and Bits (www.pitsandbits.co.uk), which can be used without water. The idea is that you use the product and then simply towel off afterwards. Simple... and a 200ml (6.8fl oz) bottle of body wash can save over 300 litres (66 gallons) of water (when compared with a bath). The products use 100% recycled packaging, recycled bottles, compostable wipes and packaging. They're worth looking at for an off-grid adventure.

Chemicals in your face (avoid, avoid, avoid)

Cosmetics and personal grooming products may contain any number of chemicals or additives to give the product different qualities. Some of them, including parabens, triclosans, triclocarbans and phthalates, have been banned by the EU because of issues with human health. Others, like microplastics and liquid polymers, may affect the aquatic environment.

↓ Take a trip to your local waste-free shop to pick up all kinds of Earth-kind products, from toothpaste tablets to flannels and make-up removers. It should be possible to get hold of most of the basics for most washing stuff, for boys and girls. What's interesting about waste-free products like shampoo bars or toothpaste tablets is that using them can also help save weight when lightweight camping.

Friendly
SOAP

NATURAL BALANCE

Detox Bar
Rosemary & Lime

PLASTIC · CRUELTY · SULFATES
FREE from
PALM OIL · PRESERVATIVES

NATURAL ALL IN ONE

Travel Soap
Lemongrass, Lavender, Tea Tree & Peppermint

Friendly
SOAP

PLASTIC · CRUELTY · SULFATES
FREE from
PALM OIL · PRESERVATIVES

NATURAL SOAP

Aloe Vera
Fragrance Free

Friendly
SOAP

PLASTIC · CRUELTY · SULFATES
FREE from
PALM OIL · PRESERVATIVES

NATURAL SOAP

↑ According to the British Dental Association, we dispose of as many as 200 million plastic toothbrushes a year in the UK. Many of them find their way on to our beaches.

Parabens are used in a wide variety of shampoos and conditioners, moisturisers, face and skin cleaners, sunscreens, deodorants, shaving gels, toothpastes and make-up because of their antimicrobial properties. Studies have suggested they can act as hormone disruptors and may affect fertility and reproductive organs, birth outcomes, and increase the risk of cancer. They can cause skin irritation too. Some parabens have been banned by the EU.

Triclosans and triclocarbans have been used in home, beauty and personal care products for a long time. They can be irritating to the skin and eyes and are very toxic to aquatic organisms.

Phthalates, which have been linked to a variety of health effects in animal tests and some human studies, including hormone disruption, altered male genital development, diabetes, asthma, attention disorders, learning disabilities and obesity, are found in products such as soap and shampoo. Some types of phthalates have been banned by the EU.

While the UK has banned microplastics in shampoos and conditioners, they are still used in products that are left on the body, like lipsticks and make-up. Liquid polymers, which are liquid plastics, are still used in hundreds of products such as hair products, suncreams and nail polishes. They do not degrade in water (even though they dissolve) and cannot be filtered out by sewage plants, so end up in the ocean where they can attract pollutants.

Towels and drying

Microfibre towels might be light and dry you effectively, but they are still plastic and shed plastic fibres. Around water courses and shower blocks this is extremely troublesome as the fibres can wash down drains and then go straight to the rivers and sea (filters in sewage plants are not fine enough to contain them). Turkish towels, which are made of cotton, are light, packable and dry quickly. Bamboo towels also dry quickly and are absorbent, as well as being light.

Cleaning your teeth

According to the British Dental Association, we dispose of as many as 200 million plastic toothbrushes a year in the UK. Many of them find their way on to our beaches. A further 300 million toothpaste tubes go to landfill each year.

Bamboo toothbrushes will rot down in the compost (once you have taken the bristles out). Toothpaste tablets can replace toothpaste and can be bought plastic packaging-free, and bamboo flossers are also available, so helping to reduce your single-use footprint.

If you use an electric toothbrush then it is possible to buy compostable or 'recyclable' heads and there are some bamboo brushes on the market, but these still need to be recycled as WEE (waste electronics and electricals), even though the bamboo is, in theory, compostable.

Shaving for men and women

Sixty million razors are sold each year in the UK, which means that around that number are going to landfill or escaping into the environment. This applies to both men and women.

Razors are the ultimate in marketing guff. The shaving 'industry' is one of those industries whose model is constant improvement and inbuilt obsolescence, creating more and more ludicrous additions to their products, and passing them off as innovation. The name of the game is to get you to buy more products, to be unsatisfied with the products you already have and to shame you into feeling inadequate if you don't constantly upgrade. As a result, 'disposable' razors litter our beaches and fill up our landfill each year.

Using a safety razor is the simplest and easiest swap you can make, and it will reduce your waste to a couple of razor blades a month, if that. Shaving with a safety razor isn't that easy to perfect if you are used to shaving with a five-bladed pseudo race car of a razor but it is possible and an awful lot cheaper. You can pick up a safety razor and a pack of blades for as little as £15. The blades could last as long as a year. The razor will go on for years. It is also a lot easier to carry on camping trips as it will take up a lot less space. Brushes are light and can be used with tins of soap that are mess free, light and last for ages.

The alternative, of course, is to let nature take its course. Nothing wrong with that.

Plastic-free periods

Most period products – regular tampons and pads – are single use. And many of them are made with plastic and packaged in plastic. They are also often treated with chemicals that can cause dryness and irritation.

Using menstrual cups means you only need to buy one item that will last for years to come. They are rising in popularity, possibly because of the money saved and the fact that they can stay inserted for up to 12 hours, which is good for camping.

Period underwear is underwear that you can wash and reuse, again and again. It comes in a variety of styles accounting for different body types and flows, so that you can really choose what works best for you. You could also try reusable pads, which are another great alternative to single-use pads as they can be washed and used repeatedly.

Smelling sweet
(Deodorant and antiperspirant)

Deodorants and antiperspirants are different things. Deodorants neutralise smells while antiperspirants work to stop sweating, so reduce smells. The

YOUR NATURE - £8.99

ORANGE
& PATCHOULI
NATURAL
DEODORANT

your
nature®

NATURAL
DEODORANT
UNSCENTED

your
nature®

www.yournature.life

5 06060

your
nature®

CEDARWOOD
& GRAPEFRUIT
NATURAL
DEODORANT

your
nature®

LAVENDER
& BERGAMOT
NATURAL
DEODORANT

YOUR
nature®

LEMONGRASS
& TEA TREE
NATURAL
DEODORANT

↑ Aerosols are problematic because they release volatile organic compounds, contribute to air pollution, are difficult to recycle and can affect the planet's energy balance. Stick deodorants offer a good, plastic-free alternative.

↓ Shampoos and conditioners are available in bar form, which makes them lighter and less messy to take camping, with less waste.

trouble with traditional methods of either using an aerosol or roll-on is that they are single use and contain plastic and metal, so are hard to recycle and often end up in landfill.

Aerosols (fine particles in the atmosphere caused by natural events as well as manmade pollutants) are problematic because they release VOCs (volatile organic compounds), contribute to air pollution, are difficult to recycle and can affect the planet's energy balance (causing absorption of heat or reflection of heat).

According to an article by NASA from 2009, 'By reducing aerosol (soot) emissions, we can buy ourselves some climate time – about five to ten years – while we work on reducing emissions of greenhouse gases such as carbon dioxide (CO_2) in parallel. CO_2, you see, hangs around in the atmosphere for an extremely long time, from decades to centuries, so even if we implement cuts today, it will take years for them to take effect. Aerosols, on the other hand, have much shorter lifetimes.'

In addition, aerosol cans are bulky and difficult to dispose of, so are not ideal for camping. Plastic roll-ons are equally difficult to dispose of as they are composite, which means they are made with different types of plastic. While they are light and often very effective, they do produce waste.

There are lots of eco deodorants on the market, with some offering refills, others coming in cardboard and others offering subscription services whereby refills are sent regularly. Your local waste-free shop should provide a good range.

Shampoo, conditioner, soap and lotions

Most waste-free shops will have a selection of moisturisers, balms and lotions, as well as shampoos and conditioners in bulk. You take in your old bottle to refill with as much or as little as you need and only pay for what you take. If you don't have old bottles to use, you can often buy rucksack-friendly (some call them airplane friendly) 100ml (3.4fl oz) aluminium bottles. These kinds of bottles are durable, can be refilled until they die, can be recycled (infinitely), are lighter than taking a whole bottle and take up less rucksack space – so you only take what you need.

Lots of shampoos and conditioners are available in bar form, too. They can be stored in tins (or old takeaway containers) so they create very little mess and won't leak in your rucksack. If you are concerned about weight, you can chop bars up to take just what you need.

Laundry strips

Lightweight and easy to stash away until you need them, laundry strips like those made by Tru Earth (www.truearth.uk) save packaging and contain no parabens or phosphates, are biodegradable, hypoallergenic and vegan.

The green camper's washbag
(choose what you need!)

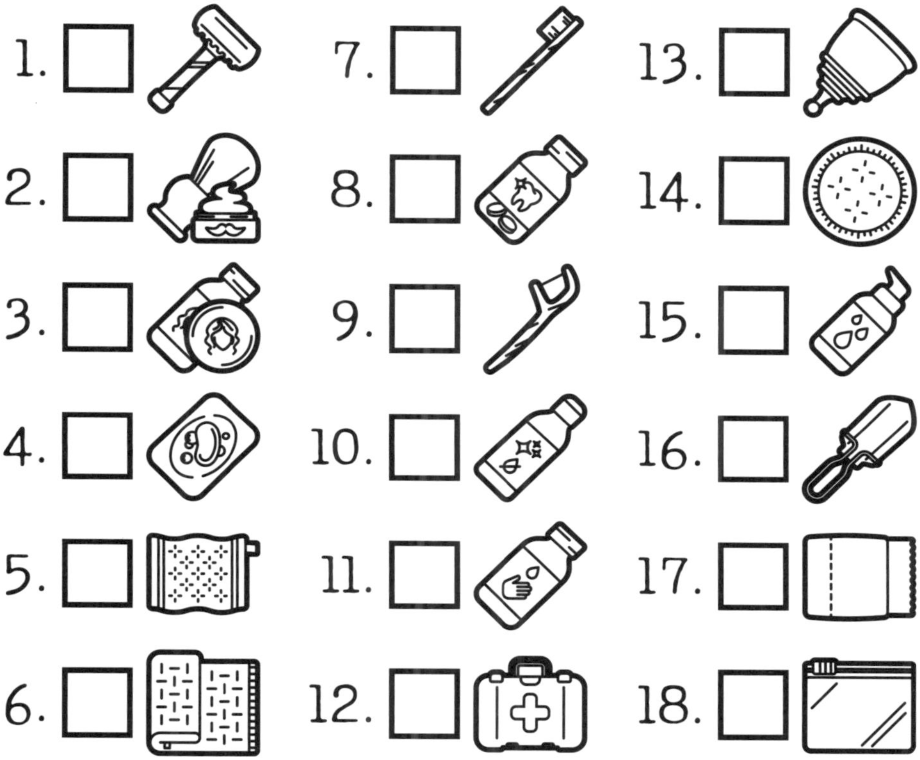

1. ☐
7. ☐
13. ☐

2. ☐
8. ☐
14. ☐

3. ☐
9. ☐
15. ☐

4. ☐
10. ☐
16. ☐

5. ☐
11. ☐
17. ☐

6. ☐
12. ☐
18. ☐

1. Safety razor
2. Brush and tin of shaving soap
3. Biodegradable shampoo and conditioner in bottles/bars
4. Biodegradable soap in a tin
5. Flannel
6. Cotton Turkish towel
7. Bamboo toothbrush
8. Toothpaste tablets
9. Bamboo flossers
10. Dry wash
11. Plastic-free hand sanitiser
12. First-aid kit
13. Menstrual cup/plastic-free tampons/pads
14. Washable make-up removal pads
15. Refillable moisturiser
16. Foldable trowel
17. Toilet paper
18. Ziplock bag

↓ You might call talking to people socialising, but it can also be called campaigning, as long as you don't ram your views down anyone's throat. Activism doesn't have to be about lying in front of bulldozers or delivering petitions to Number 10. It could be as simple as chatting with your neighbour and just being nice.

16

Who are you talking to?

This chapter is about spreading the word and campaigning for greener, more nature-rich camping experiences for everyone, on the basis that the more of us that get to love the outdoors, the more of us there will be to protect it. In some ways that relates to the rest of our lives too: the lessons we learn on the campsite don't stop when we pack up and the planet doesn't stop hurting just because we went home on Sunday.

This chapter is about getting the message out there and using your influence to inspire others. This starts with what you do and the way you do it and spreads out from there. Ultimately, this could be getting involved with camping clubs, societies, councils or even government. It could be protesting or playing 'them' at their own game by stepping up to join 'The Establishment' or it could mean changing your life to set up a new business in the camping industry. If there is something that you believe in, carry on doing it and tell others about it. If there is something that bothers you, tell others about it and, ultimately, try to take steps to do something about it.

The lore of the campsite
(And other campfire stories)

Camping is a great way to meet and influence, or be influenced by, other people. You get to chat with people at the dishwashing area, on the trail, while sitting outside your tent or unit and at the campsite bar in the evening. This is when tips and ideas can be exchanged, myths debunked, and positive actions welcomed and championed.

Camping is a sociable activity where good times can lead to meaningful interactions and change can happen. You might call talking to people socialising, but it can also be called campaigning, as long as you don't ram your views down anyone's throat. Activism doesn't have to be about lying in front of bulldozers or delivering petitions to Number 10. It could be as simple as chatting with your neighbour and just being nice.

Equally, activism can be about posting positive news on social media, doing small positive acts, telling people about companies doing the right thing, writing to your MP, getting involved with a camping club to instigate change at board level or just supporting those who are doing good.

Ranting and raving
(Might not work)

It's easy to get worked up about the state of things. There is plenty to be upset about, from the state of nature to the fossil fuel industry's continuing exploitation of the planet, to plastic pollution and government inaction. While it might feel like shouting is the best way to do things, a lot of people are overwhelmed by climate change and environmentalism. It is too big a problem and they feel they cannot solve it.

Some people don't like change because they fear it will put their 'way of life' under threat. This is maybe because they are sitting pretty and really, genuinely feel that they couldn't improve their lot, are concerned only with themselves, or simply because they fear the unknown. Either way, we need to treat them with care and get them onside. It's easy to lose support by doing things that are branded as woke, lefty activism (blah blah blah) by the media – crimes against the hard-working people of Britain – even though it might be an act that was done for the benefit of us all.

> Camping is a sociable activity where good times can lead to meaningful interactions and change can happen.

I admire those who block roads or throw paint over BP's HQ, because they have the courage to directly confront those who are largely responsible for climate collapse and who could, but don't, take enough action. However, I have long known that my strength lies in trying to bring people along with me: to help create a groundswell of activism and microactivism that, I hope, may add up to a tsunami. I don't have the patience for changing things from within (I was a local councillor and found it to be depressingly slow and difficult to make anything happen) so the power I choose is the power to influence, through books like this or through social media.

When I was working on the 2 Minute Beach Clean project I found that offering an easy way into environmentalism was more effective than browbeating people into doing something that made them uncomfortable. We welcomed activism (and microactivism) with love and gratitude, accepting that any action, as a first action, is a powerful act.

That's what I am asking you to do. Find your drum – whether that's about creating more diverse spaces, working towards better access to the countryside for people of colour, renting a tent instead of buying, shopping local, donating your old gear or staying on sites that have incredible environmental credentials – and bang it. Keep banging it. You don't have to achieve it all at once, of course, you just have to start. That's how change happens.

Influence others
(Use your cool)

Influencer marketing is a powerful tool that allows brands to infiltrate your feeds with products by gifting them to people you might follow on social media. It's another of the weapons marketers can use to get products in front of you in the hope that you'll be impressed enough to buy them. They pay people you trust to tell you about things they think you will like. A bit like a celebrities flogging perfume, for example, but much more insidious and closer to home.

I understand that it's exciting being gifted stuff. It feels special to be singled out as worthy of such attention. You're important. Sadly, it's never as simple as a gift and there is always something to be paid back, whether that's a mention of the product on Instagram or wearing the kit in a photograph.

Of course, some influencers set themselves up for this and make it their business to take money and products in exchange for access to their online following. Their 'celebrity' has a value that could be the odd free can of drink or a whole new wardrobe, plus a couple of grand per post. That's decided by how much chutzpah you have got or how much the marketer wants to get to your audience.

I see so much of this from the camping world. I can't blame anyone for wanting to make a living and for playing the game, but I do worry about people selling their souls for a bit of flattery and some new clothes when we have more pressing issues to work on.

That said, influencers who are selective, and who push brands that are doing the right thing, are having the kinds of conversations with their followers that we can all have.

You are important
(Please don't forget it)

You might not think it, but you are an influencer too, whether you have ten followers on social media or 10,000. Or none at all. What you say and do matters in every aspect of your life. Small conversations can have lasting and profound effects for everyone concerned. A bit of advice here, an opinion there. It all matters.

What this means is that you have a say in the future, just by being you and by camping in the way that's important to you. By 'being the change that you want to see', you can influence and educate other people, as long as you stay true to yourself. That, I believe, is the only way to do it. Do what you do with love and conviction and the rest will follow.

This time it's personal
(And political too)

You might not think that camping and the outdoors has much to do with politics, but it has everything to do with politics, I am afraid. It was politics that led to the mass trespass of Kinder Scout in 1932, which ultimately led to the formation of the UK's National Parks, and it is politics – and the wielding of the power of the wealthy and well-connected 'ruling classes' – that ended wild camping on certain parts of Dartmoor in January 2023 (even though the High Court overturned the ruling in July 2023).

Politics sets the tone of the landscape, whether by supporting landowners' rights, implementing (or not) green policies, taking action against polluting water companies, or supporting those who would like more access. It decides the law and where and how we are permitted to camp – it was politics that introduced the Land Reform (Scotland) Act in 2003, which opened up the Scottish countryside to everyone and made wild camping legal. Politics decides how each and every one of us is treated, the rights we have and, ultimately, the way we feel about our country. It is vitally important.

As we know, what is right for politics, and those in power, isn't always right for everyone else. The thing is that we all have the right to decide, collectively, who is in power, at every level of government. You can elect people in your local council, in the district council and in Westminster who you trust to take care of our country for all of us and not for themselves or you can choose NOT to vote for the people who cannot be trusted with our country's laws and way of life. Your vote matters.

Write letters
(Hold them to account)

Whatever your political persuasion, politicians and councillors work for you. You pay their wages and you are effectively their bosses. So, if there is something that bothers you, write to them or go and see them. Keep on at them. Let them know how you feel. Get others to do the same.

The UK's government is shrinking in favour of corporations taking the reins and we need to make sure that what we get in return for our vote is decent, green and won't destroy the planet.

It's the same with camping clubs and organisations. Generally, they are keen

↓ You decide. If you want more access to nature and the countryside, more land reform and more public spaces given over to nature, ask for it. Vote for the people who will deliver it. And if they don't, demand to know why not.

to hear from their members and will try to keep everyone happy because they won't want to court controversy. So, if you have problems, write to them. Tell them how you feel. Make your voice heard.

Change your preferences
(Just stop oil)

Whatever you think of Just Stop Oil, Extinction Rebellion or any of the other climate movements, there is little doubt that the oil industry, if anything, is the major cause of climate collapse. Its sidekick, the chemical industry, is also culpable.

You may not realise it but aside from all the ways you support the oil industry by buying plastic, sleeping in a nylon tent and driving a camper van, you may also be inadvertently supporting them through your choices and, in particular, your investments, if you have them.

Divesting from companies that invest in fossil fuels isn't that hard and will begin to show them that you think it's toxic. If you have a Nest pension you can change to an ethical pot (your money gets invested in 'ethical schemes') in about five minutes by choosing the type of pot. If you have a broker, for shares or investments, you can ask them to move your money to ethical pots.

If you bank with a company that bankrolls oil and gas or chemicals, then you can switch to ethical banks. It's a bit of a pain in the arse, but it can be done. Check out the Current Account Switch Service (www.currentaccountswitch.co.uk) for more information on UK banks that are signed up for the service.

Support the good
(Not the bad or ugly)

It's often quite difficult to know who funds what in this day and age. Fossil fuel companies have a long history of sponsoring football clubs, sporting events, museums, art galleries, events and university research projects. It's something they do to buy goodwill so that they can deflect from the harm their business models do to the planet. After the void left by the tobacco industry's departure from world commerce (after years of denial) it's time to ensure the same fate lies with the oil companies (after their years of denial).

You can do this by simply refusing to take part in any kind of activity that is sponsored by oil companies or the people who fund them.

At the time of writing, the British Museum had ended its sponsorship deal with British Petroleum (BP) after 27 years of taking its money. But there are plenty of examples where the organisers of events – particularly sports events – are still taking oil money. And the reason oil money is so keen to get into sports sponsorship is because of people's emotional connection to sports teams and clubs and the association with health and vitality that it brings. It was the same with tobacco. An act of denial that's really, when you think about it, quite audacious.

Oil sponsorship is everywhere. Even COP27 was sponsored by a fossil fuel company in 2023.

What can you do? See it. Call it out and boycott if you can. It won't be easy. Oil is so embedded in our culture that it's hard to do anything environmentally positive without involving oil in some way. Even the keyboard I am using is plastic. Ironic, huh?

As it says on the Ban Fossil Fuels in Advertising website (www.banfossilfuelads.org): 'For the very first time, the latest Intergovernmental Panel on Climate Change (IPCC) report stated that corporations have attempted to derail climate mitigation by targeted lobbying, doubt-inducing media strategies and through corporate advertising and brand building to deflect corporate responsibility to individuals.'

> What can you do? See it. Call it out and boycott if you can.

Ignore the haters
(Who are greener than you)

There is something I find very difficult about environmentalism and that's the piety of those who see themselves as greener than you. They call you out for not being as green as they are. Ultimately this is very unhelpful as it makes people feel stupid and useless and may lead them to abandoning their green journey.

Going green takes determination and energy and anyone who does it should be praised. So, if someone tries to call you out as an insincere environmentalist by saying you wear shoes made of oil or have a phone or drive a car, ignore them. It's nothing more than 'whataboutery'. And if someone else tries to call you out because you aren't vegan enough or are using the wrong soap, ignore them too. Do what you do and keep on doing it. And if you can, make a few changes as you go. But don't give up just because someone tries to shame you into doing more.

↓ Something about camping will never change: the pull of the coast and country and the need to be out in nature.

Afterthoughts
(Don't screw it up)

Camping has come a long way since the tepee and the Sibley tent (the forefather of the classic bell tent). But not really, when it comes down to why we do it. The love of the outdoors and wide-open, wild places has never left us.

We did have a period there, in the late 20th century, when we worshipped oil and plastics, convenience and chemicals. Unchecked innovation – something humans do so well – brought good as well as bad. This showed in the way we camped as well as in our everyday lives. In the search for comfort and triumph over elemental disquiet we stayed dry with the use of chemical water repellent coatings, coated our tents with PCBs and wore and then threw away a lot of stuff that's still in landfill right now. Today, we know better. We have started to understand the destructive course we've been on and have begun to make changes. Whether or not that's going to be enough is for anyone to guess.

But the thing that hasn't changed is the feeling that we need to get out there and explore, if not for the first time, certainly for ourselves. We still feel the pull of open spaces, the forest, the cool mountain stream, and the ocean.

We haven't entirely lost our fascination with nature, even though we may have hastened its demise by believing it's ours to exploit. We can still see the beauty in flowers, in snow, in sunshine in spring and in clean water, as if our lives depended on it. And it does.

Despite all the doomsaying and the tragedy, I still believe that we have the power to make changes – on a personal and planetary level – that will help to alter the course we have inadvertently set ourselves or that has been set for us by those who care for nothing but money. Don't let anyone tell you otherwise.

Camping is a part of that story. It may have changed because of the trappings we cosset ourselves with, but the emotion and joy that takes us into summer fields remain the same. The bikepackers of today are the same bicycle tourers of the 1900s who went on to form the Camping and Caravanning Club. Motorhomers are just latter-day motorised vagabonds.

We are still the same. We are still in love with the stars, nature and the wilderness. And that's a fine starting point to begin a new journey with lighter footsteps and even more wonder than ever. As we uncover land, racial and climate injustice, fight for access to our own countryside and make better choices in the way we enjoy the outdoors, we can begin a new relationship with it. We have an opportunity – now – to make sure everyone is included in this new beginning, irrespective of their race, physical ability, sexuality or gender.

We need all of us, together, to rise up and take a stand for nature and the natural world as if our lives depended on it. Because they do. And the more

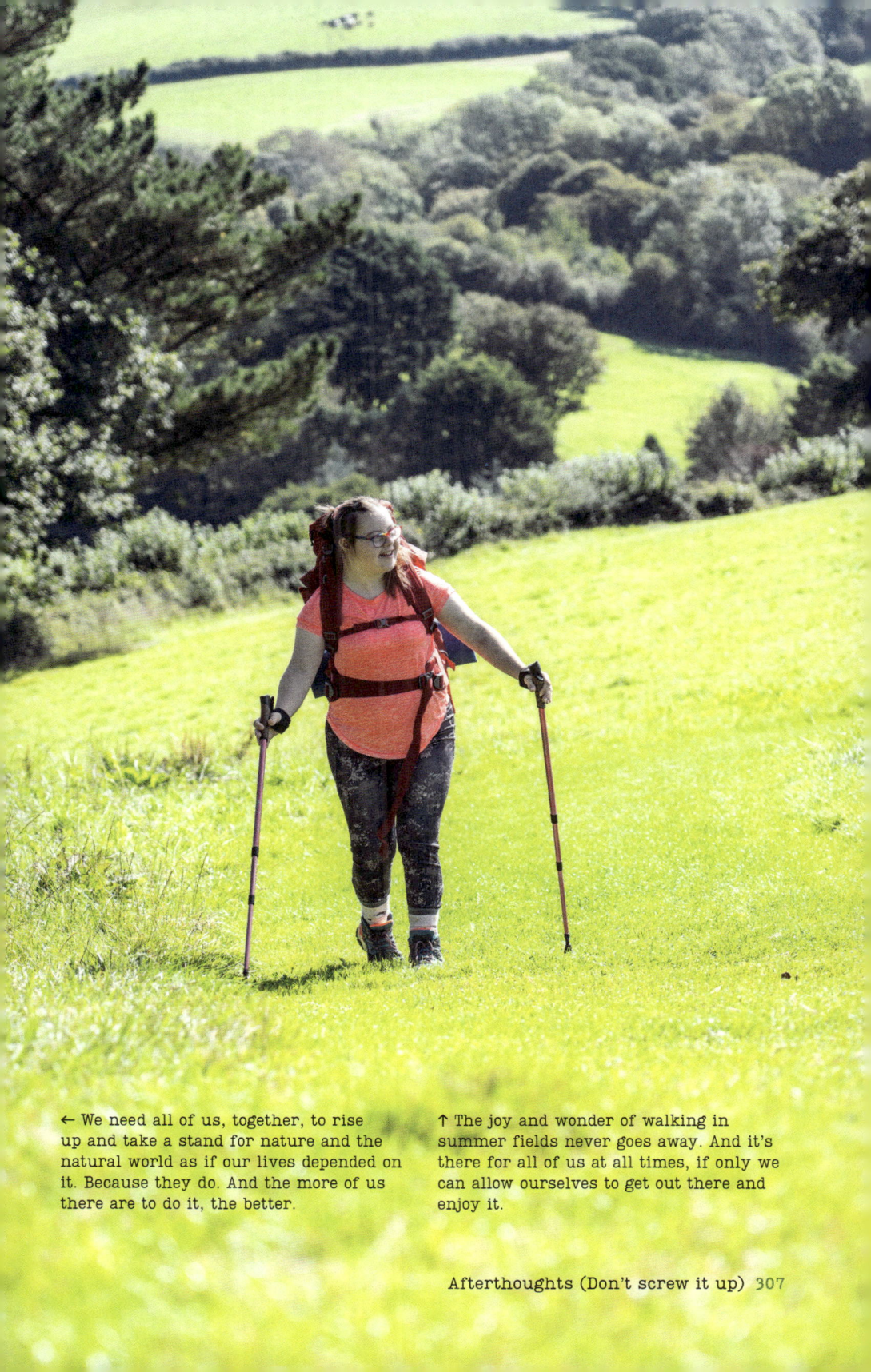

← We need all of us, together, to rise up and take a stand for nature and the natural world as if our lives depended on it. Because they do. And the more of us there are to do it, the better.

↑ The joy and wonder of walking in summer fields never goes away. And it's there for all of us at all times, if only we can allow ourselves to get out there and enjoy it.

of us there are to do it, the better. The oil, pharmaceutical and agricultural giants are looking to rinse it for a few more years because they feel their money will save them. Governments are in their pockets, unwilling to change course because that's where their campaign cash comes from. The arts, sports events and universities are still taking oil money because they depend on it. The media distorts and contorts in order to ensure its billionaire owners remain offshore and out of touch. Corrupt, sleazy, stupid, self-interested. So, it's up to us.

How we want to do it is up to us, too. We have so many choices in front of us – and not all of them are bad. Any choice that makes a positive contribution is the right choice as far as I am concerned. Don't let the zealots believe you aren't doing enough. You are.

If you have a garage full of old camping gear, you can donate or lend it to people who don't have such luck but who will still get as much from a camping trip as you did when you first used it.

If you are someone who cherishes silence and simplicity, then you can pull on your boots and set off to find it without worrying about the PCBs and microfibres you leave in your wake. You can get as far off-grid as you like, with kit that will support you, which isn't doing more harm than the good it's doing to your mental health.

If you don't have the personal resources (and by that I mean a garage full of old camping kit or the cash to buy a brand-new tent) you can borrow or rent equipment. Your experience will be just as meaningful as the person who has it all to hand.

If you have a garage full of old camping gear, you can donate or lend it to people who don't have such luck but who will still get as much from a camping trip as you did when you first used it. Their voices matter in this fight too.

The days of powering camping trips with a bunch of batteries that you have to chuck away when the lights go out are also over. You now have options for powering your campsite. Solar charging and lithium-ion have superseded wind-up torches, diesel gennies and AA batteries. What this means is that we can now have renewable power at the flick of a switch, wherever we go. People who need power to run medical devices so they can live can now step into the unknown without worrying about where the next socket is going to be. For them, as testified by my friend Karla, this is ground-breaking. A true freedom that adds more voices to the roar.

While it's easy to dismiss solar and battery technology as being the Trojan horse of 'business as usual', I feel that the benefits of these kinds of gadgets may be felt more acutely in the longer term. If they help us to embrace change, make us realise that self-reliance is possible and that living unsupported, away from

↓ We can now have renewable power at the flick of a switch, wherever we go. People who need power to run medical devices so they can live can now step into the unknown without worrying about where the next socket is going to be. For them, as testified by my friend Karla, this is ground-breaking. A true freedom that adds more voices to the roar.

↓ We have to work out how we can coexist with nature so we can simultaneously thrive, protect one another and heal each other. The first step is to enjoy nature responsibly. If we need to check our social media while we do it, so be it. It is possible to be an environmentalist *and* own a phone.

societal pressure and the grasping, greedy power of the grid might be possible, then it's a good thing.

With electricity to charge our phones, tablets, laptops, cameras, fridges and gadgets we can begin to imagine a different relationship with nature. I don't think it's about taming the wild like never before, but more about making camping more comfortable, more accessible and more enticing for those who might have struggled under candlelight. And that will mean more people can get out there, learn to love the countryside and become stewards of nature, giving it a voice, and fighting to help save and restore it. A charged phone is a powerful weapon in the right hands.

While those who deny climate change and ecological collapse will claim they aren't yet ready to give up their cars and phones and go and live in a cave, I would argue that we don't have to unless we want to. We just have to work out how we can coexist with nature so we can simultaneously thrive, protect one another, and heal each other, too. The first step is to enjoy nature responsibly and encourage as many people as possible to be active in its survival. If we need to check our social media while we do it, so be it. It is possible to be an environmentalist *and* own a phone.

But of course, those precious moments of life in the outdoors (when our phones are tucked away) will always be there to inspire us if we care to take the time to enjoy them. For some it'll be one step at a time, gently and slowly, without fossil fuels, without plastics, without chemicals and without causing havoc. For others it'll be boots first, yomping into the backcountry without a care (or a gadget) in the world.

That's fine. The most important thing about camping – and being green about it – is that we go do it.

When we do, the next thing we need to do is to let ourselves fall head over heels in love with nature and the natural world. That's our safety net. The oxygen tent. The dialysis. The CPR. And we can't afford to screw it up.

Thank you for reading and for coming on this journey with me. I have loved every minute of researching and thinking about this book. I hope it shows.

Best wishes

Martin

↓ What we need to do now let ourselves fall head over heels in love with nature and the natural world. That's our safety net. The oxygen tent. The dialysis. The CPR. And we can't afford to screw it up.

Endnotes

INTRODUCTION

1 Trash Free Trails: www.trashfreetrails.org
2 International Panel on Climate Change (IPCC) AR6 Synthesis Report: www.ipcc.ch/report/ar6/syr/
3 The 2 Minute Foundation: www.2minute.org

CHAPTER 1

1 Protect Our Winters: www.protectourwinters.org
2 www.besjournals.onlinelibrary.wiley.com/doi/10.1002/2688-8319.12197

CHAPTER 3

1 www.store.mintel.com/report/uk-camping-and-caravanning-market-report
2 *Ibid.*
3 MCZ Lundy study: www.iucn.org/sites/default/files/import/downloads/marine_protected_areas_lundy.pdf
4 Plantlife No Mow May study: www.plantlife.org.uk/campaigns/nomowmay/
5 2019 American study on urban grassland: www.sciencedirect.com/science/article/abs/pii/S1439179119302932
6 www.meadows.plantlife.org.uk
7 Soil Association: www.iarc.who.int/featured-news/media-centre-iarc-news-glyphosate/#:~:text=In%20March%202015%2C%20IARC%20classified,of%20%E2%80%9Cpure%E2%80%9D%20glyphosate) and www.soilassociation.org/causes-campaigns/reducing-pesticides/the-pesticide-problem/
8 www.metoffice.gov.uk/about-us/press-office/news/weather-and-climate/2022/joint-hottest-summer-on-record-for-england
9 University of Ghent study: www.researchgate.net/publication/366430154_Laser_scanning_reveals_potential_underestimation_of_biomass_carbon_in_temperate_forest and www.eurekalert.org/news-releases/974703
10 www.rspb.org.uk/birds-and-wildlife/helping-birds-and-wildlife

CHAPTER 4

1 High Weald Area of Outstanding Natural Beauty in the South Downs National Park of England: www.tinyurl.com/mr2j9hsm

CHAPTER 7

1 www.pannier.cc/journal/jack-thurston-a-history-of-cycle-touring-part-1/ and www.bicycleassociation.org.uk/mds-2020-covid-impact-report/

CHAPTER 8

1 NOTE: At this point I reach for an outdoor magazine lying about in the office and skim through it, counting the number of white faces (127) versus the number of Black or brown faces (2) in any editorial or advertising (about 1.57%). The general UK population, by contrast, according to the census of 2021, is made up of around 14% ethnic minorities. Advertisers, graphic designers and picture editors take note: you need to represent people properly if you are to be part of this positive change.

2 NOTE 2: She's right: from my lived experience, I was only able to build and run the 2 Minute Beach Clean project because I already had a business to support me. I was able to build that business because of the advantages I have had throughout my life, thanks to my background. Not everyone could have done that.

3 www.cpre.org.uk/wp-content/uploads/2021/08/August-2021_Access-to-nature-in-the-English-countryside_research-overview.pdf

4 www.london.gov.uk/press-releases/mayoral/bame-londoners-bear-brunt-of-climate-emergency

CHAPTER 9

1 www.bikeradar.com/features/long-reads/cycling-environmental-impact/

2 researchbriefings.files.parliament.uk/documents/POST-PN-0691/POST-PN-0691.pdf

3 www.ourworldindata.org/emissions-by-sector; www.gov.uk/government/statistics/transport-and-environment-statistics-2022/transport-and-environment-statistics-2022 and www.ourworldindata.org/travel-carbon-footprint

CHAPTER 11

1 www.gov.uk/government/publications/common-misconceptions-about-electric-vehicles/common-misconceptions-about-electric-vehicles

CHAPTER 12

1 www.europarl.europa.eu/news/en/headlines/society/20201208STO93327/the-impact-of-textile-production-and-waste-on-the-environment-infographic

2 www.gov.uk/government/statistics/transport-and-environment-statistics-2022/transport-and-environment-statistics-2022

3 www.greenpeace.org/static/planet4-international-stateless/2016/01/d9343da2-leaving-traces.pdf

4 www.link.springer.com/article/10.1007/s11356-017-0528-7

CHAPTER 14

1 www.theguardian.com/environment/2022/mar/18/recycled-plastic-bottles-leach-more-chemicals-into-drinks-review-finds

2 www.sciencedirect.com/science/article/abs/pii/S0890623813003456

CHAPTER 15

1 www.unpckd.com/blogs/lesseverydaywaste/spotlight-on-razors

2 www.tapwarehouse.com/blog/latest-news/bathroom-waste-legacy

Index

Acknowledgements

Inspiring people, as always, can't help but inspire. During the writing of this book, I had the pleasure of talking to (and being inspired by) some amazing people at wonderful organisations doing good things for the planet and for camping. Each one of them gave me the gift of their time and knowledge, sparking conversations and ideas that helped me gather my thoughts and put them down on paper. I am always grateful.

Andy Middleton, Adam Hall, Nikki Nichol and Natasha Shane at The Caravan and Motorhome Club; Chris Bishop at Vango; David Hanney at Alpkit; Tom Kay at Finisterre; Kieran Bosch at Camplight; Rebecca Heap at Tentshare; Rob Fearn at Alan Rogers; Steve Evison and Lee Barton at Nearly Wild Camping; Kevin Bird at The Greener Camping Club; Dom Ferris at Trash Free Trails; Simon McGrath at the Camping and Caravanning Club.

As always, the whole team at Peter Fraser Dunlop, including Tim Bates and Daisy Chandley, making it happen.

Without the team at Bloomsbury none of this would happen either: Jenny Clark, Kathryn Savage, Austin Taylor, Elizabeth Multon, Alister Savage.

Massive thanks to the Supermodels for letting me take their pictures: Lizzy Kay, Izzy Colwill, Malikiah Harris, Tom and Sophie Fox, Daisy Green, Maggie Dorey, Sian and Rowan Dearing, Lee and Matt at Rooted Ocean.

To the essayists, sharing their thoughts on where we need to go next: Alex Gibbon, Shell Robshaw-Bryan, Jeantique Hommel, Karla Baker, Sarah Riley.

And, finally, to the people who allowed me to take pictures on their wonderful slices of our beautiful planet: Rob Bird at OA Surf Club, Anna at Bakesdown Farm, Charlotte Veale at Wooda Farm Campsite.

Thank you all.